The Show
Starts
on the
Sidewalk

Yale University Press

New Haven and London

Maggie Valentine

The Show
Starts
on the
Sidewalk

An Architectural
History of the
Movie Theatre,
Starring S. Charles Lee

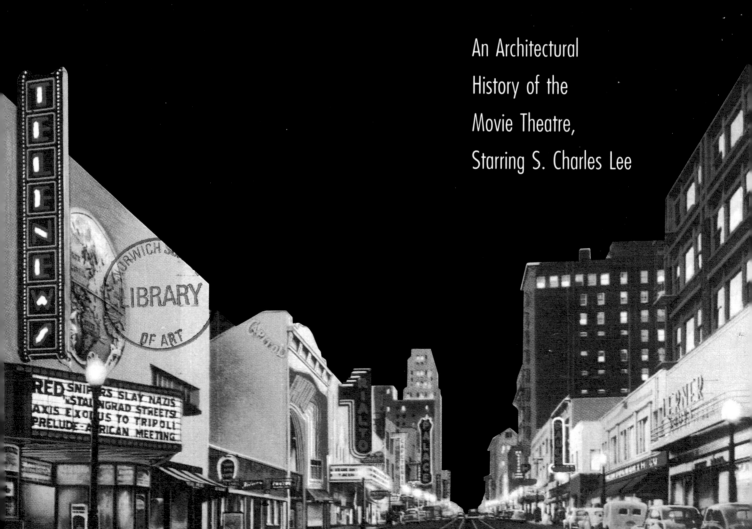

Designed by Nancy Ovedovitz. Set in Adobe Garamond type by The Composing Room of Michigan, Inc., Grand Rapids, Michigan. Printed in Hong Kong by Everbest Printing Co., Ltd.

Library of Congress Cataloging-in-Publication Data

Valentine, Maggie
The show starts on the sidewalk : an architectural history of the movie theatre, starring S. Charles Lee / Maggie Valentine.
    p.   cm.
    Includes bibliographical references and index.
    ISBN 0–300–05527–7
    1. Lee, S. Charles—Criticism and interpretation.   2. Motion picture theaters—United States.   I. Title.
NA737.L42V36   1994
725′.822′092—dc20   93–24977
                                    CIP

A catalogue record for this book is available from the British Library.

The paper in this book meets the guidelines for permanence and durability of the Committee on Production Guidelines for Book Longevity of the Council on Library Resources.

10 9 8 7 6 5 4 3 2 1

For Paul, for his faith in me
and in this project

Contents

Acknowledgments   ix

Trailer   xi

Coming Attractions   1

Short Subjects
The Theatre and the Architect   12

Double Feature
**Chicago to Los Angeles, and the Introduction
of the Movie Palace**   34

Teaser
Lee's Movie Palaces   53

Feature Presentation
The Movie Theatre Takes Shape   90

Newsreel
The Impact of World War II   128

Intermission
From Architecture to Business   163

Epilogue   183

Souvenir Program
Appendixes   195

Notes   209

Bibliography   223

Index   229

Photo Credits   232

Acknowledg-ments

I could not have written this book without the assistance and support of many individuals. In particular, I wish to thank the librarians at the Department of Special Collections at the University of California, Los Angeles, especially David Zeidberg, Dale Trelevan, Anne Caiger, and Jeff Rankin. This book began as my dissertation at UCLA, and I thank the members of my committee for their encouragement. S. Charles Lee not only designed the wonderful buildings shown here but gave generously of his time to answer my many questions and share the details of his life and work with me. Hildy Rabinovich, who worked in Lee's office, cheerfully accommodated all my requests. Most of the information about Lee comes from the oral history on file in the Department of Special Collections at UCLA. Marlene Laskey, Elaine K. S. Jones, and Dolores Hayden continually challenged and supported my thinking and gave me ideas they made me think were my own. John Miller and Deac Rossell were of great assistance, even though they did not know it. The following individuals carefully read the manuscript in its different versions and kept me on the right track: Paul Gleye, Marshall Croddy, George Talbot, and Pamela J. Hill. The schools of architecture at UCLA and Montana State University supported my work and made it possible for me to pursue these ideas. Friends and family, often coerced to go miles out of their way to track down a theatre, understood why I was too busy to play but rescued me when necessary. Joanna Valentine's help came in many forms. My editors at Yale University Press, Judy Metro and Karen Gangel, balanced enthusiasm with meticulousness in a very even-handed way. I thank them all. For the advice I did not take and for errors of fact as well as judgment, I assume full responsibility.

In 1988 I presented a portion of chapter six at the "Americans and the Automobile" conference sponsored by the Society for Commercial Archeology and the Henry Ford Museum. It was later published as "Of Motorcars and Movies: The Architecture of S. Charles Lee," in *Roadside America: The Automobile in Design and Culture,* edited by Jan Jennings (Ames: Iowa State University Press, 1990). I gratefully acknowledge permission to reprint sections of that material.

The American movie theatre as it developed into a unique building type during the first half of the twentieth century was both a product and a symbol of its time. It created an emotionally charged atmosphere in which millions of Americans learned about life, culture, politics, romance, and sex through what was shown and implied and what was both said and suggested on screen. Movies contained archetypes who represented ideals, possibilities, and pitfalls. The theatre housing these models reflected a tangible expression of hope and dreams. Theatre buildings formed the visual centerpieces of major commercial streets in every American city and in most small towns. In addition to creating an atmosphere appropriate for synesthesia, the theatres are remembered decades later for the purely sensory pleasures they provided. Even after many years, people recall the feel of the nap of the seat fabric, the smell of popcorn and chocolate mixed with stale cigarette smoke, or the distinctive feel and sound of folding seats edged in cold metal going up and down.

In this book I explore the evolution of the American motion picture theatre through the work of architect S. Charles Lee, who designed approximately 250 movie theatres between 1920 and 1950. Movie theatres were a national phenomenon; each was unique and typical at the same time—that was part of the architectural program. Lee designed theatres across the country and internationally, most of them in the movie capital of the world (see appendix B). The cultural climate of the West Coast fostered experimentation and innovation. From the start, Lee's theatres were at the vanguard of theatre design throughout the nation. Using Lee's career as a window and tracing the development of the building type through the work of one architect, I examine the role of the movie theatre in America and its place in contemporary architecture.

S. Charles Lee's life and career coincided with the rise and fall of the American movie theatre in the twentieth century. Although the development of the movie theatre, especially in its early forms, is usually associated with a group of eastern and midwestern architects—the best-known of whom were John Eberson, Thomas Lamb, and Rapp and Rapp—the history of the building type, especially in the post–movie palace era, can also be explored through Lee's work, which spans the evolution from movie palace into neighborhood house. From the late 1910s through the late 1940s the image of Hollywood glamour replaced the notion of European culture in the design of theatres, and commercial modernism became an accepted norm, due in large part to the movies.

Born in Chicago in 1899, five years after the first commercial showing of motion pictures in the United States, Lee received an architectural training founded in the Beaux-Arts. He lived in the environment of Louis Sullivan, Frank Lloyd Wright, and

Trailer

burgeoning American Modernism and apprenticed in the offices of early motion picture theatre architects. The American movie theatre as a building type drew on all these trends—Beaux-Arts styling, functional modernism, and popular design. In his own architectural career, Lee specialized in motion picture theatre design, but even his nontheatre commissions were infused with the same theatricality and emphasis on functional innovations.

I parallel the development and evolution of the American movie theatre in general with the architectural career of Lee, as a specific study of theatre design at its peak. This is a work about the history of film that focuses on consumption rather than on production. I pay little attention to the titles of films and even less to their content. Instead, I argue that the experience of the film—that is, the reality for the observer—was largely influenced by the surroundings. The experience of "going to the movies" equaled, and often surpassed, what was seen on the screen. The theatre was central to the experience and, therefore, to the memory—which is, in fact, what movies were selling. Theatres influenced everything from the movies themselves to the cityscape to the life-style of the individual.

The book is neither a typology nor a biography in the traditional sense but a combination of the two. Although Lee was an influential architect, I offer few details about his personal life and no psychological analysis of his personality. Rather, I have chosen to look at a body of work that was dominated by one person's ideas and came out of one office.

I chose this approach for several reasons. The full story of the movie theatre as a building type, focusing on architectural expression from penny arcade to multiplex, has not been recorded. Consequently, there is no single context for examining the work of an individual architect or period. It is also difficult to compare Lee's career with that of other theatre architects because of the dearth of such studies. Lee's work is significant in its own right as an expression of the "joy in architecture" associated with this twentieth-century genre; but it is also worth uncovering for the significant parallels with the development of the type and for its exceptional quality and originality. Furthermore, the specific characteristics of his work and career choices reveal certain truths about the film industry, about the popular audience and, perhaps, about American life.

Lee donated what remained of his professional papers to the Research Library at the University of California, Los Angeles, including original plans, renderings, and photographs. In writing this book, I was granted access to the Lee Collection, and it served as the primary source material for studying his architectural career. Piecing together a coherent picture of Lee's work and its role in theatre development was particularly challenging, because there existed virtually no correspondence, office files, memoranda, or other kinds of information about the office or clients. To the detriment of architectural history, all such records were purged from Lee's files in the 1950s when the office saw no further use for them. This part of the picture therefore remains incomplete, and I was forced to corroborate the surviving evidence with the professional literature of the period.

By the time I began this research in 1984, most of Lee's clients had died. I interviewed Lee extensively between 1984 and 1989, but the events we discussed had taken place thirty-five to sixty-five years before. He had no memory of some things, such as specific events, people, or buildings, whereas some recollections were the result of years of anecdotal editing and retelling. They were what might be called polished chestnuts, charming stories that had been honed in retelling until the wording was memorized and calculated to promote the desired image. More revealing were his offhand comments and candid answers to questions. It was also possible to triangulate facts and theories through the use of primary and secondary sources, including the manuals of theatre exhibitors and trade journals.

The methodology for this book is not the usual one for architectural history. It goes beyond a stylistic typology to include social, economic, and political forces as well as aesthetic choices. Motion picture theatre design was often a direct response to these forces and changes in American society. Interwoven in the text are discussions of the film industry and its organization, laissez-faire attitudes and economic legislation, world wars, civil rights, and popular fads and trends. To separate these developments is to ignore much of the commercial impetus and success of the genre and to miss many of its lessons. Because of the nature of the topic and the approach, I explore Lee's work in a national context. Although 90 percent of his work was in California, the characteristics common to the motion picture theatre were more national than regional.

I have organized chapters according to general chronological periods, which are determined by significant transitions in Lee's career that coincide with developments in the evolution of the type. The two stories have parallel beginnings, then become intertwined, and then return to a parallel route. The chapters weave together a discussion of Lee's work during each period through an analysis of specific examples, as well as general trends and themes, with changes in the exhibition and distribution of motion pictures. The primary focus of each period and chapter is how Lee responded to changes in the motion picture industry. The evolution of the type is drawn from analyses of changes in site plan, layout, theme, cost, materials, innovations, and attendance patterns, all related to historical, social, and economic developments. The significance of Lee's contribution is determined from an evaluation of how typical (or atypical) and how successful his work was in that context. The title, *The Show Starts on the Sidewalk,* is taken from Lee's philosophy and applies to the genre itself. It is also a literal description of the building, the function of which was to provide escapist entertainment, beginning with the colorful terrazzo sidewalks. Architecture played an intrinsic role in the motion picture business—a fact that Lee recognized and capitalized on.

An analysis of Lee's work is instrumental in developing an appreciation of popular architecture of the twentieth century. In his use of historical, contemporary, and futuristic references and ornament, his work serves as a lesson in commercial imagery.

This book is especially timely in that much of Lee's work, and the nation's stock of movie theatres, still exist, albeit in various degrees of maintenance and original fabric and against increasing odds. Given the changing nature of film exhibition as home video rentals and multiplexes come to dominate the movie-viewing experience, the future of these theatres is at severe risk. Many of the survivors are now old enough to have been awarded historic landmark status, if warranted, or to have been threatened with demolition.

Many movie theatres, including some of Lee's, are listed on the National Register of Historic Places or have been designated as local landmarks. But the majority of American movie theatres remain unrecognized as cultural markers of historical importance. With this book, I hope to document the importance of the motion picture theatre in social, architectural, and cultural history, to provide support for preservation efforts, where warranted and before it is too late, and to bring the movie theatre, especially post–movie palace theatres, into the body of film and architectural history.

The jargon of the motion picture is worth noting here. Moving pictures came to be known simply as the "movies," a term first applied to patrons. There were many attempts to upgrade the image of the industry through more elegant labeling. Biograph, for example, referred to its studio as a "laboratory." Essanay Studios sponsored a contest to find a better name than movies and paid the winner twenty-five dollars for coining "photoplay." Although a magazine adopted that term as its moniker, most people continued to use the word *movies,* which reflects the relative informality and accessibility of this art form. Thereafter, the industry embraced its popular audience, and show business reveled in Variety-ese (an abbreviated lingo used in the self-proclaimed "Bible of Showbiz") with words such as *fan, Tinseltown, pix, ballyhoo* (promotion), and *boffo BO* (high gross receipts). I have occasionally used some of this language to capture the flavor of exhibition practices. I have also used the historic spelling of the word *theatre* throughout the book because that was the spelling used in the literature of the period and in most of the proper nouns for the buildings under discussion; I have tried to use the more recently accepted *theater* when that is the correct proper noun. When the dates of buildings are known, the years given refer to the time the projects were in the architect's office, that is, from design through completion.

The Show
Starts
on the
Sidewalk

American heroes and celebrities in the twentieth century have been predominantly movie stars; details of their personal and professional lives fill the tabloids, talk shows, and best-seller lists. Shortly after their crude beginnings, movies began to cross over the proscenium to include the audience (fig. 1). Plots are commonly described through the personae of the actors rather than through the characters, implying an intimacy between performer and viewer, as though the film were shared, not watched. Public expression of this sense of intimacy ranged from collecting memorabilia to emulating vogues made fashionable on screen to postulating with great authority what the Academy was thinking when handing out awards. Veronica Lake's hairstyle, a blonde mane that dipped across one eye, created safety hazards for female factory workers; as a result, she agreed to pin it back for the duration. Clark Gable nearly destroyed the men's underwear market when he revealed his chest without benefit of an undershirt in *It Happened One Night.*

What Americans learned at the movies also influenced their lives and values in deeper and longer-lasting ways. Memories from a cross-section of Americans transcend nostalgia to reveal the magic, the dreams, and the vivid realities of life at the movie theatre. Author John Updike recalled a favorite moment from his boyhood, "the instant when the orange side lights, Babylonian in design, were still lit . . . the curtain was closed . . . [and] the camera had started to whir . . . that delicate, promissory whir."[1] Despite the racist versions of life on screen, black actor Morgan Freeman recalled fondly: "All my life I've been going to the movies. When I was 9, living in Chicago, you could sell a milk bottle for a nickel and a beer bottle for 2 cents, and if you sold enough to make 12 cents, you had entree into those huge movie palaces. They had velvet ropes and vaulted stairs and chandeliers and darkness. And for 12 cents, you could enter that magical world. I'd stay all day—you could see two features, cartoons and newsreels."[2]

Writer John Charyn bemoaned that "Hollywood ruined my life," referring to Loew's Paradise, a Venetian palazzo in the Bronx, where he fell in love with Rita Hayworth. "It's left me . . . searching for the kind of love that was invented by Louis B. Mayer."[3] Finally, in 1925, a recent immigrant wrote that the Capitol Theatre in New York City was "the first thing that made me realize I am in America."[4] Implicit in these memoirs is an understanding of the contribution of the physical surroundings of going to the movies—the place constituted much of the experience.

In the 1980s, legal and ethical arguments abounded over colorization, editing for television, and the restoration of infamous lost reels of classic films. Distributors and cable television companies promised to present movies "the way they were meant to be seen," choosing to ignore the physical environment in which they were meant to

1
Coming Attractions

I can remember a time when where we went to the movies was just as important as the movies we went to see. . . . From the moment moviegoers arrived to buy their tickets, there was a sense of something special, a feeling that to step inside was to enter another time and place.
Gene Kelly, in Naylor,
Great American Movie Theaters

be seen. Unlike the family room, the traditional motion picture theatre, with its broad screen, made the audience feel part of the action. The lessons of the screen had a greater impact because of the design of the auditorium in which they were taught. Through the collective and manipulative experience within the motion picture theatre, the audience was emotionally, psychologically, and physically drawn into the action and immersed in a total environment that excluded all reminders of the outside world. Viewers were not outside looking in, or at, but were participating in a drama that was magnified before them. They moved through a stage set, interacting with the fantasy and romance through the theatricality of the architecture itself.

Most historians and critics have overlooked the significant contribution of the theatre environment in social, film, and architectural history. Film historians have tended to focus on the history of the industry—namely, the economic and substantive development of film production and distribution—describing the exhibition process only in vague or generalized terms.[5] They have examined the content and evolution of specific films primarily from the perspective of the creator, whether auteur, studio, or period, as though the films existed in a vacuum. The success of the genre also clouded scholars' eyes in the uneasy truce between art and commerce. Production could be considered art, but exhibition was clearly commercial, and commercial motives, at the very least, were thought to compromise art.

Architectural as well as theatre historians have either benignly ignored and critically

1 "You Are the Star," Hollywood, 1993 (Thomas Suriya). In this wall mural, depicting the movie theatre as set design, moviegoers and movie stars reverse roles. It was commissioned by the Los Angeles Citywide Murals Project in 1984.

dismissed the architectural style of the movie theatre as mere folly or have described it as a variant or derivative of legitimate or live theatre and European opera-house architecture.[6] The very word *legitimate* implies that movies are illegitimate—a bastardization of centuries of drama. A more accurate analysis reveals that the American movie theatre largely derived its form from, and in turn had much impact on, the experience of watching a film. The development of the movie theatre was closely allied to changes within the film industry and remained unrelated to traditional theatre design.

Motion picture theatres were not only the product but also the victims of twentieth-century ideology. Culturally, this resulted in the denigration of movies as not being "high" art. Architectural criticism and theory grounded in minimalism and rationalism had no place for the movie theatre, just as drama criticism reflected disdain for the movies. Modernist architecture emphasized the merging of form and function; by implication, these theatres were seen as false and trivial instead of being read as an ideal expression of the function of film—which may be serious or not but should not be assumed to be false simply because it is not "real." When ornament was crime, honesty meant the expression of the materials—steel frames, not set design.

Since the 1920s and 1930s, most architectural criticism has been linked with the ideology of Modernism. This trend coincided with the period in which motion picture theatres were declaring their independence as a building type. The Bauhaus philosophy taught that history and style must be ignored and that new architecture should be allowed to emerge based on contemporary needs and possibilities. For decades, historical references in architecture were disparaged. It was not until the late 1960s that American architects, designers, and critics began to question the values of the Modern movement and the sparsity so characteristic of it. Up until that time, the *Chicago Tribune* Tower competition of 1922 had symbolized the good versus the bad (Eliel Saarinen's Modern proposal for the new building took second place to Raymond Hood and John Mead Howell's neo-Gothic design). Revisionists eventually forced a reevaluation of the meanings of these forms. By that time, however, theatre architects had changed to reflect the contemporary ethics and aesthetics of economy.[7]

To dismiss movie theatre architecture as trivial is to deny the economic and social reality of one of the nation's largest industries and the role of mass entertainment in urban life.[8] The motion picture theatre served as a significant architectural experience for millions of people. To consider it a derivative or variant of traditional theatre design is to miss the point as well. The movie theatre is a separate architectural type, distinguished by program, emphasis, imagery, and history; one must read the building as such, as an architectural type, rooted in popular culture with its own symbolic program, to appreciate the architecture. The movie theatre is not merely an apologetic footnote in the history of theatre. In fact, the architecture owes little to European precedents, with the exception of period revival details loosely rearranged and reapplied. The movie theatre should not be judged by the same criteria as the playhouse any more than live theatre should be judged by the standards of religious buildings, even though all three overlap in form.[9]

Both types of theatre, along with churches, concert halls, opera houses, and sporting arenas, share a central feature: rows of seats pointed in the direction of the ritual. And both can be divided into public space in front and support facilities backstage (fig. 2). There are fundamental differences, however. Traditional theatre design focused on the production of live entertainment; because of this requirement, backstage facilities were given precedence in terms of space, design, money, and energy. In motion picture theatres, which had little or no need of a backstage, support facilities were reduced to a two-dimensional wall and a projection booth. Thus, the need for an expensive fly tower and wings in which to store scenery was eliminated, as were dressing rooms, rehearsal halls, greenrooms, and shops used for set carpentry and for storage of wigs and costumes.

With this shift in concept, the audience then becomes the focus, and comfort and view become the primary considerations. Measurements that govern seating arrangements are less crucial, because there are no "bad" seats, given the size and angle of the screen. Sight lines are inherently better, acoustics clearer, and there is no stage lighting to interfere with either. Seats are not only better but cheaper. The show consists merely of shadows of light on a screen, which can be manipulated to create an intimate experience and to enable each viewer to see clearly.

Psychological differences also exist between the two types. In the movie theatre, ticket buyers take with them only a mood and a memory, which is reinforced by the physical surroundings. In live theatre, the audience and actors interact, feeding off each other and creating a new experience each time. But in a movie theatre, the film is always the same. The experience of moviegoing is shaped by interaction among members of the audience and by the environment itself.

In fact, the link between the motion picture theatre and the playhouse is more conceptual than programmatic. Those who dismiss movies as being frivolous or unreal are usually willing to accept the same "flaws" in drama, where certain theatrical conventions requiring suspension of disbelief are considered traditional. Motion pictures on the surface appear to be more realistic because of the nature of photography, its potential, and its accepted use in documenting events and reporting news. If one is also willing to suspend disbelief within the walls of a movie theatre, the architecture takes on new meaning. Theatrical conventions—including exaggeration, heroics, set design, abstraction, and entertainment that reveals truth—are, in fact, more clearly expressed in movie theatres than in traditional theatre design.

In watching drama through the "fourth wall," the audience in the playhouse accepts the fact that it is watching a story acted out by exaggerated characters. The set design,

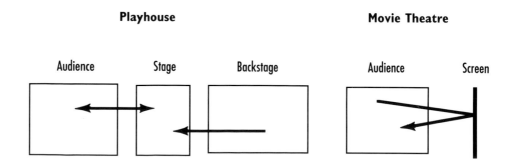

2 Playhouse versus movie theatre.

admittedly only painted canvas, uses distortion and false perspective to create effect and suggest place. Time is shortened or lengthened, and the "dead" time between scenes and acts does not interrupt the action except as dictated on the program. A good drama, comedy, or farce not only entertains but also reveals some truth about the human condition. These same conventions underlie motion picture theatre architecture.

Thomas Suriya's wall mural in Hollywood entitled "You Are the Star" illustrates this attitude (fig. 1). When walking through the lobby at the cinema, the audience is passing through the fourth wall and becoming part of the experience in a way that is not true in traditional theatres. It is sitting in a set design that extends beyond the screen. Individual architectural elements are exaggerated or taken out of time historically; or they are mixed to create a mood or an attitude. Members of the audience become actors in this set. The architecture uses easily recognizable archetypal forms, such as Chinese, Egyptian, or modern motifs. Time is collapsed, extended or, more often, suspended completely in that the environment is all-encompassing. Day becomes night, night is day, outdoors and indoors are confused. It is always surprising to leave a matinee and find the sun shining. The shock of the outside world jolts the senses back to reality.

As with good drama, good architectural entertainment reveals certain truths. These truths have to do with the quality of the space. To be true, the space should stimulate, delight, and create an appropriate mood; it should reveal or create a sense of place in the landscape.

The aesthetic roots of the motion picture theatre can be traced to nineteenth-century popular entertainment and live theatre, as well as to religious and commercial building traditions. But the structure was also dictated largely by the mechanical needs of motion picture projection and the economic forces that shaped theatre ownership.

Indeed, the fabric of the movie theatre is woven from three concurrent strands: the history of film exhibition and the organization of the studio industry; the development of a new building type; and the evolution and evaluation of architecture in the United States. The theatres of S. Charles Lee illustrate the relationships of these three components.

AN OVERVIEW OF MOTION PICTURE THEATRE HISTORY

The motion picture theatre is an American phenomenon. Historically, theatre attendance was consistently higher in the United States than elsewhere, and American cities contained more movie theatres per capita than any other country. The architectural trends discussed in this book began in the United States and were copied throughout the world. Furthermore, the semiotics of the motion picture theatre were also unique. In the United States, movie theatres were equated with egalitarianism and democracy, expressed originally through appropriating European symbols of social status and class differentiation and later through commercial modernism.

Motion pictures began to be shown commercially at the turn of the century, as part of other established forms of popular entertainment, such as the penny arcade and vaudeville theatre, which had evolved their own built forms and traditions. The earliest movies were "shorts," lasting only a few minutes and cast with a few stock actors portraying a single scene or event. Gradually, shorts became popular by themselves and began to be shown in a new milieu, away from the penny arcade and vaudeville. The first movie theatres were established in existing buildings—either converted retail shops or vaudeville theatres—which were adapted for film projection. As the medium became more popular, buildings were designed exclusively for the special needs of motion picture exhibition. Stylistically, these designs evolved from incidental or accidental beginnings (buildings intended for other purposes, for example, suddenly became theatres with the addition of posters and signs) into an original building type based on the realization that architecture could be an important advertising feature (fig. 3).[10]

Popular entertainment forms catered to a mass audience and focused on novelty and mechanical devices. Their architectural forms, based primarily on functional requirements, went in and out of vogue rapidly. By comparison, the roots of legitimate theatre went back hundreds of years, and its architecture was dictated as much by culture and custom as by pragmatic concerns. Once established, the motion picture theatre evolved in both type and style, drawing from popular as well as elitist traditions, though clearly belonging to the former. As I shall demonstrate, certain architectural features are characteristic of the movie theatre type, regardless of the style of the building.

The appearance of feature-length films, which told an artistically edited story, coincided with the development of "feature" motion picture theatres—the "moving picture theatre" and early palaces that celebrated the theatre form through conscious design and architectural distinction. Movies in the 1910s and 1920s were silent adventures and romances, seldom very realistic and often set in an imaginary, exotic locale. Movie palaces were equally exotic and romantic in mood so as not to break the spell until the patron left the building. Customer amenities, such as nurseries, lounges, ushers, and elaborate gathering spots, reinforced this pampering. Architects of this period employed then-popular historicist styles, stretching these styles to their limits in unheard-of romantic fantasies (figs. 18–20, 29).

Modern architecture, however, also found acceptance in the motion picture theatre, which, in keeping with trends in Moderne set design, always aspired to the new. The intricate Busby Berkeley musicals and glossy Fred Astaire and Ginger Rogers romances were at home in the Art Deco palaces of the late 1920s and 1930s. Again, the spell remained, though the mood had shifted from historical adventure to romance. As movie stars emerged in the 1910s and 1920s, so did star theatres, announcing their uniqueness through architecture and marketing.

Movie attendance peaked in the 1940s as the public embraced messages of patriotism and romance, and theatre chains responded to the demand. Neighborhood movie houses reflected America's new emphasis on family by showing up in suburban locations. As "movies" became "films," with more serious attitudes, the seemingly anachronistic ornate architecture and design disappeared from the building. Both product and process were stripped of their artificial decoration in favor of a more honest, if brutal, examination of life.

In the 1950s, with the introduction of television, the disbanding of studio-owned

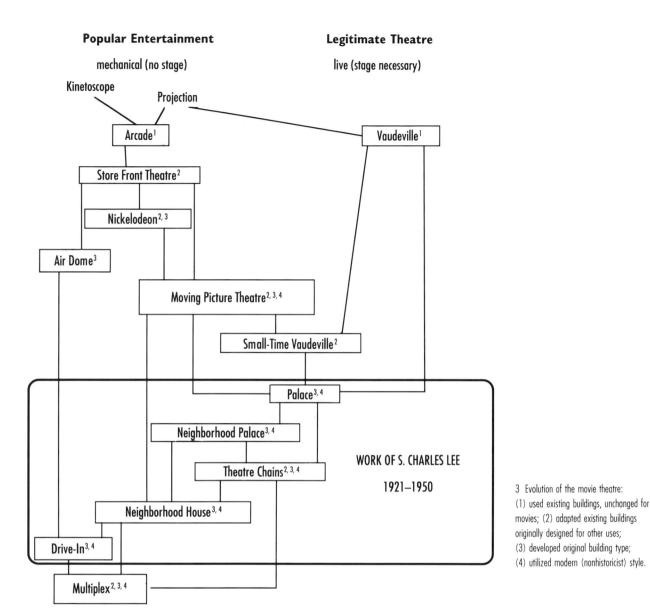

Popular Entertainment

mechanical (no stage)

Legitimate Theatre

live (stage necessary)

Kinetoscope

Projection

Arcade[1]

Vaudeville[1]

Store Front Theatre[2]

Nickelodeon[2, 3]

Air Dome[3]

Moving Picture Theatre[2, 3, 4]

Small-Time Vaudeville[2]

Palace[3, 4]

Neighborhood Palace[3, 4]

Theatre Chains[2, 3, 4]

WORK OF S. CHARLES LEE

1921–1950

Neighborhood House[3, 4]

Drive-In[3, 4]

Multiplex[2, 3, 4]

3 Evolution of the movie theatre:
(1) used existing buildings, unchanged for movies; (2) adapted existing buildings originally designed for other uses; (3) developed original building type; (4) utilized modern (nonhistoricist) style.

theatre chains, and the emphasis on suburbanization, movie attendance declined, and the theatres became much simpler. Eventually, customer amenities were reduced to nothing more than the refreshment stand. The vestiges of lighted marquees were all that gave away the presence of a motion picture theatre, as the buildings evolved back into storefront-like spaces. Commerce won over art. In the late 1980s, however, architects, builders, and owners began to recognize that a vital part of theatre attendance had been lost in both quantity and quality—and that there was a correlation. The career of S. Charles Lee spanned this transition from talkies to television. A celebrated motion picture theatre architect, Lee influenced and defined the style and type of the motion picture theatre for three decades.

S. CHARLES LEE

The birth of S. Charles Lee in 1899 was contemporaneous with the birth of commercial moving pictures in the United States (fig. 4). Lee grew up in Chicago, a city that shaped his interest in both architecture and the movies. Following his studies at the Chicago School of Architecture, he worked as an office boy for Henry Newhouse, who designed nickelodeons and small motion picture theatres, and later as a draftsman for the firm of Rapp and Rapp, noted for their grand movie palaces.

Lee moved to Los Angeles in the 1920s, at the time Hollywood studios were acquiring chains of theatres and beginning to build neighborhood theatres. Although Lee designed many types of buildings in his thirty-year career as an architect—among them, office and commercial structures, residential hotels, houses, and factories—his most distinctive and creative energy was expressed in the movie theatres he designed, which constituted most of his work. His commissions ranged from 1920s movie palaces and Depression-era storefront conversions and remodelings to postwar neighborhood theatres and drive-ins. He worked extensively for Fox West Coast Theatres as it established an empire of theatre chains, doing his best work in the 1940s, at the peak of the industry's popularity. Stylistically, his career spans the transition from Beaux-Arts Neoclassicism and period revival to non-historicist Modernism. He retired from architecture about 1950, when the economics of theatre building were altered by antitrust legislation and television; thereafter, he focused his professional energies on a career as a developer.

4 S. Charles Lee, ca. 1920.

Lee designed approximately three hundred movie theatres throughout the United States, as well as a few in Latin America.[11] Most of these were scattered throughout California, the home, if not the birthplace, of the film industry. The pattern of Lee's career parallels not only the evolution of the motion picture theatre into a distinct American archetype but also the growth and decline of the industry as measured by theatre attendance. His work exemplified the maturation of the movie theatre and reflected changes in American life, architectural theories, and the film industry.

Certain motifs are repeated in the history of the building type and, specifically, in Lee's work, including such characteristic elements as the marquee, the box office, and organ grilles. Features that started as functional requirements evolved into symbolic canons. Likewise, the quality of movie theatre as set design can be seen throughout this history. The customers were the actors, the primary users-participants, and the building was a backdrop.

Lee's unofficial motto, "The show starts on the sidewalk," had both a literal and symbolic meaning.[12] It is, in fact, a distillation of movie theatre design and philosophy. The physical environment of the theatre began, literally, at the sidewalk, where a colorful terrazzo pattern set it apart from the usually dirty concrete sidewalks of the surrounding commercial district; overhead, a marquee formed a canopy. Symbolically, the theatre was set apart from all other adventures of the city. Cinema was an industry that sold an experience and a memory, not a product. The psychological environment had to be part of the successful sale, offering the patron an event worth remembering and repeating. The architecture thus shaped the experience and reinforced one's memory of it. Lee was a master of manipulating space and form to create an atmosphere that was profitable for the client, comfortable for the user, and distinctive in setting.

In discussing his theatres, Lee frequently referred to the "psychology of entertainment" to describe the physical attributes and amenities that seduced customers and made them feel a part of the theatrical experience. As used here, the term refers to the mental and emotional processes involved in using and moving through the space. Lee translated this psychology into specific design features, which he then exploited as ready-made advertising to serve his clients and to further his career. Such elements as visibility, comfort, luxury, and seduction came to define the genre and were incorporated to varying degrees into virtually all motion picture theatres.

Another theme that emerged in the Lee's designs was his pragmatism. Although one notices his exuberant imagery first, the plan and technical innovations were primary to his work. Plans were designed for efficiency and cost control. Often spaces were organized to accomplish several ends with a minimum of effort, such as simultaneous supervision of the parking area and the interior, or the accommodation of various social needs within the lobby.

The outside, however, was designed for fun. The facade of the theatre was intended to stand out in the streetscape, allowing Lee to be flamboyant in his designs. He understood the need for ballyhoo in the theatre and translated it successfully into architecture. His buildings sold his skills as an architect, and he capitalized on their inherent salesmanship, using publication and promotion to secure additional clients.

Like any other building, theatres represented first and foremost an investment for the owner, who hoped for a financial return. Clients were capitalists, not philanthropic patrons of the arts. If Lee could create an artistic commodity in addition to a sound structure, so much the better. Architecture was serious business, but he was also able to provide joy and wonder for the users.

Stylistically, the movie theatre was to be the newest, most fashionable expression of civilized living. It was important to owners that theatres be at the cutting edge of popular architecture. Style sold tickets and gave a theatre identity. In the 1920s, this meant interpretations of the Paris Opera, Versailles, Spanish Colonial villas, or other forms that could be advertised as unique, exotic and, above all, cultural. From the late 1920s through the late 1930s, Art Deco and Streamlined Moderne designs carried modernistic lines to their commercial extremes. Period revival theatres, exotic in the 1920s, were remodeled to appear futuristic in the 1930s. By the 1940s and 1950s, the movie theatre had lost most of the now-extraneous flamboyance, and what was left were the key elements of shape, light, and color.

Movie theatres enhanced city life as well, providing the latest architectural interpretation of elegant and sophisticated living and drawing all classes of people to urban or suburban downtowns after dark. The buildings not only defined and adorned the skyline but also lent a touch of Hollywood glamour to staid commercial districts. In small towns, the single movie theatre, modest as it may have been, was a microcosm of the allure and excitement of the big-city theatre district.

Between 1920 and 1950, the role of the motion picture theatre in community life expanded. Besides being one of the most glamorous buildings in town, it served as a source of public information, a gathering spot for neighbors, and a landmark of the physical and social growth of the city and its inhabitants. New buildings and remodelings revealed fluctuating business cycles, migration patterns, and changing standards of beauty. The movie theatre captured both the positive and negative social values that characterized the first half of the century. Although promoted as democratic institutions that made culture and luxury accessible to all classes, the theatres were often segregated. Staff assignments exposed further racist and sexist values (white male managers and ushers; white female ticket sellers; black male janitors and shoe shine attendants).

During World War II, newsreels brought reports from the front and shaped public opinion, encouraging patriotism while stimulating ethnocentrism. On a more intimate level, theatres became a primary place for courting. Feature films educated the nation about sex roles and practices—as approved by the studios and the Hays Office;[13] these messages were filled with innuendo about sophistication, wealth, and sexual exploration. The dark rows of the balcony or the "passion pits" at the drive-in became well-known testing grounds for such exploration.

A catalog of S. Charles Lee's motion picture theatres reflects the aesthetic and social progression from the palaces of the 1920s to the independent and chain theatres of the Depression to the postwar neighborhood houses and drive-ins of the late 1940s. The product may have been flashy, but beneath the surface was a solid foundation based on economics and common sense. For Lee, the art of architecture was built on business. His relationship with clients was grounded in the practical, from determining the maximum return on an investment to making the most efficient use of the site and building materials. The client, he believed, should always get the most show for the money. The movie theatres he designed during these three decades rank among the most beautiful, inventive, and creative in the United States. They are symbols of time and place that incorporated a sense of wonder and personal involvement, which have been too often overlooked in the study of twentieth-century architecture.

**11
Coming
Attractions**

2
Short Subjects
The Theatre
and the
Architect

S. Charles Lee was born Simeon Charles Levi in Chicago on 5 September 1899 and was very much the product of his family and birthplace. His father, Julius Levi, known as Billy, was born in Springfield, Missouri, in 1865. His mother, Hattie Stiller, was born in Portland, Oregon, in 1870. Both families were of German ancestry. The Stillers moved to Chicago via covered wagon and railroad just after the fire of 1871. There they bought a furniture store named Goldstein's, and rather than change the handsome and costly sign over the door, they changed their surname to Goldstein.[1] Whatever emotional attachment they had to the family name was secondary to their sense of pragmatism, economics, and business; this precedent influenced Lee many years later when he too decided to change his name.

Billy Levi and Hattie Stiller married sometime around 1890 and had two children, Hazel and Simeon Charles, nicknamed "Sim." Although the Levis were not what Lee referred to as "church people," they were proud of their Jewish heritage and its values, stressing to their children the importance of integrity, morality, and irreproachable character. At Hattie's insistence, the family went to temple once a year on High Holy Days; as Lee later remarked, "As long as she was alive I had to go."[2] Billy was a traveling salesman for a wholesale ready-to-wear business and Hattie was "a perfect thirty-six," traveling with him and modeling the merchandise for department store buyers in such faraway and exotic places as Walla Walla, Washington, and Los Angeles, California.

Lee recalled a very happy childhood. "If I had to design a life for a child—I had the best." He remembered his father as being patient, kind, and soft-spoken, never violent. Billy was an experimenter and inventor—he patented an idea for a hat-pin holder—and the son acquired his father's inquisitive mind. His mother, he recalled, was patient and encouraging with her children. "She always had a saying on her lips like 'Hitch your wagon to a star.'"[3] He inherited her pragmatic outlook on life and her longevity. She lived to be one hundred years old; Lee lived to be ninety. He and his sister were close, he said, even though she was seven years his senior and they had few friends in common.

The older Levi taught his son business values at an early age, encouraging him to go into business for himself. He lent his son five dollars to buy a box of cigars at the wholesale price of three cents each. The father promised that if the boy stored the cigars correctly at the proper humidity, he would buy them from him at the retail price of five cents each. After repaying the five-dollar capital investment, Sim had earned a small profit and learned a lesson about the basic structure of American business that stayed with him the rest of his life. Other ventures of the young businessman included selling eggs door-to-door and delivering the *Saturday Evening Post.*[4]

Another influence on him was the city of Chicago, birthplace of the American skyscraper and the commercial Chicago School and the showplace of architects Daniel Burnham, Louis Sullivan, and Frank Lloyd Wright. Chicago's architecture combined grand plans, functional design, and artistic innovation to express the power of commerce in uniquely American department stores and office towers. Less than twenty years old at the turn of the century, the city was new and modern and the center of architectural innovation for the rest of the country. Louis Sullivan, one of Lee's mentors, said, "The passion to *sell* is the impelling power in American life."[5] With partner Dankmar Adler, he expressed this power in Chicago buildings such as the Auditorium (1886) and the Schiller Theater Building (1891–92), multiuse buildings housing culture with commerce.

Lee was familiar with these Chicago landmarks as a child. His favorite, he said, was the Schlesinger and Mayer (Carson Pirie Scott) Department Store. Its bold massing contrasted with delicate cast-iron filigree motifs to provide a setting of respectability designed to attract women shoppers.[6] In discussing the building, Sullivan biographer Willard Connely commented: "His aim was to court unhurried femininity, to lure the susceptible women. . . . The effect was festive . . . but the psychology of it was that an individual shopper should feel that her own visit was being celebrated."[7] From this approach, Lee learned early about the use of architecture as a sales incentive. His philosophy about the psychology of entertainment and the show starting on the sidewalk may have subconsciously been grounded in downtown Chicago.

Like Sullivan's and Wright's, Lee's mature work emanated from the plan. It was modern but not stark, simple but not dull. A building by Lee was rational and integrated, an entity in which each part served the whole. Ornament consisted of focused expression and often symbolic quotation, not a hodgepodge of applied decoration.

While Lee was growing up, Chicago was also an important focus of the early motion picture industry. At the turn of the century motion picture production was centered in New York, Philadelphia, and Chicago, which was the home of the Essanay and Selig Polyscope companies, although both moved to Los Angeles in 1911. It was also home of the first legislative attempts to censor films and to regulate motion picture theatres. In 1907, Chicago's 116 nickelodeons, 18 ten-cent vaudeville houses, and 19 penny arcades counted a daily attendance of 100,000. An editorial that year in the *Chicago Tribune* attacked the theatres collectively, saying, "They cannot be defended. They are hopelessly bad."[8] Reformer Jane Addams prompted legislation to suppress them. The ordinance she secured requiring the superintendent of police to issue permits for motion picture exhibition was, however, overturned by the Supreme Court.[9] Chicago's theatre district, like those in all major cities, had both live houses and motion picture theatres and distinguished between them both legally and socially.

Before the mid-nineteenth century, the American theatre catered to all social classes. Upper- and lower-class patrons (if they could afford admission) were separated only by seating arrangements and ticket prices. During the second half of the century, various forms of popular entertainment developed in counterpoint to the traditional forms.

Designed to appeal to an uneducated mass audience, these new diversions included the circus, traveling show, "dime museum," melodrama, midway, penny arcade, and phonograph parlor. To create a sense of cultural legitimacy, some of these forms pretended to the title of "serious" culture. The dime museum, for example, an American institution developed by P. T. Barnum that was popular by the 1840s, utilized a museum format set in a circus midway atmosphere.[10] Similarly, melodrama exaggerated and simplified drama to present moral lessons through overdrawn characterizations and sentiment. Both dime museums and melodrama were housed in traditional commercial blocks in the prevailing downtown style. Penny arcades and phonograph parlors, full of coin-operated games and vending machines, were located in storefront amusement halls.[11]

The modern circus, another popular entertainment format dating from the late nineteenth century, featured a tent show with animals, acrobats, and clowns, in addition to a midway, which hosted sideshows. The circus created its own architectural forms based on practical and economic needs: tents could be packed and moved quickly; circulation paths encouraged patrons to take in everything.

All of these forms were aimed at providing low-cost entertainment and novelty to a mass audience. That audience consisted of a new urban population created by the industrial revolution, including immigrants and people with little higher education but increasing amounts of leisure time. Garish advertising and barkers, who stood at the entry and teased passersby with promises of the marvels inside, attracted paying customers. The featured talent, ranging from midgets to popular singers, capitalized on the emergence of a mass, nonintellectual market that was not following the Broadway season. Newly invented machinery, amazing phenomena, and sensationalized murderesses on display proved to be appealing and highly marketable assets.

Serious theatre in the United States, on the other hand, focused on the opera, drama, and concerts. Each of these presented different architectural requirements in terms of acoustics, orchestral needs, stage size, and the relationship of the audience to the performers. The opera house, developed in Europe, required elaborate stage facilities, a large hall with excellent acoustic resonance that blended music appropriately, and an orchestra pit that could accommodate the large-scale productions of European opera. Playhouses needed absorbent surroundings, so that each word could be heard distinctly, and less-elaborate stage facilities. The acoustics of concert halls depended on the type of music performed and were most effective when each member of the audience was equidistant from the source of the music; the only backstage facilities needed were dressing rooms and occasional rehearsal halls.[12]

Functional needs were frequently sacrificed, however, for the decorative and status-filled conventions of boxes and balconies. The opera house and concert hall appealed to a cultural and educated elite and employed symbolism in the appointments of a building to assure the presence of high culture. Such trappings were borrowed from European prototypes. In American small towns, the local auditorium was often called the Opera House, Town Hall, or Academy of Music, giving it an aura of respectability, even if opera and classical concerts were seldom heard (fig. 5). More often, it housed melodrama, circuit vaudeville, or Chatauqua, a lecture circuit of educational and morally uplifting speakers.[13]

In contrast to traditional theatre design, whose lineage could be traced to antiquity, motion picture theatre architecture drew on these popular forms. It selectively merged old conventions with new symbols, recycling the architectural remnants of each. The mechanical and acoustic considerations of motion picture theatres differed substantially from those of the playhouse because of the need to accommodate a loud, dangerous projector and a piano or organ, which accompanied silent films. The two types of theatre shared certain theatrical customs, however. In the 1910s, many live houses were converted into motion picture houses, and before the introduction of sound movies, some exhibitors offered a combined program of live performance and film. The buildings that housed such performances resembled the playhouse—with rows of seats facing a stage with an apron—and were referred to in the professional press as "moving picture theatres."

But this relationship is somewhat misleading. Mature motion picture theatre architecture also derived from other nineteenth-century forms, including storefronts, churches, hotels, royal palaces, and period revival styles. Conceptually it had sources in the twentieth-century machine aesthetic, a passion for the exotic, and the desire for novelty. Both traditions utilized popular contemporary images of respectability and glamour, whether their targeted audience was the wealthy or the middle-class patron. But the architectural elements of the motion picture theatre went beyond its legitimate counterpart. Features such as the box office and marquee combined elements associated with both popular and serious entertainments. Marketing and advertising techniques were borrowed from commercial traditions and the circus. The iconography of wealth

5 Opera house, Lowville, New York, ca. 1900.

and conspicuous consumption in the form of grand fountains and statuary in niches was reminiscent of the palatial homes built for the robber barons in the late nineteenth century. Rich materials and fabrics, plush seats, draperies, chandeliers, lounges, and smoking rooms echoed grand hotels, government institutions, and private monied clubs.

THE KINETOSCOPE

Such grandeur, however, evolved from a much simpler setting. On 14 April 1894, Thomas Edison's Kinetoscope, a moving picture machine, was shown for the first time at Andrew M. Holland's phonograph parlor at 1155 Broadway in New York City. Viewers dropped a coin into the machine and, by peering through a peephole, saw "moving pictures." Although Etienne-Jules Marey, a French physiologist, had invented the camera equipment in 1882 and various inventors and tinkerers had made changes and improvements in both the camera and viewing equipment, Edison's Kinetoscope was the first commercial version. The 4-foot contraption cost $250 and ran short films for individual viewers. Holland's phonograph parlor was a former shoe shop decorated with a plaster bust of Edison, giving it a pseudoscientific ambiance. It featured advertisements in the window, a ticket booth in front, and two rows of machines inside. Each 25-cent ticket entitled the patron to view one row of machines. The venture was immediately profitable, earning $120 the first day.[14] By the end of the year, the Kinetoscope Company had installed more than 60 machines in parlors, department stores, drugstores, hotels, barrooms, and phonograph parlors in major cities throughout the United States.[15]

Films were also exhibited in tents at traveling shows and fairs. These early films were short and without plot, focusing simply on the "magic" of three-dimensional movement in a two-dimensional medium—for example, people walking, horses running, trapeze artists, and circus performers. Although initially brisk and profitable, business dropped off after about a year and a half, and by the turn of the century the apparatus had all but disappeared.[16] Viewing remained a solitary event, and the magic machines were soon taken for granted. During these early years the European development of film exhibition paralleled the American phenomenon. The impetus quickly moved to the United States, however, in part owing to the established market for popular entertainment, including vaudeville, that easily incorporated and supported motion pictures.

The success of the Kinetoscope parlor between 1894 and 1900 suggested, even in its crude beginnings, the inherent power of the industry. As time went by, motion picture actors would become some of the world's most famous personages, and motion picture theatres would emulate the world's most opulent architecture.

VAUDEVILLE

Vaudeville, the most popular entertainment form at the turn of the century, emerged from the variety show and music hall in the United States, England, and Canada of the

1850s and 1860s. Both of these forms were rooted in working-class traditions but had been cleaned up to be "suitable for ladies" by the 1880s.[17] Vaudeville shows comprised a variety program featuring singing, dancing, comedy skits, and novelty acts. Organized and operated by several national chains, the largest being the Orpheum and Keith-Albee circuits, the shows traveled from city to city and were booked in vaudeville theatres owned or leased by the circuit. "Continuous" vaudeville meant that shows ran all day long; "big-time" or "two-a-day" vaudeville had scheduled performances and reserved seats. By 1900, there were sixty-seven vaudeville theatres operating in the United States, two in Canada, and two in London.[18]

Because competition was keen, managers continually sought novelties to attract customers. Vaudeville was therefore a perfect venue for the new motion picture. The Vitascope, an improvement on the Kinetoscope, projected the pictures onto a screen remote from the projector, allowing an entire audience to share the experience. Thomas Armat's invention, marketed by Edison, premiered on 23 April 1896 at Koster and Bial's Music Hall at Union Square in New York. Front-row patrons were said to have ducked to avoid being splashed by the waves on the twenty-foot screen.[19] The effect was so spectacular that in one month attendance doubled from thirty-five hundred to seven thousand a week.[20] By June, other vaudeville theatres had added motion pictures, thrilling audiences with the new medium. Vaudeville operators advertised not the subject, performers, or title of the film, which would not have made any difference to the viewer, but the machinery itself, emphasizing the distinct features of each. The machines carried a variety of brand names, such as Lumière's Cinématographe, reflecting both the sense of novelty and the entrepreneurial state of the film industry at that time. (In 1908, however, Edison organized the Motion Picture Patents Company trust, which consolidated film production and distribution.) The new toy, introduced as a novelty act, continued as a staple of vaudeville for the next ten years.[21] Film of the Spanish-American War, often shown within hours of the actual event, helped to establish the popularity of films.

In 1900, B. F. Keith and Edward Albee, along with other theatre owners, organized the United Booking Office to control vaudeville bookings and split the 10-percent agent's fee between agents and owners. Performers, organized into a group named the White Rats (*star* spelled backward), responded to this and other perceived abuses of management by going on strike. To keep the theatres from going dark, managers dimmed the lights and relied increasingly on the mechanical entertainment. This forced reliance on motion pictures helped to establish a market in the United States long before it took a comparable foothold in Europe.[22] The timing was perfect for motion picture producers; the strike created a demand in real theatres, which required no capital investment, not in penny arcades, which had a lesser reputation and required the frequent purchase of new equipment. When the strike failed that same year, however, movies were once again relegated to a single spot on the bill. Although still very popular, they were also used as "chasers" to indicate the end of the program and to chase the audience out of the theatre.[23]

Vaudeville theatres reflected their communities in scale and architectural style; between 1880 and 1920 they were designed in the tradition of legitimate theatres, which was understandable since vaudeville was an offshoot of the legitimate theatre, even though it was not considered part of that tradition. Beaux-Arts buildings faced in brick or stone, they usually had simple square marquees and sandwich-board posters set in front. The Orpheum Theatre in Los Angeles and the Colonial Theatre in Chicago are representative of the type (figs. 6, 8). Unlike the later freestanding version, the ticket booth was located along the recessed wall of the outer lobby or inside the lobby in the tradition of live theatre design. Because reserved-seat tickets were sold in advance, the ticket seller needed to be near the business office. The buildings typically supported huge roof signs announcing the name of the theatre, often spelled out in lights and framed in a decorative motif, thus emphasizing the large scale of these buildings (fig. 7). In smaller cities, the shows might be housed in the Town Hall auditorium.

Many vaudeville theatres were deliberately made ornate in order to attract a more refined audience that would associate them with high-class entertainment. B. F. Keith's theatres, for example, were nicknamed the "Sunday-School Circuit." Lavish vaudeville theatres, beginning with Keith-Albee's "de luxe" Colonial Theatre in Boston in 1894, appeared in major American cities, invading the theatre districts formerly dedicated to the playhouse. As applied to these theatres, the term *de luxe* translated into ornate architecture, lavish interior design, and a barrage of customer services, including refreshments (figs. 8–10). Until that time, such appointments and services had been found only in private, monied environments—and certainly not in playhouses. Forerunners of the movie palaces, the vaudeville palaces were also built during a period of severe economic depression. In the 1890s, when people were losing their jobs or having their salaries cut, the palaces provided escape and luxury. Such appointments as marble ticket

6 Orpheum Theatre, Los Angeles, ca. 1920 (Albert Lansburgh, 1911). Vaudeville theatre on the Orpheum Circuit.

537 — Orpheum Theatre, Los Angeles, California.

7 Orpheum Theatre, Los Angeles, 1989 (ca. 1911). Huge rooftop signs such as this, lighted at night, were used to create excitement and to announce the location of the theatre.

8 Colonial Theatre, Chicago, 1903. Vaudeville theatre.

9 Keith's Theatre, Boston, 1894. De luxe vaudeville palace.

10 Keith's Theatre, Boston, 1907 (1894). This promotional postcard demonstrates the theatre owners' dependence upon both the performances and the architecture to draw customers.

GRAND STAIRCASE, KEITH'S THEATRE

Boston,   1907
Dear
    We are pleased to learn that you will be in Boston Old Home Week, July 28th. Remembering how much you enjoyed the performances and admired Keith's Theatre when you were last here, we have secured seats for Old Home Week.
    Keith's is more beautiful than when opened thirteen years ago.
    Cordially yours,

booths, mirrored foyers, oil paintings, plush auditorium seats, and personal services boosted attendance. For example, E. F. Proctor's Pleasure Palace (New York, 1895, McElfatrick and Sons) featured a Romanesque facade and housed an auditorium, roof garden, café, library, barbershop, and Turkish bath.[24] Described as "palaces for the people," the vaudeville palaces were rivaled only by grand hotels in luxury and service. They were like private clubs suddenly opened to the middle class.

The ultimate measure of success on the vaudeville circuit was to "play the Palace," meaning that the act was booked at the eighteen-hundred-seat Palace Theatre in New York, the flagship of the Keith-Albee Circuit, designed by Kirchoff and Rose in 1913.[25] The numerous uses of the word *palace* linked to this genre indicate the importance of the image being cultivated. Originally the word referred to ancient imperial residences on the Palatine Hill in Rome. The implications of magnificence, ornateness, and access to a special place in the city—all rights of royalty from the Renaissance on—were thus passed on to the masses when the term was applied to vaudeville palaces and movie palaces.[26]

By World War I, a formula of fanciful design for popular entertainment that was calculated to enhance yet balanced by economic considerations had already begun to be applied to theatre design. A 1918 guide to building and managing a vaudeville theatre reminded its readers: "In particular does the vaudeville house draw from both the classes and the masses. A theatre should represent to the less favored of its patrons, something finer and more desirable than their ordinary surroundings; and to the better class, it should never present itself as inferior to the environment to which such persons are accustomed."[27] The site was chosen so as "to cater to all classes of people" and to encourage spontaneous ticket purchases by being locating on main transportation lines downtown. Theatres frequently were designed to accommodate irregular lots because land was cheaper at the rear of a prime downtown site.[28]

The exterior lobby, recognized as the front yard of the theatre, read like an index of the conditions one could expect to find inside. A good first impression was important and maximized advertising potential. Color schemes and fixtures came directly from the opera house and concert hall: plush red velvet seats, bronzed fixtures, brass railings, and murals of historical or allegorical scenes. Expensive galleries and second balconies were generally avoided because the seats generated less revenue than boxes, which, poised on the side walls overlooking the stage and orchestra seats, added dignity and a decorative effect. Significant remnants of the opera house, boxes served primarily a social purpose: it was important to be seen or to feel worthy of being seen, regardless of the terrible acoustics and poor view of the stage. Movie palaces would later include boxes that served the same impractical purpose.

Believing that the novelty would soon die, vaudeville producers did not originally consider film a threat to live entertainment. By the 1910s, however, vaudeville houses were being converted into motion picture theatres. Vaudeville had become increasingly expensive to produce; movies and radio were cheaper mass entertainment. By the 1920s, vaudeville was in its last days as a major force in the theatre. Each week big-time theatres were being locked up or converted to movie houses. If the movies killed the vaudeville show, they retained trophies of the kill in the form of buildings. Converting vaudeville theatres established a precedent of lavishness and excess that would reach its apex in the grand architectural expression of the fantasy world of entertainment, the movie palace.

At the turn of the century small cities and towns not included on the vaudeville circuits welcomed itinerant film exhibitors equipped with portable machines and a few reels of film. These entrepreneurs would rent vacant stores and equip them with folding chairs often borrowed from the local undertaker, the only person in town with a sufficient supply (fig. 11). With a muslin sheet hung on the back wall, windows darkened, and a box set up in the doorway to serve as an "office" for selling tickets, the motion picture theatre was born—a space designed or redesigned solely for the purpose of showing movies.[29] The box soon became a permanent ticket booth but retained the name box office.[30]

Even before Los Angeles established itself as the film capital, it was home to the first theatre devoted solely to movies. Tally's Electric Theatre at 262 South Main Street, which opened in April 1902, was advertised as a:

NEW PLACE OF AMUSEMENT
Up to date high class moving picture
entertainment, especially for ladies and
children. See the *Capture of the Biddle Bros.,*
New York in a Blizzard, and many other
interesting and exciting scenes. An Hour's
amusement and genuine fun for
10 CENTS ADMISSION[31]

The Electric was so successful that Thomas Tally abandoned his other arcades and phonograph parlors and went exclusively into the business of motion picture theatres.[32] Others followed suit.

11 Hopper's Opera House, Cimarron, Kansas, ca. 1911. Hardly what one would expect to see in an "opera house," this auditorium resembles the itinerant film exhibitor's temporary movie theatre.

Many of these storefront theatres became permanent fixtures rather than temporary rentals. Promoters and critics searched for new names to describe the new form, including "spectatorium" and "theatrelet." Blaring music boxes, garish posters, and barkers—traditions of the circus, the midway, or the traveling show—filled the lobby to entice customers. The overhead for these storefront theatres was low: the buildings were simple, there were no performers to pay, and only two or three salaried employees were needed to run the operation. An admission price of ten cents catered to a mass audience and eventually drove vaudeville, with an admission price of two to five dollars a ticket, out of business.

Some owner-entrepreneurs reinvested their profits to improve the building and attract more customers. Innovations included more-comfortable surroundings, enhanced sound effects produced from the back of the screen or from the orchestra pit, and narrators for silent films, who sat perched on a shelf by the screen. Between pictures, singers would appear onstage and render a musical selection accompanied by a "stunt" organ that produced sound effects.[33] By 1912, most remodeled storefront theatres had disappeared, replaced by small theatres built for motion pictures after the model of Tally's. The Cameo Theatre in Los Angeles, which opened as Clune's Broadway in 1910, was built to show motion pictures and operated continuously for over eighty years doing just that; having been kept intact, it was a wonderful example of the interiors of these early theatres until it closed in 1991.

THE AIR DOME

An offshoot of the storefront theatre was the open-air theatre, sometimes referred to as an air dome, which consisted of four walls, without a roof, and seats placed directly on the ground between a projector coop and a simple screen (fig. 12).[34] This relaxed structure catered to summertime entertainment much like the rooftop gardens, restaurants, and theatres found in some of the larger vaudeville theatres in New York.[35] Stale air, produced by hot machinery and warm bodies, was always a problem in the unventilated storefronts. Open to the sky, the air-dome structure was economical, requiring only an open lot with a high fence, and less of a fire hazard than enclosed theatres.

THE NICKELODEON

In 1905, John P. Harris and Harry Davis added another innovation to the new motion picture scene; in the process they coined a name that identified an entire genre of theatres during that period and continues to be used as a show business reference in the 1990s. Instead of scheduling nightly performances at their storefront theatre in Pittsburgh, Harris and Davis began showing a program of movies that ran continuously from 8 A.M. until midnight, in the tradition of continuous vaudeville Charging a five-cent admission, they called this new format a "nickelodeon." The ninety-six-seat theatre, originally a store room, was cheaply redecorated with stucco, burlap, and paint to convey a sense of

12 Airdome Theatre, Danville, Illinois, ca. 1910. The air-dome theatre was a roofless structure that from the exterior resembled a traditional movie theatre.

pseudoelegant interior design. Opera chairs arranged in rows served as seating, and a white linen sheet as a screen.[36]

Thousands of customers were soon paying to watch a fifteen-minute film, *The Great Train Robbery.* "Nickel madness," as it was called, seemed to sweep the nation.[37] Within two years, there were three thousand nickelodeons.[38] One year later, in 1908, an estimated eight thousand nickelodeons occupied former stores and new buildings throughout the United States (fig. 13). By 1910, five years after their introduction, nickelodeons were taking in $91 million nationally.[39] They were so popular that the gross revenue of a single theatre per week could be estimated by multiplying 3.5–4 cents by the population of the city.[40]

At the same time, film distribution became more efficient and less costly through the development of film exchanges. An exchange purchased films from the producers and rented them to exhibitors for one-fifth of the list price. Previously films had been ordered from a catalog and purchased outright by the foot, requiring major investments to keep new titles before the public. To recover their expense, theatre owners ran the same film until it disintegrated. Exchanges solved those problems and decreased the costs. By 1907, there were nearly 150 film exchanges operating in the United States.[41]

The first nickelodeons were no different physically from the storefront theatres (fig. 14). What was unique was the marketing strategy, which resulted in increased attendance and a building boom (fig. 15). References to "Ladies and Gentlemen with their families" is indicative of the attempt of advertisers to upgrade movies and theatres from their saloon-hall roots.[42] The glass front and framing for doors and windows of vacant stores were frequently removed to afford greater visibility and easier access to the auditorium. This was replaced with a closed front set back from the sidewalk, creating a lobby or vestibule accompanying the box office.[43]

Speculative builders and local carpenters erected new buildings using supply house

Charleroi, Pa. Palace Theatre.

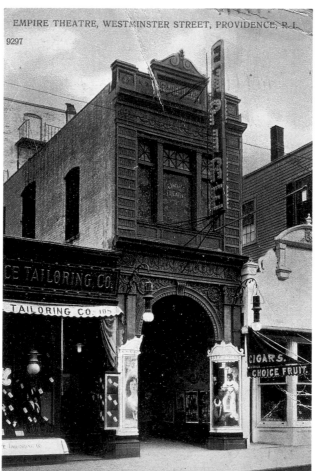

EMPIRE THEATRE, WESTMINSTER STREET, PROVIDENCE, R.I.

9297

13 Electric and Palace theatres, Charleroi, Pennsylvania, ca. 1908. Side by side in the theatre district of Charleroi were the Electric, a nickelodeon, and the Palace, a vaudeville house. Both the name "Palace" and the reference to "refined vaudeville" were deliberate attempts to clean up the image of this entertainment format.

14 Empire Theatre, Providence, Rhode Island, 1908. A storefront, which became a nickelodeon when the shop windows were removed and a lobby was carved out of the ground-floor space. Many of these nicks were converted back into stores a few years later.

Grand Opening
for LADIES And GENTLEMEN at
384 Myrtle Ave.
Near Vanderbilt Ave.   Brooklyn, N. Y.

I take pleasure in announcing to the public that I have opened at the above address a first class **Moving Picture** place, where Ladies and Gentlemen with their families can have a pleasant time for a little money. It will be my special duty to procure the **Latest and Best Pictures** obtainable; such as will be fit for the youngest and oldest of my patrons to look at and enjoy. Come and be convinced yourself. **The price is small, the FUN is great**

Laugh and Be Merry

Admission only **5 Cents**
Open daily at 3.30 p. m.   Our pictures do all but speak.

15 Announcement for the grand opening of a new nickelodeon theatre in Brooklyn, New York, ca. 1908, aimed at attracting "Ladies and Gentlemen with their families."

catalogs. The plan was straightforward and standardized, yet quite different from that of the opera house. Nickelodeons were small, typically measuring twenty by eighty feet, and usually had a center aisle leading to the screen; appointments included short straight rows of straight-back chairs or wooden benches and a projector located at the rear. There was no balcony. An announcement from the period advertises "only a plain, neat hall, scrupulously clean, with the usual uniformed group of ushers as in an ordinary theatre, and a 'ticket-chopper' at the door."[44] The language used reveals that movie houses were beginning to be considered part of the world of theatre, out of the world of parlor entertainment.

The number of seats in a nickelodeon often depended on the locale and on the municipal regulations defining a theatre, for which an amusement license was required.[45] To avoid paying the fee, "nicks" would contain one seat less than the municipal definition of a theatre. In New York City, for example, a theatre license cost five hundred dollars, whereas film exhibitors only paid twenty-five dollars. The weekly cost of operating a theatre that presented only one show a night was twenty-five hundred dollars, as compared to five hundred dollars to run a nickelodeon that ran several shows a day.[46] Although food was not allowed inside a theatre, vendors sold popcorn, peanuts, and candy in the aisles of the nickelodeon and "song pluggers" provided musical accompaniment. Music publishing companies employed pluggers to sing new songs to the accompaniment of a piano in the hopes of selling sheet music. Between films, illuminated slides informed patrons of the accepted norms of conduct in the theatre, including clichés that stereotype the sex roles of the period: "Ladies, remove your hats" or "Gentlemen—No Spitting." Although there were no carpets, no upholstered chairs, and no orchestra, the prototype of the movie theatre was nonetheless emerging.

The manipulation of design to entice patrons inside was again employed on the exterior of nickelodeons. Facades consisted of square storefront windows used for posters and advertising as well as a recessed lobby at least six feet deep that contained the box office, with entrance and exit doors on either side. Although six feet was not a large space, this defined area began to separate the form from the earlier storefront plan. According to an adviser, however, a even deeper front was desirable because "it gives the opportunity for decorative effects without the expense of decorating the entire front of the business house; it suggests retirement in the theatre, and when the prospective patron steps off the sidewalk he feels he is already within the theatre, even before he has purchased his admission ticket."[47]

Another important innovation was the decision of designers to separate the box office from the building, placing it in line with the sidewalk. The change in position functioned as a device to indicate that immediate seating was available and to encourage spontaneous attendance. As Charlotte Herzog has pointed out, the new box office closely resembled the barker's position outside the sideshow, where he could actively encourage ticket sales rather than passively wait for them.[48]

Above the entry lobby were massive electrical displays in unusual shapes, flamboyantly advertising the uniqueness of the building design and the theatre. The Liberty Theatre in Seattle featured a forty-foot-high Statue of Liberty made up of twelve hundred lights in eight colors. According to reports, the sign caused such excitement that police were required to control the crowds.[49] Distributors, exhibitors, and theatre managers encouraged such publicity as part of the promotion that has always been an important part of motion picture and movie theatre advertising. Spectacular events, in addition to creating free advertising, sold tickets and etched the architectural imagery on the mind of the public. Whether true or not, fantastic tales became part of the mystique of early motion picture theatres and were linked to other heavily promoted myths and anecdotes that made klieg-lit opening nights worthy of coverage in the newspapers—creating advertising not available at any price. This was architecture as set design.

Nickelodeons blossomed virtually overnight, flourished for nearly a decade, then disappeared almost as quickly as they arrived. Overshadowed, outclassed, and physically dwarfed by the larger and more pretentious movie palaces being built by the mid-1910s, most nickelodeons were eventually converted back into restaurants, hardware stores, cigar stores, and haberdasheries.

During the era of the nickelodeon (1905–14), the design of the building and the story line of the films improved, but the technology for producing and showing film remained primitive. Given the highly flammable nature of silver nitrate film, the inadequate ventilation in the buildings, and the poorly designed equipment, fires and panics occurred frequently. In fact, many popular entertainment forms of that period were considered dangerous because of flammable materials, large crowds, and poorly planned exits. Movies, however, were additionally denounced in the pulpit and the press as socially dangerous and degrading to morals and culture.[50] One of the first films in 1896, for example, was *The Kiss,* featuring a chaste, innocent kiss when presented onstage that became shocking due in part to its enormous scale when projected onto a screen. Movie theatres abetted their questionable reputation by turning off the interior lights and using dangerous machinery. The crudely fashioned projectors, which ran sixteen hours a day, frequently overheated, sending sparks flying. The only exit, moreover, was underneath or next to the main source of fires. Beginning in the 1910s, municipal codes required asbestos, metal, or other fire-resistant materials for the construction of projector booths in order to contain the dangerous machines.[51] Licensing fees were raised, fire exits became mandatory, and children were often required by law to be accompanied by an adult chaperone.[52]

Typical theatre names, such as Gem, Bijou Dream, Nickelet, Big Nickel, or Electric, further conveyed a message of uniqueness, fantasy, and expansive experience. Nickelodeons were generally found not in the prestigious sections of downtown but on side streets, where the rent was cheaper. Such locations may have helped keep costs down and may have attracted a different audience than live theatre, but they also gave the theatres, and the movies with them, a bad reputation. For many owners, the nickelodeon was a get-rich-quick scheme; others saw greater profits in improving the physical environments.

SMALL-TIME VAUDEVILLE

To compete with nickelodeons while charging a higher admission, and to compete with vaudeville while keeping costs down, movie showmen introduced small-time vaudeville acts into the motion picture theatre, reversing the host-and-guest relationship between live and film performances of the previous decade. The show consisted of several reels of film punctuated by a short program of vaudeville acts that could not get billing in the big time. Film became the focus of the bill rather than a ten-minute diversion.

The link between small-time vaudeville and the later movie palace was both substantive and physical. Small-time vaudeville theatres were generally large (with between five hundred and one thousand seats) and ornate and offered such amenities as uniformed attendants.[53] To attract both nickelodeon and vaudeville devotees, admission ranged from ten cents up to fifty cents for reserved seating. During the 1910s, while studios were being consolidated and an oligarchy of film production and distribution was being established, nickelodeon and theatre owners, including William Fox, Marcus Loew, and Adolph Zukor, began buying theatres with the intent of building exhibition empires. Architects were commissioned to create new buildings at the same time that vaudeville theatres and other large-capacity auditoriums were being recycled. For example, the Tivoli in San Francisco, built in 1910 for grand opera costing from one to five dollars a ticket, was being used five years later to show movies at fifteen to twenty-five cents a ticket.[54] The names given to these theatres no longer suggested quaint, ephemeral qualities but reflected the zeitgeist of World War I, with names that described places (Seventh Avenue, Lexington, 59th Street) or persons (Warfield, Ringling) or referred to government (Royal, American, National, State, Capitol, Columbia).

The move from storefronts into small-time vaudeville houses brought about better safety conditions and an improved public image of the movies. As a result, patronage, and therefore box office revenue, increased. By World War I, theatres were ranked in a hierarchy according to size and quality, a process that separated first-class theatres from the "cheap" nickelodeons. Theatre-chain operators, such as Zukor and Loew, encouraged this distinction to avoid competition within their chains. This classification eventually resulted in the demise of the nickelodeon and led to the larger, more ornate theatre built with historical imagery, the movie palace.

The labels "nickelodeon" and "palace" refer to types of entertainment and broad generalizations about building structure, including size and the economics of construction. The architectural transition, however, is more gradual than these categories would suggest. Not all nickelodeons were small, gaudy fairground facades. The Knickerbocker Theatre (New York, 1907) was described in *Moving Picture World* as "one of the prettiest picture theaters in America. The lobby is done in Italian marble, plate glass mirrors with mosaic floor."[55] The cream-and-gold auditorium featured Corinthian pilasters and plaster swags along paneled walls. Numerous other descriptions suggest nickelodeon theatres decorated in equally rich materials.[56]

During the era of the movie palace, the psychology of design and architectural imagination turned into a frenzy. The building of the palaces coincided with the death of vaudeville and the postwar economic boom in the United States, a period in which the tremendous growth of American cities created an enormous market for entertainment. America had emerged as a world power politically and *the* world power in terms of film production. Every major city soon boasted a palace worthy of the nation's and the movies' new prominence.

MOVING PICTURE THEATRES

In addition to small-time vaudeville, other changes were taking place in film exhibition techniques. As a result of improved municipal code regulations, buildings were being constructed more carefully. At the same time, there were changes in film production. In 1915, D. W. Griffith's twelve-reel *Birth of a Nation* became a major financial and artistic success. Thereafter, feature-length films became the norm, replacing shorts. The impact of this expanded format came in the form of higher ticket prices, reserved seats, scheduled showings, and longer runs. Concurrently, theatres developed increased respectability with the introduction of the term "moving picture theatres."

For the first time, builders and managers gave serious consideration to safety, sight lines, maximum capacity, heating, lighting, and ventilation. Some buildings were no more than nickelodeons "in drag"—one-story boxlike buildings all dressed up, such as Tally's Broadway Theater in Los Angeles (fig. 16). Others were two- or three-story buildings that copied traditional theatre facades. Prominent architects were commissioned to create practical works of art to rival the vaudeville houses that were fierce competition for the motion picture houses.

Theatre designers also took a serious approach to the genre. Whereas the traditional theatre had been designed around the stage and live performances, the new movie theatre was planned around the projection booth. Although the stage area sometimes accommodated a fly tower for hanging flats, there were virtually no backstage facilities. Most of the space was devoted to the comfort of the audience, not to the production. Design competitions, such as the *Brickbuilder*'s Architectural Terra Cotta Competition

16 Tally's Broadway Theater, Los Angeles, ca. 1910. One of the first theatres designed especially for movies.

HOME OF THE FINEST THEATER PIPE ORGAN IN THE WORLD

TALLY'S BROADWAY THEATER

FAMOUS PLAYERS   LOS ANGELES   IN MOTION PICTURE

in 1914, were beginning to be held to encourage innovation. This period in the early 1910s that bridges the nickelodeon and the palace has been little noticed but was an important transition from practical showiness to ostentatious showmanship in theatre design—a balance that took several years to rediscover.

Vaudeville, storefronts, nickelodeons, and movie houses—these were the theatres that Simeon Levi knew as a child in Chicago and as he began his career in architecture. In an interview he recalled this period of his childhood:

> Children were admitted free [with adults] so we used to stand in front of the theatre and when grownups came along we'd ask them to take us in as their kids. My greatest memory of the picture shows at that time was the attempt to have talking pictures. They had actors back of the screen that would talk the lines. Of course, there was a piano in front of the screen, and they attempted to create talkies in that way. The early pictures in those days were *The Great Train Robbery* and *The Perils of Pauline.*
> Vaudeville came in and I had a seat in the front row of a certain theatre every Friday night. It used to cost fifteen cents.[57]

Observers have examined the traits and motivations that characterized young persons destined to become architects. Frank Lloyd Wright played with Froebel blocks, and Richard Neutra created cavelike shelters beneath the family piano. In the case of future movie theatre designer Simeon Levi, it was a childhood not only of silent movies and vaudeville but of discovering, inventing, tinkering, and building. As a teenager, he set up a workshop in his bedroom, complete with lathe, band saw, and power saw, all driven by motors he had scavenged. His parents ignored the six inches of wood shavings on the bedroom floor so that he could be free to experiment. Between the ages of fourteen and eighteen, he built three automobiles in these surroundings. The first consisted of a wheel base and gasoline engine with an external flywheel. When it was completed, however, he was unable to negotiate it down the stairway in his home, which persuaded him to move some of his industry to a backyard shop. Receiving support from a family friend who owned a stock of parts from a defunct automobile company, he built another car, this one with a four-cylinder engine and standard transmission. His last car was a racing model, built from another car, using modified Ford parts. It was in this racing car that he drove to California in 1921.

When Simeon was about fourteen years old, the family decided that he should pursue his obvious mechanical aptitude as a career. As part of a prevocational experiment, he had already been selected to attend Lake Technical High School in Chicago, where he studied engineering. Rejecting a suggested career in mechanical engineering as too boring, he chose architecture instead, which would allow him to combine his artistic and mechanical abilities. Chicago architect Henry Newhouse was a family friend and served as his role model, allowing him to apprentice in the office. Newhouse was a theatre specialist, designing nickelodeons, remodeled storefront theatres, and small motion picture theatres. Sim began working there as an office boy in 1915, at the age of fifteen, and later became a draftsman in the firm.[58]

Although the theatre designs of the mature architect S. Charles Lee were notable for their visual extravagance, he insisted that the force behind the aesthetic creativity was a practical business sense. Indeed, his early creative thinking revealed a concern with efficiency over aesthetics. While visiting a garment-manufacturing factory in Chicago's Loop with his father, Sim observed the wasteful method of moving piece goods between machines using belts and pulleys aided by small boys pulling baskets. He measured the factory area, made paper models of the machines and tables, drew the floor area on a piece of paper, and rearranged all the parts and pieces, increasing the efficiency of the operation. The superintendents were sufficiently impressed to close the factory temporarily and rearrange the facilities according to the designs of the salesman's son. Other manufacturers followed suit, and Simeon Levi soon discovered he had a lucrative consulting practice at the age of sixteen.[59]

After graduation from Lake Technical High School, he attended Chicago Technical College, where he undertook an intensive two-year architectural and engineering course, graduating with honors in 1918 at age eighteen. While there, he developed an interest in the innovative use of materials and began to explore the realm of design. He learned that the Chicago park authorities were holding an examination for senior architect, the requirements for which included a minimum age of twenty-one. Lying about his age, Levi passed the examination at the top of the list and was appointed senior architect for the South Park Board, where he primarily designed bathing beaches.[60]

Although the eighteen-year-old supervised several junior draftsmen, they had one thing that he did not: a draft card. With World War I in full force, he decided to enlist in the navy before his employer discovered he was under age for the job. At Great Lakes Naval Training Station, he earned the rank of carpenter's mate and was assigned to the engineering department, where he designed cantonments (temporary quarters for the troops) and navy buildings. He also built hundreds of coffins for navy victims of the flu epidemic in that area.

After Armistice Day, the government announced that anyone going back to school would be eligible for an early discharge. Sim applied to the Armour Institute of Technology to study architecture and was discharged from the navy in February 1920.[61] Armour Institute, founded in 1892, offered a course of study that combined engineering, art, and architecture. Engineering classes were held in the mornings on campus, and students took architecture and drawing classes at the Art Institute of Chicago in the afternoon. The Art Institute subscribed to the Beaux-Arts program, as did most architecture schools of the time, but in Chicago it was especially popular following the 1893 World's Columbian Exposition.

The educational principles derived from the Ecole des Beaux-Arts in Paris included rational design theory, a study of history that focused on Classical ideals, supremacy of the plan, and a grand and monumental approach to design. Much of the course work involved competitions in drawing and design. In fact, the Chicago students' work was reviewed in Paris by officials of the Ecole, and Levi received two honorable mentions.[62] One of them, "A Naval Pantheon," which later hung in the library of the Graduate School of Architecture and Urban Planning at the University of California at Los Angeles, reveals his Beaux-Arts training as an artist. It was drawn with a careful hand and an educated eye regarding color and variations on a theme; the subject matter utilized historicist imagery and vocabulary; great attention was paid to the imagery, the vocabulary, and the composition of the drawing. Even when he distanced himself from traditional imagery in his later work, he kept with him the compositional aspects of presentation drawings, which can be seen in his drawings—how they are placed on the page, usually framed in pencil lines that pick up the structural or decorative motif (see figs. 98, 102, 113).

Growing up in and studying architecture in Chicago may have been redundant, because Chicago and the surrounding suburbs of Oak Park, River Forest, and Evanston provided a tangible architectural education. The work of Frank Lloyd Wright stimulated Levi, and like Wright, he was strongly influenced by Louis Sullivan. In addition to Sullivan's Schlesinger and Mayer Department Store, Levi was impressed by Wright's own residence and Midway Gardens. Sullivan's lectures to Levi's architecture classes shaped his thinking about the nature of buildings, spaces, shapes, and ornament. Another powerful influence on the young architect was the 1922 *Chicago Tribune* competition and the resultant debate between the winning historicist entry of Hood and Howells and the modernist designs of Saarinen, Walter Gropius, and Adolf Loos. Sixty years after the competition, Lee could still sketch the second-place Saarinen building from memory, so impressed was he with the philosophical point of view for the modern skyscraper.[63] His experience of architecture as a child, reinforced by a Beaux-Arts education, focused on the plan rather than on decoration or style. Style expressed the building but did not define it.

Lee later described his attitude: "I was born to be a modernist."[64] His architectural career would reveal both the Beaux-Arts discipline and emphasis on planning and the modernist functionalism and freedom of form. His work also encompassed his belief in business efficiency—as measured in increased profits—as the motivating force behind commercial architecture. Helpful, too, was his understanding of popular culture, developed from the movies and from playing the banjo in an orchestra for five dollars a night in "questionable places" to support himself through school.[65]

Even while growing up, his choices and attitudes were pragmatic. He was not an ungrounded visionary but a practical businessperson, as evidenced through his childhood experiences, student projects and, later, the underlying program of his buildings. Like Sullivan, he successfully merged commerce with art, and engineering with architecture, and made ornament a servant of the structure. Lee's family, the city of Chicago, the early forms of motion picture theatres, and the debates in American architecture in the early twentieth century helped shape his thirty-year career.

As Simeon Levi was growing up, so were the movies. Following years of experimentation and attempts to find a niche in the entertainment arena, the motion picture industry came of age and established itself as a leading economic, social, and entertainment force in American life. Attendance boomed from the start. The improvement of films in terms of content, storytelling techniques, and the quality of the physical product was accompanied by improved distribution and exhibition techniques.

From its beginnings, the motion picture theatre differed inherently from live theatre, promoting innovation, technology, machinery, and entertainment, not drama and tradition. Advertising for this new form tended to identify the equipment and the building rather than the film titles or actors' names. The original buildings, and therefore the type itself, were inherited from other forms of retail or popular entertainment. The early buildings focused on business, expressed in economy and efficiency. When movies absorbed vaudeville houses, part of that legacy was the image of escape, fantasy, and fun not generally associated with other legitimate theatre. Live theatre was threatened both economically and geographically by the territorial infringement of the movies, as the latter moved from side streets to downtown theatre districts in less than twenty years.

It was this tradition of popular culture embellished with the trappings of highbrow culture that the motion picture theatre embraced. The purpose of the building was to lure the customers inside, to create an atmosphere of increasing respectability yet accessibility, and to be part of the entertainment. The conventions of the motion picture theatre—the layout, symbolism, iconography, and opulence—had been established.

3
Double Feature
Chicago to
Los Angeles,
and the
Introduction
of the Movie
Palace

After graduating from Armour Institute in 1921, Simeon Levi began working for Rapp and Rapp, an architectural firm best known for elaborate motion picture theatres, commonly referred to as movie palaces. The movie palace, which dominated motion picture exhibition from the late 1910s through the 1920s, glorified the monumentality of the film experience. The surroundings created a palpable emotional atmosphere for the movies, extending the fantasy of the film to include the physical environment in which it was viewed. It was no coincidence that this extravagant architectural expression accompanied the increasing acceptance and popularity of film as an entertainment medium. What Lee learned about theatre design in the offices of Rapp and Rapp would be further developed in his own practice in Los Angeles.

In the late 1910s and early 1920s, the typical movie palace was an ornate, period revival extravaganza, with references to live theatre in its architecture and entertainment program. In the early movie palace, the silent film was almost incidental to the live show, the architectural appointments, and the entertaining qualities of the large staff that served the theatre. With the introduction of talkies in 1927, however, the movie palace no longer needed to supplement the mechanical equipment with live entertainment. By the 1930s, the program focused almost entirely on the film. These two entertainment formats had different architectural requirements.

In 1929, movie palace architect John Eberson explained the architecture of the grand palace: "Here we find ourselves today creating and building super-cinemas of enormous capacities, excelling in splendor, in luxury and in furnishings the most palatial homes of princes and crowned kings for and on behalf of His Excellency—the American Citizen."[1] The theatre that marked the beginning of the trend for the type known as the movie palace is generally considered to be the 1,845-seat Regent (New York, 1913), built for Henry Marvin, founder of the Biograph Company. In creating an architectural image that would give the desired effect, architect Thomas Lamb modeled his theatre after the Doge's Palace in Venice, an architectural landmark that educated Americans would recognize and that the less-educated would regard as classy. Lamb's copy of the Venetian palace was outrageous on two counts. First, it was in New York City, outside the traditional theatre district; and second, it was a de luxe theatre designed especially for the movies. The facade of white terra cotta with green trim was designed to compete architecturally for the middle-class patrons of the nearby vaudeville houses. The auditorium even resembled a conventional vaudeville house with an elaborate proscenium and full backstage facilities.

In spite of the Venetian trappings, however, the theatre was not successful at first.

It may be that the public did not know how to react to this environment until Samuel "Roxy" Rothafel assumed management and told the public what to expect. He remodeled the theatre, introduced an eight-piece orchestra, and capitalized on the opulent interior as an important part of his marketing technique. In the words of a contemporary critic, the pipe organ and red velvet curtains created "an environment so pleasing, so perfect in artistic detail, that it seemed as if the setting were a prerequisite to the picture, that to an educated audience the two should, and must hereafter, go together. . . . The handsome and comfortable interior . . . has much to do with the success of the performance. There is no finer theatre in New York . . . an interior not to be equalled in a single other theatre here."[2] This observer anticipated the sumptuous quality sought in the movie palace. The reviewer's only criticism was that the Regent was not charging enough admission.

Large theatres were not new, of course. In the 1820s, one could see melodrama at the Park (New York, 1821), with three tiers of boxes, a gallery, and 2,500 seats; at the Bowery (New York, ca. 1820s–1830s, 3,500 seats); and at the Broadway (New York, ca. 1830s–1840s, 4,000 seats).[3] The Hippodrome (New York, 1905, J. H. Morgan), with more than 5,000 seats, had the capacity to present extravaganzas. There had also been lavish and expensive motion picture theatres, such as Lubin's Palace (Chicago, 1908) or Swanson's Moving Picture Theatre (Chicago, 1909).

The movie palace overwhelmed all other theatres because it *combined* all these features—the live entertainment, courteous service, and generous seating capacity. Palaces were, indeed, huge (with approximately two to six thousand seats), complete with balconies and mezzanines. They were frequently referred to as cathedrals or shrines and, in fact, did display relics such as costumes or footprints in the sidewalk. The halls, filled with the resonant chords of huge organs, even sounded like sanctuaries.

As movie palaces expanded into prime downtown areas previously reserved for office buildings and legitimate theatres, romantic and exotic architecture began to appear as adornment. To recoup the expense of a large office building, developers frequently included movie palaces on the first floor. Lee's work with Rapp and Rapp involved planning the layout for multistory office buildings that housed ground-floor movie palaces; one of his first independent commissions was also for such a building, the Wurlitzer Building and Theatre (see fig. 42).

Throughout the 1910s and 1920s, movie palaces still featured live entertainment to make the silent movies a more theatrical experience. An impresario-showman often oversaw the theatre in a tradition that combined the talents of Oscar Hammerstein I and P. T. Barnum. The most famous of these showmen was Roxy Rothafel of the Regent, who eventually managed a series of New York movie palaces. His background had trained him for just such an opportunity. Born in Minnesota of German and Polish parents, he combined Old World charm with Yankee ingenuity and had the skill of a circus barker. Before managing theatres, he spent seven years as a Marine drill sergeant and played minor league baseball in Pennsylvania, where he got his nickname. His contribution to the genre started with an attempt to bring respectability to the nickelodeon theatre he ran by adding moving curtains, colored lights, and a pianist and vocalist. As he discovered, this inexpensive formula paid off at the box office and made his theatres unique. He worked for the Keith circuit, supervising films in their vaudeville houses, before moving to New York to become theatre manager for the Regent.[4]

Rothafel understood a fundamental requirement of the movie palace—namely, to put on a show that would attract large crowds—and exploited it. He realized that people were curious about the exotic and played on that curiosity. As he explained it, "All you hear about these days is the everlasting cry of theatre managers that they are looking for 'what the people want.' That idea is fundamentally wrong. The people themselves don't know what they want. They want to be entertained, that's all. Don't 'give the people what they want'—give 'em something better."[5] Later, he refined his philosophy: "We make no attempt to 'please our public.' . . . [We provide] a program based on the fundamentals of good taste, honesty, and sincerity and within the bounds of average intelligence."[6] He was credited with democratizing culture while improving the status of motion pictures by banning reserved-seat policies and keeping admission prices as low as possible. In 1927 Robert Sherwood wrote about Rothafel: "Although movie audiences were supposed to be composed entirely of incurable lowbrows, Roxy gave them highbrow entertainment and made them like it. He gave them grand opera . . . ballet . . . operetta . . . [and] violin solos."[7] Roxy's influence on the motion picture theatre was so great that he became the eponym for hundreds of motion picture theatres across the United States. He managed his first namesake, the 5,920-seat Roxy (New York, 1927, W. W. Ahlschlager). There is also a Roxy Theatre in Choteau, Montana, in Carney, Kansas, and in hundreds of other towns across the United States. He had no involvement with these enterprises and probably never visited the towns, but small-town America knew the name Roxy long after he was forgotten.

Just as Rothafel excelled in the showmanship of place, Sid Grauman, his West Coast counterpart, excelled in publicity stunts. Grauman commissioned several theatres, including the Million Dollar Theatre (Los Angeles, 1918, William Lee Woollett and A. C. Martin), the Egyptian Theatre (Hollywood, 1922, Meyer and Holler), and the Chinese Theatre (Hollywood, 1927, Meyer and Holler). Grauman's particular contribution was to pioneer "first-run premieres," extravagant social events that featured searchlights and red carpets, all to celebrate running a roll of celluloid through a machine. He also introduced the "prologue," a live act related to the theme of the feature film, to give the people more for their money and to compete with other theatres. More sophisticated prologues, consisting of an overture and a live production number accompanied by an orchestra, were soon standard fare at non-Grauman theatres as well. In smaller theatres, live prologues were replaced by film prologues.[8] With the advent of talkies, prologues became a thing of the past, but their influence can be traced through selected shorts, coming attractions, and eventually commercials.

Grauman's attitude was, "The public doesn't *demand* anything. . . . It is only after a thing is created that the public demands it."[9] And he was adept at telling the public what they thought they wanted. One of his stunts was the idea of having actors leave their footprints in cement in front of his Chinese Theatre. People still come to see these consecrated blocks of concrete, often without going inside to see the film. There were many apocryphal accounts of how this custom started, and Grauman let all of them proliferate.

The movie palaces reflected the emerging "star" system, which encouraged loyalty to names, whether it be that of an actor, a studio, or a theatre. The uniqueness of the movie palace environment was matched by a staff well drilled in courtesy and service. The Capitol (New York, 1919, Thomas Lamb) employed 350 people trained by ex-marine Rothafel. The fresh flowers in the lobby and the retinue of doormen, maids, and nurses were more in keeping with fancy hotels than with ten-cent entertainment. There were also the usual ushers, now trained in military precision. Where else could the middle class have access to an obedient staff so cheaply (fig. 17)? Newspaper advertisements bragged as much, or more, about the building as they did about the films being shown, as seen in a full-page advertisement for the Roxy in the *New York Times* of 6 March 1927. Although the copy claimed that "we cannot find adjectives strong enough to describe the thousand and one wonders and innovations of The ROXY, truly the most sumptuous and stupendous theatre ever erected," it did manage to summon sufficient superlatives to describe the size, beauty, luxury, and technology of the theatre. Cathedral chimes of twenty-one bells were mentioned, lest anyone not understand the iconography of "The Cathedral of the Motion Picture." Advertising and showmanship were intended to inspire a loyal following. As Marcus Loew explained, "We sell tickets to theatres, not movies."[10]

The image presented to the public and the message of in-house publications, such as the 1926 *Pep Club Yearbook,* showed that owners and managers took their theatres very

17 Meeting of RKO ushers, Cincinnati. Mayor James Garfield Stewart (center) addresses the first meeting of ushers of the Cincinnati RKO Theatres.

seriously. John F. Barry, director of the Publix Theatre Managers' Training School, wrote of the Paramount (New York, 1926, Rapp and Rapp):

> For generations yet unborn it will stand as a monument to the motion picture industry as an ever-lasting tribute to the vision and genius of a leader [Adolph Zukor]. . . .
>
> Within the foyer of the Paramount Theatre there will be a panel in which will be set a stone from every country of the world. This is symbolic because nothing has done more to develop a common understanding among the peoples of the world than the photoplay. The celluloid film threading through the projection machines of the world is knitting into closer unity the peoples of every language. . . . This "Hall of Nations" will be a silent reminder that the peoples of the world have helped to build the monument whose tower will carry the Paramount trademark.[11]

Here was the language and tone of wartime propaganda and the cultural equivalent of a League of Nations, whose arguments had filled the headlines less than ten years before. In a decade of economic boom and political isolationism, when, according to the President of the United States, The Business of America Was Business, it was not surprising that this fervor spread to consumer advertising. And what better commercial product than motion pictures to symbolize international leadership and goodwill in the American mind. The individual businessman as hero replaced the statesman. As with wartime slogans, in which patriotism and propaganda fed each other, so it was with movie hyperbole, to the point that the purveyors believed every word of their own publicity.

THE LEADING MEN

The movie palace was the first motion picture theatre for which architects were consistently consulted and their talents exploited. Owners had moved beyond the solely functional requirements of the building in search of artistic enhancements that called for architectural expertise. Theatre builders sought out architects experienced in the design of large vaudeville houses, and an oligopoly of palace architects soon formed. Many of the early motion picture theatre architects were born in Europe, received a Beaux-Arts education, and equated theatricality with European opera house traditions. They excelled in period revival excess. Each firm was known for a particular style and was usually connected with a specific network of chain theatres. In addition to John Eberson, the best known architects nationally were Thomas Lamb, who worked with Marcus Loew; Marcus Priteca, with Pantages; Albert Lansburgh, with Orpheum; C. Howard Crane, with United Artists; and Rapp and Rapp, with Balaban and Katz, which later became Paramount. By the time the studios began to use local architects to build their theatres, the design standards developed by these firms had been canonized (fig. 18). In contrast, the next generation of motion picture theatre architects, including S. Charles Lee, was born and educated in the United States and worked in a more modern vein.

Indiana Theatre, Terre Haute, Ind.

18 Indiana Theatre, Terre Haute, Indiana, ca. 1930. Movie palace.

Thomas Lamb (1871–1942), the first well-known architect associated with the movie palace, designed over three hundred motion picture theatres during his career. He was born in Dundee, Scotland, and his theatre designs evolved from Baroque to Neoclassical, inspired by the work of Robert Adam in eighteenth-century England. The Cort (1909) was modeled on the Petit Trianon, whereas the American Theatre Roof Garden (1909) was a rustic Adirondack lodge with structural columns disguised as tree trunks. He also designed several vaudeville houses for William Fox. He designed the first movie palace, the Regent, as well as the Strand (New York, 1914) in conjunction with Rothafel. The Rialto (New York, 1916) was billed as a "Temple of the Motion Picture; Shrine of Music and Allied Arts"; and the Rivoli (New York, 1917) may have been a copy of the Parthenon on the exterior, but the interior was a temple to the movies (fig. 19).[12]

The mature Lamb utilized Beaux-Arts principles and materials—symmetry and balance, clarity, and classical motifs expressed in limestone, granite, and marble. Materials included patterned brick and terra cotta, which was inexpensive and had sculptural qualities of color, sheen, and plasticity. Lamb's theatres featured opera boxes set between columns on both sides of the auditorium, flattened domes, relief ornament, and lobbies resembling the Fontainebleau gallery. He described his work for Loew's State (Syracuse, 1929): "The Grand Foyer is like a Temple of gold set with colored jewels. . . . These exotic ornaments, colors, and scenes are particularly effective in creating an atmosphere in which the mind is free to frolic and becomes receptive to entertainment."[13]

John Eberson (1875–1954) was born in Austria and educated at the University of Vienna before coming to the United States in 1901. He built over five hundred theatres throughout the world and was credited with the creation of the atmospheric theatre, which gave one the impression of being seated outdoors (fig. 20). Eberson, like Lee, was adept at promoting himself and his work, keeping his name in both the popular and professional theatre press. He later served on the War Production Board during World

War II and for many years wrote a column on theatre architecture in *Film Daily Year Book,* always using his own work as an example of what was new, appropriate, and most desirable.

Marcus Priteca (1889–1971), the only movie theatre architect named a Fellow in the American Institute of Architects (FAIA), made famous a style known as "Pantages Greek." The organ screens and proscenium arches were the same in most Pantages theatres, but each had a unique ornamentation and ceiling-cove design. Priteca typically used a triple-domed ceiling, the center of which was a stained art-glass panel surrounded by two cove-lit domes that lighted the main ceiling. One entered the loges from the front of each balcony. He remarked of the design process: "The decision finally rested upon an original treatment that would best exemplify America of the moment. Effort centered upon motifs that were modern, never futuristic—yet based on time tested classicism of enduring good taste and beauty."14

Lamb, Eberson, and Priteca were all respected, European-based architects employing conservative styles, credentials that guaranteed the acceptance of these fantasy empires into downtown American cities in the 1910s and 1920s. Although the scale, massing, and detail of the Beaux-Arts facades were harmonious with surrounding banks and office buildings, the flashing lights, marquees, and vertical signs were highly visible. The theatres were therefore contextual yet at the same time exploited the psychology of design as a marketing tool.

The Neobaroque trend, exemplified by Rapp and Rapp, introduced curves and graceful arches in contrast to the straight commercial lines of other downtown buildings. In 1915, shortly after making the grand tour of Europe, brothers George (1878–1942) and Cornelius Ward (1861–1927) Rapp were commissioned to design the Al Ringling Theatre, a motion picture–vaudeville house in Baraboo, Wisconsin. The 804-seat theatre was a small-scale palace inspired by the Royal Theatre at Versailles. By the time

19 Rivoli Theatre, New York, ca. 1922 (Thomas Lamb, 1917).

20 Tampa Theatre, Tampa, Florida, ca. 1926 (John Eberson, 1926). Atmospheric auditorium.

Simeon Levi was hired, the firm had already completed, in addition to vaudeville theatres, the Central Park Theatre in Chicago. Built in 1916–17, it was Chicago's first movie palace and the first Balaban and Katz (B&K) theatre. In 1919 Rapp and Rapp also designed for B&K the Riviera Theatre in Chicago, a French Renaissance Revival extravaganza. Typical Rapp treatments included a triumphal arch motif, a grand lobby with marble Corinthian columns, in the tradition of the Paris Opera House, and a monumental stairway.

As Ben Hall wrote, "Rapp and Rapp put one idea above all others: eye-bugging opulence. . . . Their stock in trade was a grandeur that spelled m*o*n*e*y to the dazzled two-bit ticket holder."[15] The names of their theatres describe their sources of inspiration: the Tivoli, the Versailles, the Palace, the Oriental. When commissioning the Spanish Renaissance Uptown Theatre (Chicago, 1925), which covered an entire city block, B&K instructed them "to leave patrons awestruck."[16] They did. W. A. S. Douglas, no fan of the pretentious movie palace, mocked this Neobaroque trend, which he claimed created "gaudy horrors" that "stink with class."[17]

The Rapp office was organized into several departments, each of which was responsible for a specific part of the building process; Levi was assigned to the design department. Most of the firm's work consisted of large office blocks with theatres on the ground floor. Levi's responsibilities included taking programs directly from Cornelius or George Rapp and developing preliminary drawings and detailed floor plans. His ability to think in plan enabled him to make a name for himself in the firm very quickly. "I was always the originator of the concept," he later said of his duties there.[18]

From Rapp and Rapp he learned about the "theory of the theatre."[19] The firm understood the psychology as well as the economics of the business and was able to express both in architecture. During the time Levi was there, the office was completing two Tivolis (one in Chicago, one in Chattanooga) and was putting the finishing touches on the Chicago, a 3,800-seat French palace with grand staircase and the flagship theatre for the B&K chain. The office was also working on the Palace (Cleveland), housed in the twenty-one story Keith Building. Both the offices and the theatre were built by Edward F. Albee and dedicated to his vaudeville partner, B. F. Keith. This was the kind of project Simeon Levi would have worked on.

In 1921 Levi passed the three-day licensing examination in architecture and engineering for the state of Illinois. He was now prepared for a career in designing motion picture theatres, but it was to be interrupted for five years. That same year, he took a leave of absence to drive to California in his home-built racing car, in spite of the fact that the roads between Chicago and San Diego were not designed for such a vehicle. In fact, there were no roads at all across the desert between Yuma, Arizona, and El Centro, California, merely a track of railroad ties laid across the sand to try to keep it from shifting. The car broke down on several occasions, which meant unscheduled stops for repairs. Levi, and the car, did make it to San Diego and then to Los Angeles, however, arriving in December 1921. There Levi called on his father's sister, who lived in the seaside resort community of Venice, fourteen miles from downtown Los Angeles. After staying with his aunt for a while, he rented an apartment in Venice on "The Speedway," so named because it was just wide enough for two cars to pass and the speed limit was seven miles per hour.

The business of Los Angeles in the 1920s was real estate. And Levi's first business venture was with Walter G. McCarty, a real estate developer he met shortly after arriving. The firm of McCarty, Vaughan, and Evans held an option on seventy-two acres of land along the south side of Wilshire Boulevard in the "mid-Wilshire" area, a few miles west of downtown Los Angeles. Invited to join the firm, Levi sent word to Chicago that he would not be returning to his job. Instead, he sold his racing car and invested the proceeds in McCarty's venture. The firm purchased the land for seventy-five hundred dollars an acre, which Lee understood to be the highest price paid up to that time for such property in Los Angeles. The new owners subdivided the land and set up an office, including a drafting room, designed by their architect-partner.

Wilshire Boulevard, later the principal traffic artery through the city, was then a two-lane highway with a dirt shoulder and a sign that read, "Wilshire Boulevard to be widened to this point."[20] Using a sales gimmick typical of many Los Angeles–area real estate salespeople of the 1920s, McCarty and his partners would block Wilshire Boulevard with a tractor on Sundays and holidays, stopping all traffic. Salesmen would then jump on the running boards of the cars and direct the drivers through the dirt streets of the subdivision, selling the lots to the hijacked drivers. As part of the sales pitch, they would come back to the office and introduce potential customers to the architect, who for one hundred dollars would draw plans for a house of any size. The firm sold many lots and architectural plans in this manner, and so began Lee's architectural career in Los Angeles.

Levi, the junior member, soon quit this partnership, displeased that street and sidewalk improvements were assigned to the brother of one of the syndicate members without any competitive bids. He sold his interest to the syndicate for a profit, reinvesting the money in a lot near La Brea Avenue. On that lot he built a duplex, which he traded for a bungalow in Hollywood; he then sold the bungalow for a profit. Thus he established a career in real estate as well as in architecture from his earliest days in Los Angeles.

Simeon Charles Levi opened his first Los Angeles architectural office in the Douglas Building, near Third and Spring streets, circa 1923, paying the bills by subcontracting drafting for other architects, assisted by one junior draftsman. He recalled that one day early in his career, he saw a shadow through his office window, pacing back and forth in the hallway. Finally the person entered the office and asked to see "Architect Levi." When told that he was addressing Levi, the visitor exclaimed, "I expected to see an old man with a beard and a big hat. You can't be him!" Levi's reaction was, "What kind of nonsense is this? I'll change my name."[21] The decision was motivated more by a desire to avoid the potential threat of anti-Semitism to his business career than by an actual experience with it. The stereotype of a bearded old man was not what the movie-star-handsome architect had in mind. As with actors and actresses whose names were changed to "look good on the marquee," the architectural office of S. Levi became the offices of S. Charles Lee, who was always known as Sim to his close friends.

Lee moved to a hotel on Bunker Hill, where he paid rent of approximately fifteen dollars a month, and later moved to a bungalow court near Western Avenue and Pico Boulevard, which his parents purchased when they moved to Los Angeles soon after their son. By 1925, Lee's practice had grown sufficiently to warrant a move to the new Petroleum Securities Building, "where I had a small but well-decorated office and quite a few clients, mostly speculative builders for whom I designed numerous apartment buildings."[22] Lee had become a permanent resident of Los Angeles, establishing long-term business and personal connections. In April 1927 he married Miriam (Midge) Aisenstein, the daughter of a friend of his mother's.

To obtain commissions, he joined civic organizations and made speeches before community groups. Advertising was considered unethical for professionals, but because self-promotion was a necessary part of business, he supplied the *Los Angeles Times* with sketches and floor plans without charge to get his name before the public. He also wrote the column "Ask the Architect" for the Sunday edition, in which he responded to readers' questions and presented sketches and plans, resulting in some commissions.

Although he engaged in a few joint ventures over the course of his career, he never established a lasting partnership or promoted himself in the architectural profession. He was too busy promoting himself in the business world and the motion picture industry. Real estate, investments, and commercial success appeared to be more important than recognition by his peers, which was one reason he was able to retire in mid-career with no regrets. He did, however, believe in professional standards. He joined the American Institute of Architects in the early days of his practice but soon resigned, disgusted by a "knock-down-drag-out argument" among the contenders for the Los Angeles City Hall commission. He felt that the institute at that time was not representing the best interests of the city, nor of the profession. It did nothing, he maintained, to further the business of the architect; instead it restrained architects.[23] He later joined, and was subsequently named a Fellow of, the Society of American Registered Architects, a smaller professional association that he found to be "a much more practical and tractable organization."[24]

His initial commissions were for small speculative houses, duplexes, and apartment buildings, and for a few custom-designed houses, all in and around Los Angeles. The diversity of his clients resulted in projects that ranged from small bungalows to large mansions. The Cohen House (1926), for example, was an eight-bedroom Italian Renaissance Revival home perfectly comfortable in its Hancock Park surroundings. The Philip Hunt House (1927), an elaborate Italian palace based on the Duke of Alba's estate in Seville, featured a fifty-foot vaulted dome and cathedral art-glass windows, revealing Lee's theatrical flair. Others were simple four-room bungalows, usually designed in period revival styles—most often Spanish Colonial Revival but also English Tudor, Italian, and American Colonial. Evidenced in all of this work was the quaint detailing that made these homes picturesque.

The speculative apartments built in Hollywood and Los Angeles followed a typical pattern of combinations of singles and doubles. The singles contained a living room with kitchen area, a bath, and a closet with a foldout Murphy bed; the doubles had an actual bedroom. These apartments were, to quote the architect, "nondescript, no special style."[25] On the contrary, however, some of them were quite handsome, such as the El Mirador (fig. 21).

Although the exteriors of these buildings may not have been unusual, the interiors revealed innovations in planning, layout, technology, and efficiency. Lee included, for example, parking facilities, steam heating, and iceless refrigeration, replacing the weekly delivery of ice by truck with the recently invented electric icebox.[26] Haddon Hall (1926) featured a central refrigerating system for the kitchens, which consisted of a complex process of chilling water with ammonia and pumping it through insulated pipes to individual apartments.[27]

The shape of the DuBarry Apartments was the result of his desire to relocate the kitchen in the traditional apartment floor plan (fig. 22). This variation conflicted with the building code in Los Angeles, which required that the kitchen be on an outside wall; thus, additional outside walls had to be created.[28] The DuBarry Apartments were a modern building in terms of plan and technology, but the owner, Jacob Kalb, insisted on traditional architecture, so Lee gave him a mansard roof. There is, nonetheless, a theatrical detail, in the form of a French Renaissance motif, adorning the facade. Stylistically Lee gave his clients what they wanted, whether the commission was a residence or a theatre; functionally he created modern structures, thereby increasing the value of his clients' investments and satisfying his own architectural curiosities. But most important to the client, he managed to stay within the budget. Satisfied clients, he knew, led to more commissions and to new clients.

Sometimes he served as his own client. In 1926 he joined forces with two friends, forming the Universal Holding Company (UHC). Together they built speculative

21 El Mirador Apartments, Los Angeles, 1929 (S. Charles Lee, 1929).

houses, duplexes, and apartments in various parts of the city, including the Carthay Circle area, where they created a community of duplexes. Lee built one of the two-story duplexes for his wife and himself, renting out the other half as a showcase for his work and as a source of income. The duplexes cost approximately $12,000 to build, including the land. UHC would take a trust deed of $10,000, sell the units for $15–16,000, with approximately $2,000 down; UHC carried the balance. Their profits were included in a second trust deed. When the Depression affected the real estate market, however, and the houses went through foreclosure, UHC was left holding the second trust deeds. The buildings sold for $6–9,000 each on the courthouse steps, while the maker of the trust deed was liable for the balance between the remainder of the deed and the proceeds from the sale. All Lee's available cash, as well as his home, went to pay off the deeds and protect his credit.[29]

This financial setback was short-lived, however. Gradually he attracted wealthier clients and larger commissions, including several people in the motion picture industry. He designed two homes each for directors Irving Cummings (1925) and Tod Browning

22 DuBarry Apartments, Los Angeles, 1929 (S. Charles Lee, 1929). The period-revival exterior belied the innovative interior.

(1927–28). Other Hollywood clients included Louis B. Mayer and Irving Thalberg (1928), C. B. DeMille (1930s), Charles Skouras (1935, 1942), theatre muralist Anthony Heinsbergen, and screenwriter Al Boasberg (1934). He noted that he enjoyed working for clients such as these. They could afford large residences; their homes typically cost $5–6 per square foot compared to typical frame and stucco houses, which were built for $2–2.50 per square foot. They also understood set design and styles and appreciated the effectiveness of materials. "No money or convention stopped these people from building what amused them."[30] Referring to both the residential and theatrical buildings he designed in Los Angeles, Lee said in hindsight: "From the time I decided to plant my roots in Southern California in 1921, I came to the conclusion that there were two factors that would allow me to adjust architecture to my own point of view . . . 1) the climate, and 2) the free spirit of the general working population due to the influence of the making of moving pictures in the area."[31]

Although most of his residential designs in Los Angeles during the 1920s were period revival styles, Lee experimented with modern innovations and modern lines, too. He ran into trouble with the banks, however, in attempting to secure financing for flat-roofed houses. "The bank said that modern architecture would never last," he recalled, "and they did not want to have a mortgage on them."[32] Modernist ideas were also bucking the trend toward Mediterranean and Spanish Colonial design that was part of the historicist styling so popular for residences in that decade. Some subdivisions, such as Beverly Estates, had restrictions against roofs of any material other than Spanish tile, which then dictated the rest of the architectural treatment.

Lee's design of these projects displayed his theatrical flair, and his comfort with these period revival trends revealed his Beaux-Arts training. Their set-design quality reflected his experience with theatre architecture and predicted his future work. Lee commissioned theatre muralist Anthony Heinsbergen to demonstrate the technique for painting the interior of one of the houses. Residences were adorned with arches, columns, and Churrigueresque ornamentation; the duplexes and hotels featured heraldic shields, balconies (both real and false), interior courtyards, and colonnades. There were also a few commercial buildings decorated with medallions, cartouches, and garlands. Even when a tight budget dictated a simple exterior, the facade was enlivened with interesting details.

In 1928, Louis B. Mayer and Irving Thalberg commissioned Lee to design the Hollywood-Western Building on a lot they owned in Hollywood adjacent to several studios. It was to be the home of the Motion Picture Producers and Distributors of America (MPPDA), the industry's trade association, organized in 1922 to counter charges that Hollywood was involved in, and was thereby inciting, immoral and antisocial behavior. The most notable scandal concerned Roscoe "Fatty" Arbuckle.[33] Former Postmaster General Will Hays, a midwestern, middle-class, Republican teetotaler, was paid $100,000 a year to head the organization. It was his responsibility "to establish and maintain the highest possible moral and artistic standards of motion picture production" as stated in the code of ethics in the articles of incorporation, so as to defuse the growing threat of legislative censorship and to "restore the bankers' confidence."[34] The building was also to house Central Casting, formed by the MPPDA in 1926 to act as a nonprofit clearinghouse for people seeking work as extras, in another attempt to clean up the industry's image. The Hollywood-Western Building was to play an important role in Hollywood, because its major tenants were involved in the business side of motion picture production. Dozens of medical offices and ground-floor shops would pay the rent.

Headlines in the *Hollywood News* of 8 December 1928, the day the $200,000 building was dedicated, read: "Design Shows Modern Trend/Architecture of Block Symbolizes Spirit of Hollywood."[35] Lee's four-story Art Deco building celebrated the motion picture as the merging of art and business, with the latter being the superior spirit of Hollywood (fig. 23). The Lee Lawrie-esque cast-stone figures across the top of

23 Hollywood-Western Building, Hollywood, 1928 (S. Charles Lee, 1928). Commissioned by Louis B. Mayer and Irving Thalberg to house the Motion Picture Producers and Distributors of America.

the facade represented the arts of the motion picture industry: music, drama, literature, architecture, and the motion picture director. The larger figures looming over them were the producers (figs. 24, 25). In the keystone over the entry was a cast-stone figure denoting business, executed by Carlo Garrone after a design by Lee.

Described by the *Los Angeles Times* in 1928 as being in "the most modern architectural vein," the symmetrical building had a Beaux-Arts plan and massing with Art Deco decoration, demonstrating again Lee's application of Beaux-Arts traditions within a modern context.[36] The first floor, built of structural steel, formed a square; the second through fourth floors, of wood frame construction, formed an L shape, with the remaining space a skylight over the first floor. Although the building appeared to be a huge block from the front, this solution brought light into all the offices and the first floor. Rich materials adorned the lobby, including Bottecino marble, mahogany elevator cabs with gold leaf decorations, bronze doors, and a bronze lighting fixture that hung from the high groin-vaulted ceiling.

Probably the most notable features of the building were the fire escapes (figs. 26, 27). Built of cast stone rather than of conventional iron, they helped give the building a "distinctly modern [appearance] . . . decorated with the finesse of the old school." The escapes were decorated with a carved bas-relief narrative of movie making, which, according to the *Hollywood News* "can only be appreciated by careful observation. Following around the fire escape is the story of the motion picture. Actors and actresses are portrayed facing their duties before the camera. The cameraman, the property man, the director, the script girl and all combined forces are shown going about the various duties."[37]

What the reporter failed to mention to the readers was that the figures were realized as seminude, stylized Classical gods and goddesses. Lee credited himself with introducing "the first 'porno' in Hollywood."[38] On the underside of each balcony, a cast-stone Mercury held a movie camera. The irony was that on the fourth floor, just above the racy sculpture, the "Czar of All the Rushes," Will Hays, was censoring film titles and doling out or withholding stamps of approval. The Hays Office, as the MPPDA was commonly known, enforced the "Don'ts and Be Carefuls," officially referred to as Rule 21 of the Code of the Motion Picture Industry, adopted in 1927 to ensure that Hollywood movies were of unquestionable and uncompromising morality.

The dedication of this business block was a klieg-lit opening night, rivaling a Hollywood motion picture premiere (fig. 28). Lee acted as emcee as Thalberg and his wife, Norma Shearer, opened the door with a golden key. MGM's "Baby Stars" distributed souvenirs.[39] Sixty years later, on 5 January 1988, the building was designated a Historic-Cultural Landmark by the city of Los Angeles. The architecture was the only reference to

24 Hollywood-Western Building, 1989. Cast-stone figures above entrance depict directors, producers, and architects.

25 Hollywood-Western Building, 1989. Cast-stone figures along cornice line represent drama, music, and literature.

26 Hollywood-Western Building, 1989.
Bas-reliefs on fire escapes portray the art of
making movies. The figures are nude,
in the classical Greek tradition, and were
placed just outside the offices of the
movie censors of the Hays Office.

27 Hollywood-Western Building, 1989.
Winged angels on the underside of the fire
escapes are cast-stone figures of Mercury,
god of commerce, holding a movie camera.

the former glory and significance of the site, by then a run-down crime-ridden neighborhood.

During the 1920s, both Lee's work and the movie palace itself reflected a growing awareness of the importance of client amenities, which also served as advertising gimmicks. Even in his residential buildings, Lee began to combine theatricality with pragmatic concerns. Romantic, historicist facades revealed progressive ideas about space planning and an emphasis on function. His residential buildings of the 1920s can be viewed as stage sets for living, with decorative flourishes that suggest richness and elegance, primarily on their public face. He rearranged floor plans to maximize views and minimize plumbing and insisted on modern conveniences and services. The Hollywood-Western Building exploited the same qualities of showmanship but predicted the Moderne direction of 1930s Hollywood: the Art Deco movie palace. During this period, Lee became adept at the use of publicity to build a reputation for himself and his architecture, becoming a nonactivist within the architectural profession but an activist in the business community of his clients.

The introduction of talkies spelled the demise of the eclectic movie palace and marked the beginning of a building boom for theatres that could accommodate sound.

Sound motion pictures and the increasing sophistication of films made live shows unnecessary and too costly. During the construction of Loew's 72nd Street Theatre (New York, 1932, Lamb and Eberson), plans were altered to eliminate the orchestra pit. The stage house was never used, and the organ was not installed. The Art Deco Radio City Music Hall (New York, 1932, Donald Deskey), the last great movie palace, incorporated live entertainment, but this was in the heart of New York City, where such investment, though difficult to maintain, was possible.[40] The changing form of motion picture presentation, as well as the Depression economy, precluded this kind of expense in most locations.

The early movie palace, with its European styling and allusions to religious and dramatic themes, had been successful in lending an air of respectability to motion pictures through architectural connotations. During the 1920s, movie attendance in the United States doubled from forty to eighty million moviegoers per week (see appendix A). The motion picture theatre had invaded the theatre district and was competing successfully with live theatre to attract middle-class audiences. In 1914, *New York Times* drama critic Victor Watson compared opening night at the Strand to "a Presidential reception [or] a first night at the opera. . . . If anyone had told me two years ago that the time would come when the finest-looking people in town would be going to the biggest

28 Hollywood-Western Building, 8 December 1928. Opening night. In the center are Irving Thalberg, Norma Shearer, and S. Charles Lee.

and newest theatre on Broadway for the purpose of seeing motion pictures I would have sent them down to visit . . . Bellevue Hospital."[41]

The continual emphasis on being "new-fashioned" was an integral part of motion picture theatre design from the days of the storefront and was one reason why each theatre type lasted only a few years. The movie palace expressed its new presentation techniques by clothing them in the newest old styles. Historical styles were not unique to theatre design, but in the movie palace they were carried to an extreme. Eberson later stated that "the prime purpose of the design was always to satisfy the patron rather than my own aesthetic taste," which he claimed ran along more modern lines in the 1940s.[42]

The first generation of motion picture theatre architects believed that the new theatre form would be accepted more willingly under the guise of established cultural institutions; they therefore designed buildings that fit that mold. The next generation of theatre architects were younger, American born and educated, and products of twentieth-century thought. Lee had foundations in the Old School, but as a mature architect he pursued the Moderne vein. His first movie palaces were period revival pieces, but with technical innovations. He soon began to shift away from the historicist emphasis to introduce modern lines, like those in the Hollywood-Western Building.

The Oberndorff brothers, who had commissioned Lee to build the Haddon Hall hotel-apartments (1926, Los Angeles), had a friend named H. L. Gumbiner who owned a lot at Eighth Street and Broadway in downtown Los Angeles. Gumbiner wished to build a motion picture theatre on that lot, but the architects he consulted all concluded that it was impossible to contain a 900-seat theatre and commercial stores in a space that measured only 50 by 150 feet. S. Charles Lee disagreed with that assessment and believed he could do the job. The problem was how to approach the client. Investing heavily in his own salesmanship, Lee financed a champagne-and-caviar dinner party hosted by the Oberndorffs at the Ambassador Hotel, to which Gumbiner was invited. At the party, Lee cornered the unsuspecting guest and proposed not only to prepare all the plans at his own expense but to guarantee Gumbiner a building permit. Gumbiner would pay a standard fee if the efforts were successful; if not, he would owe nothing. Unable to refuse such as offer, Gumbiner agreed to the terms.[1]

At that time, the building codes for the city of Los Angeles allowed for two types of theatre construction based on the distinction between live drama and motion picture presentation in the nickelodeon tradition. The motion picture ordinance was written for theatres up to nine hundred seats, prescribed as one-story wood or masonry structures with a wooden roof, allowing for neither stage nor balcony. The legitimate theatre ordinance, on the other hand, allowed for a full stage and balcony, requiring Class A, steel-reinforced construction. Lee drew up plans for an amalgam of the two. He designed a narrow, nine-hundred-seat, Class A, steel-reinforced motion picture theatre with balcony, a small, seven-foot stage, and no fly loft (fig. 43). The plans required that more than thirty variances be submitted to the Building and Safety Commission. When the plans were completed, however, Lee recalled that the building department refused to approve them because they had no experience with such an animal. The Tower Theatre was approved by the Building Department only after appeal to the city attorney, who assured the department that it was legal, if unorthodox.[2]

The Tower was Lee's first solo theatre. Gumbiner was so pleased with it that he rewarded Lee with both a membership in the Hillcrest Country Club in Beverly Hills and another commission for the Los Angeles Theatre (1930–31) at Sixth Street and Broadway, which was to be the flagship movie palace for the city whose name it bore.[3] Before beginning the Los Angeles Theatre, architect and client made a trip throughout the United States to examine major motion picture theatres, most of which were done in various period and exotic revival styles. Gumbiner, who had come from Chicago, was acquainted with the work of Rapp and Rapp, and it was his suggestion

4

Teaser

Lee's Movie

Palaces

that both theatres should be in the French style. The Tower was a miniature interpretation of the Paris Opera House on the interior, whereas the Los Angeles emulated the glory of Versailles. The two theatres were typical movie palaces in most respects but atypical in that they were independent of any studio. The success of the Tower led to other theatre commissions.

Lee's movie palaces of this period typified the general trends in motion picture theatre architecture in the late 1920s and early 1930s, including downtown movie palaces designed for talking pictures (Tower, 1926–27; Los Angeles, 1930–31; Fox Bakersfield, 1929–30; Fox Phoenix, 1930–31) and neighborhood palaces (Fox Wilshire, 1928–30; Fox Florence, 1931), many of which were designed for Fox Studios as part of the studios' theatre-chain competition. During this period, Lee's aesthetic trademark changed from period revival to Art Deco.

By the late 1910s, a business hierarchy of motion picture theatre types had been established, defined by distribution and exhibition techniques as determined by the studios. In the eyes and bank accounts of the studios, there were six basic types of houses: first-run "de luxe"; "super"; neighborhood; third- and fourth-run; vaudeville; and double-feature. The number of the run referred to the sequence of priority rights to the exhibitor to show a particular film in a designated geographical area without competition from another theatre in that district for a designated period of time. First-run de luxe houses were usually situated in the central business or shopping area of a city. The program consisted of a first-run film, which played for as many weeks as the house was filled or until a new feature was released. The feature film was preceded by short subjects, one- or two-reel comedies, a newsreel, and sometimes an additional travel or novelty short. Studios designated a first-run house in every city where their new features premiered. In New York, Chicago, Los Angeles, and other key markets, these were the huge movie palaces, and the program was often supplemented by live entertainment. In smaller cities and large suburbs, they were the finest movie theatres, offering the same program as the palace, but without the architectural excess and without live performances.

The super, as it was called in the 1920s, was the culmination of the movie palace. A separate category from the first-run de luxe theatre, the super movie palace featured the most current architectural and exhibition trends. With a seating capacity of up to six thousand, it was "a city under one roof," with proportions comparable to public buildings of the period.[4] The lobbies and public rooms were on a grand scale; instead of one entrance lobby, there were several. Noted for spaciousness and luxury, these were the exceptional, extravagant movie palaces discussed in chapter 3, usually featuring live entertainment and overseen by a known personality such as Rothafel or Grauman.

By the late 1920s, two types of interior architectural treatments were assigned to de luxe and super movie palaces, creating substantially different spatial experiences. "Hard tops," such as Lee's Tower and Los Angeles theatres, had the character of palatial interior rooms. Legacies of live theatre, hard tops were designed in Beaux-Arts, period revival (especially French), and exotic revival styles, including Egyptian and Chinese. The other type, the atmospheric, introduced by John Eberson, had a ceiling that resembled a starry sky (fig. 20). Atmospherics exercised fantasy, imagination, and even more unfamiliar styles and special effects in a collage of paint, light, and furnishings. The auditoriums of these theatres were designed to resemble enticing exterior locations. By the late 1920s, both types had standardized formulas emphasizing new-fashionedness; only the imagery and stylistic themes varied.

Neighborhood theatres were sometimes palaces, such as Lee's Fox Florence (Los Angeles, 1931; fig. 51), and sometimes smaller nonpalaces, depending on the plan. Located in residential rather than commercial areas, they were usually considerably smaller than downtown theatres, though just as opulent, and sat as few as three to four hundred people. There was no live entertainment, and the amenities and ornamentation were scaled down. Neighborhood palaces might play first-runs or second-runs following the downtown premiere. Third- and fourth-run theatres were found wherever the population warranted them. This category also included "sensational" theatres, small houses that catered to a specific kind of movie, that is, Westerns or action pictures.

Movies continued to be shown in vaudeville-picture houses in large cities, although the live entertainment, usually five or six vaudeville acts, was still the primary focus of the show. The picture would be either a second-run or a first-run B movie, a smaller-budget, less-publicized movie than a first-run A. In small towns, the local theatre presented vaudeville acts, live theatre, or concerts, plus whatever motion pictures they could acquire.

The introduction of the double feature, consisting of two feature films instead of one feature and several shorts, was aimed at bargain hunters. This custom, which lasted for many years, was widely debated among exhibitors, however, many of whom saw the secondary movie (rated B for "bad," according to distributors) cutting into their box office revenue. They would have preferred to fill their auditoriums with a new round of ticket buyers for a second showing of the primary movie.

Motion picture producers, distributors, and exhibitors all catered to the de luxe and super theatres, because they were the greatest source of income. The economics of the studios dictated that first-run movie theatres in big cities receive preferential treatment—in the form of extensive advertising and the best movies. When studios began acquiring theatre-chain empires to keep the exhibition profits in the family, the de luxe and super theatres were their targets. They realized that by owning the first-run theatres and a handful of second-runs, they controlled the largest percentage of tickets sold and therefore made the largest profits. In 1930, the major studios owned or controlled only 13 percent of the nation's theatres but took in 70 percent of the national box office receipts.[5] What's more, the studios could afford to subsidize the building and maintenance of huge movie palaces. Independent theatre owners—those who owned from one to three theatres or who operated small houses—competed with this monopoly for the paying audience. The studios found it in their financial interest to release features only to their own theatres or to the major theatre circuits. This issue eventually led to the breakup of the studio-owned theatre-chain monopoly in the 1940s and was the death knell of the comfortable, single-screen movie theatre.

At the time Lee designed the Tower and Los Angeles theatres, Broadway was the main theatre district in downtown Los Angeles. Between the 1860s and 1890s, the first theatre district in the city had been established on the old Spanish plaza; between 1883 and 1910, it was found on Main Street, which had become the center of downtown. By the 1910s, however, Broadway boasted the most theatres in the city; there, one could see everything from motion picture premieres to the biggest names in vaudeville, at ticket prices that brought in the highest box office revenues in the city. By 1931, when the Los Angeles was built, Broadway was reputed to have the largest concentration of movie palaces in the world, with a capacity of over fifteen thousand. In addition to the seven blocks on Broadway between Third and Tenth streets, the Broadway theatre district included theatres on nearby Hill Street and was comparable in attendance and economic concentration to the legitimate theatre district of the same name in New York.[6]

The theatres along Broadway in Los Angeles ranged from small storefront nickelodeons, such as Clune's Broadway (1910, Alfred Rosenheim) and Quinn's Rialto (1917), to the legitimate Morosco (1913, Alfred Rosenheim; located in a building designed by Morgan and Walls) to classic Beaux-Arts vaudeville theatres, two of which were Orpheum houses (1911 and 1926, G. Albert Lansburgh) and one Pantages (1910, Morgan and Walls). In addition, there were twelve movie palaces, including the two designed by Lee, all competing with one another for studio releases, architectural distinction, and incredulity. Some included facilities for live entertainment, and some were limited to motion picture presentation; most were affiliated with specific studios. Downtown palaces reflected the cornucopia of revivalist styles, including the Churrigueresque Million Dollar (1918, A. C. Martin; William Lee Woollett), the Spanish Renaissance Loew's State (1921, Week and Day), the Spanish Gothic United Artists (1927, C. Howard Crane), and the Aztec Revival Mayan (1927, Morgan, Walls, and Clements). To this palette Lee added French Renaissance (fig. 29).

According to movie palace architect C. Howard Crane, the goal of a theatre architect, especially in big houses, was "the absolute pleasure and comfort of the patrons" and the ultimate in utility and beauty.[7] This was certainly Lee's goal—pleasure and comfort translated into dollars and cents. The Tower and the Los Angeles were designed as first-run de luxe movie palaces, with neither live entertainment nor studio connections. The former was the first theatre designed for talking pictures, and the latter the last downtown movie palace in Los Angeles.

Like the civic monuments built in Paris under the direction of Baron Georges-Eugène Haussmann, these two movie palaces were designed to be showplaces for the city. Even their names suggested civic importance. Although the Tower was set on a small lot, the corner spire magnified the illusion of height and kept the edifice from being dwarfed by the tall buildings surrounding it. Naming the theatre for this architectural element increased the sense of power and physical dominance.[8] The Los Angeles was named for the city itself to imply that it was the flagship theatre in the city, similar to the Chicago or the Tampa.

In 1925, E. C. A. Bullock, another theatre architect, wrote that the exterior facade of a theatre "must overshadow everything in its immediate neighborhood."[9] Although both of Lee's facades fulfilled that requirement and gave the theatres a grand sense of presence in their commercial surroundings, that shadow extended to the retail shops sharing the marquee. The Paris Cloak, Suit and Millinery House and the Smart Tie Shop, among

29 Tower Theatre, Los Angeles, 1926
(S. Charles Lee, 1926–27).

others, benefited from the advertising, traffic, and architecture of the Tower Theatre, and the business from the shops increased Gumbiner's revenue considerably, an important consideration during the Depression. The Los Angeles Theatre was built on property renting for ten thousand dollars a week, requiring that the theatre be constructed in record-breaking time. The use of prefabricated steel walls permitted completion of the building in ninety days. The basement was being plastered even before the roof was completed.[10] In spite of the speed of construction, however, the theatres were among the most expensive in the country, costing between five and six hundred dollars a seat.

Such generosity of investment paid off, at least in the short run. Critics were lavish with their praise, extolling the Tower's "undeniable feeling of beauty, luxury and charm . . . [and its] striking design" (figs. 29, 31, 32).[11] The Los Angeles was described as "breathtaking in its scale and beauty" (figs. 34, 35).[12] Edwin Schallert called it the "ultra of ultras." In an article for the *Los Angeles Times,* he commented that "such a spacious, ornate and comfortable playhouse as the Los Angeles Theatre has seldom been unveiled anywhere. . . . Sumptuousness is the note most strongly emphasized in the scheme. . . . From the time one enters the foyer with its grand staircase he is in the presence of 'sights to behold,' whose allure is only increased upon investigation."[13]

Both of these theatres not only followed the formula for the 1920s movie palace but enhanced it. The facade acted as a giant billboard, announcing that this building was a

30 Tower Theatre, Los Angeles, 1986. Stained-glass window located in lobby window behind the marquee features a strip of celluluse nitrate film, complete with the purple stripe found on early sound films, intertwined with a fleur-de-lis symbol.

31 Tower Theatre, Los Angeles, 1927.
Auditorium.

32 Tower Theatre, Los Angeles, 1927.
Detail of auditorium.

33 Tower Theatre, Los Angeles, 1927.
Workers finish plaster ceiling by hand.

motion picture theatre, the elegance of which further proclaimed that movies were now respectable. Like the canopies of grand hotels, a cast-iron and bronze marquee forming a canopy to the street announced which movie was currently showing (fig. 34). Terrazzo sidewalks swept around the marble, bronze, and etched-glass box office. By now, the box office had been firmly established at the center of a fancy outer lobby near the street "so that it would never be necessary to pass through doors or any other obstruction in order to purchase a ticket."[14] Customers may have thought they were only seeing a movie, but for Lee, the show literally started on the sidewalk: the terrazzo, box office, and marquee were previews of the luxury and escape awaiting those who purchased a ticket.

Once inside, patrons enjoyed the sumptuous surroundings of the lobby as they waited for the movie to begin. The lobbies and lounges—actually a series of spaces designed both to help pass the time while waiting for movies to begin and to manage the crowds of thousands of people—were typically appointed with overstuffed divans, marble fireplaces, oak paneled walls, and beamed ceilings (the concession stand had not yet been conceived). Architect E. C. A. Bullock of Rapp and Rapp described how the space addressed the psychology of waiting: the lobby was "a place where the waiting throng may be transformed from the usual pushing, complaining mob into a throng of joyous and contented people. . . . [It is] so designed and so equipped that the fascination resulting from it will keep the patron's mind off the fact that he is waiting."[15] Among notable examples, the lobby at the Uptown (Chicago, 1925, Rapp and Rapp) was one block long, and the marble and bronze lobby of the Paramount (New York, 1926, Rapp and Rapp) measured two hundred by forty-seven feet and stood five stories high. Bullock described it as "similar in many ways to the old famed Paris Opera House."[16] As in Charles Garnier's design for the Paris Opera (constructed between 1861 and 1874), an inordinate amount of space was given to the lobby in comparison to the auditorium, and for the same reasons. These entr'acte spaces served social purposes; they were places to see and be seen and helped make the theatre an important civic and social place. The lobby of the Tower demonstrated an even more direct reference to Garnier's cultural monument. A grand arched stairway filled the front lobby. Flanked by marble-faced Corinthian columns, the stairs were wider at the bottom, creating a place, not just

34 Los Angeles Theatre, Los Angeles, 1931 (S. Charles Lee, 1930–31). The Los Angeles Theatre opened in 1931, featuring Charlie Chaplin's *City Lights*.

providing access to the balcony. A chandelier lighted the stairway, which was surrounded by French Renaissance detailing.

The lobby of the Los Angeles, modeled after the Hall of Mirrors at Versailles, was a barrel-vaulted, draped, and chandeliered hallway (fig. 35). Mirrored walls, in addition to making the long narrow entry seem larger, reflected the gold and glitter of the plaster baroque decorations and increased the amount of light in the space. These surroundings thrust the ticket holders into the role of actors, causing them to pose and primp before the mirrors. As a final embellishment, crystal chandeliers hung from cove-lit domes. Theatre architects and showmen had learned well the lessons of seventeenth-century France: opulence symbolized social status for the owner, the architect, and the community.

Dominating the lobby of every theatre would be a grand staircase. The Tower and Los Angeles theatres were no exception. As a focal point that filled the huge lobby space, the staircase again called to mind the Paris Opera. There is something theatrical about a stairway that encourages posturing. Even subtle gradations in height were marked by graceful stairs that slowed one's entry, making it more dramatic (fig. 36). The grand stairway also enticed people up the custom-designed fleur-de-lis carpet to the balcony. An eighteen-foot, three-tiered bronze-and-crystal fountain in the Los Angeles Theatre led the eye up to the second level of mezzanine seating. Up until that time, there had been a stigma attached to sitting in the balcony in American theatres because of a nineteenth-century custom of reserving it for segregated groups: blacks, prostitutes, and rowdies.[17] Now, however, the balcony beckoned with another luxurious lobby and loge seats.

Downstairs from the main lobby in both of these theatres was a huge lounge-ballroom paneled in walnut and decorated with authentic French antiques. At the Tower this space was seventy-five feet long and twenty feet high. The Los Angeles lounge was even larger and featured a prism designed by an engineer from the California Institute of Technology that projected the movie from the main screen in the auditorium to a smaller screen in the lounge. Each of these lounges was large enough to accommodate 450 persons (fig. 36). This area provided another waiting area and allowed viewers a sneak preview, albeit a silent one, of the movie; music piped from the auditorium above made the waiting more enjoyable. Opening off the ballroom were several ancillary rooms assigned to patrons' real and imaginary needs. One could use the smoking room; music room; nursery, complete with carousel, toys, and attendant; restaurant; and elaborate restrooms (figs. 37, 38). The ladies' lounge in the Los Angeles was equipped with sixteen toilet stalls, each appointed in a different Italian marble. The makeup room contained chairs, tables, and mirrors framed in light bulbs, further enveloping a woman in her role of actress for the evening. For men, there was a shoeshine stand of pink Carrara marble. Such luxurious spaces and services, including ladies' maids and nursery attendants, pampered theatregoers of all classes and indulged them fleetingly in a life-style otherwise available only to the wealthy.

Throughout the interior, every inch of the walls, floor, and ceiling was covered in decoration, much of it handcrafted by Old World artisans (figs. 33, 39). The ornately framed proscenium had several layers of draperies, teasers, and tormentors, lush curtains

35 Los Angeles Theatre, 1931. Entrance lobby modeled after the Hall of Mirrors at Versailles.

36 Los Angeles Theatre, 1931.
Ballroom of the basement lounge.

37 Los Angeles Theatre, 1931.
Restaurant in basement.

38 Los Angeles Theatre, 1931. Nursery in basement, which offered the services of an attendant.

that dressed up the screen in the trappings of theatre and royalty and reinforced the drama and luxury of the palatial surroundings (figs. 31, 32, 39, 40).[18] Asbestos screens, installed for fire safety, were hand-painted with murals in the motif of the theatre, usually a reference to place, history, or theme. The asbestos curtain at the Los Angeles Theatre depicted a French court scene (fig. 41). Above the curtain in the center of the proscenium arch was the coat of arms of the city of Los Angeles, a direct reference to seventeenth- and eighteenth-century European opera houses and theatres. The proscenium, by tradition, was not allowed to rival the decoration of the royal boxes, but the center placement was reserved for symbolic elements, such as the French fleur-de-lis or a royal or regional coat of arms.[19]

Although the architectural details had origins in buildings designed for French royalty, the emotional inspiration for the theatres was an even stronger institution: the church. "Like the cathedral," Lee said, "the motion picture gave people what was missing from their daily lives: religion, solace, art, and most importantly, a feeling of importance."[20] To Lee, the church was "the first to combine art and entertainment and to offer it at a price the public could afford. The idea behind the big movie palaces was that people could go in for only twenty-five cents and feel like royalty. They could sit on velvet seats under crystal chandeliers, in an atmosphere that was much grander and more lavish than anything else they knew."[21]

The iconography of the movie palace in fact combined religious, royal, and theatrical imagery. Traditionally, the ceilings of European palaces, government buildings, and theatres were decorated with elaborate murals of gods or classical heroes. The ceiling mural in the eight-story auditorium of the Los Angeles Theatre, painted by the Heins-

39 Los Angeles Theatre, 1931. Side wall of
auditorium.

bergen Decorating Company, was a period piece depicting French ladies surrounded by healthy cherubs and allegorical figures, all floating on clouds and framed by fleur-de-lis panels.

Such royal and quasi-religious imagery suffused both the interior and exterior of the building. The facade of the Los Angeles loomed like a Baroque cathedral over its surroundings, and the Tower contained a stained glass window over the entry, suggesting a rose window (fig. 30). In the center of the design was a cartouche containing a fleur-de-lis pattern, across which was draped a coiled celluloid film strip, complete with the purple stripe found on early sound film. Religious connotations and references were applied freely in the movie palace in the form of chimes, domes, pulpits, and niches. Crane's United Artists Theatre (Los Angeles, 1927) copied a Spanish Gothic cathedral, and, of course, the Roxy Theatre (New York, 1927) was blatantly billed as "The Cathedral of the Motion Picture." Forty-five years after the Los Angeles was built, then-theatre manager Robert Miranda said people would occasionally pass by the theatre, look in, and kneel down, believing they were in a church.[22]

Niches, statuary, pilasters, cartouches, murals, chandeliers, and coffered ceilings with sunbursts and geometric patterns offered a veritable catalog of architectural decoration. Even the carpets were especially designed to reflect the architectural theme. Lighting added mood by subtly, yet dramatically, focusing attention on certain parts of the auditorium and reinforcing the ambiance. In covering the opening night of the Los Angeles, the *Los Angeles Times* commented: "Sumptuousness is the note most strongly

40 Los Angeles Theatre, 1931. Auditorium seating in groups of six, so that patrons had to cross in front of no more than two people. The seats were connected to a light board in the lobby alerting ushers to available seating.

41 Los Angeles Theatre, 1931. Asbestos curtain painted with a French court scene. In the center of the proscenium is the crest of the City of Los Angeles.

emphasized in the scheme of decoration. The gold that is sufficiently dazzling when the interior is fully lighted, dims invitingly when the theater is darkened, giving a rare illusion of richness."[23]

Early movie palaces incorporated large pipe organs to accompany silent films and fill the auditorium with music. The orchestra pit was frequently mechanized so that the orchestra or the "Mighty Wurlitzer" would rise through the floor on cue (Lee's Tower featured a sixty-thousand-dollar Wurlitzer). The exposed pipes provided yet another aesthetic opportunity for interior embellishment. Organ screens or grilles, set high on the walls flanking the movie screen, were ornately decorated in complex fabric, plaster, or metal patterns. Even when later palaces did away with the organ, the legacy of a decorative screen on either side of the proscenium remained.

Traditionally, motion picture theatre architecture was grounded in the modern aesthetic, which, though sometimes translated into period revival motifs, was understood to imply new technology. The Tower Theatre contained several innovations, not the least of which was a sound system that accommodated the first showing of Vitaphone in Los Angeles. The theatre opened 12 October 1927, one week after the debut of *The Jazz Singer* in New York, in which Al Jolson, his voice coming directly from the screen, promised, "You ain't heard nuthin' yet." With those words, he introduced feature-length talking motion pictures, which would revolutionize both the motion picture industry and theatre architecture.

Lee recollected that the Tower opened with the Los Angeles debut of *The Jazz Singer.* Advertisements for that night, however, indicate that the opening was somewhat less dramatic. The gala featured the premiere showing of Lois Wilson and George K. Arthur in *The Gingham Girl,* a silent feature, along with a Vitaphone short of Fred Waring's Pennsylvanians.[24] Lee enjoyed telling an anecdote concerning the sound system: while the Tower was being built, no one knew the dimensions of the speakers or understood the operations of the sound system. The horns turned out to be too big for the stage and had to be installed in holes cut in the back wall.[25]

Warners and Fox were the first studios to experiment with talking pictures as a means of competing with the larger studios. Fox, which had been exploring sound on film, applied the new technology to newsreels, which they premiered at the Roxy Theatre in New York on 30 April 1927. In 1926, working along slightly different lines, Warner Bros. developed Vitaphone, a sound system that used sixteen-inch one-sided phonograph records synchronized to reels of film. Their "Vitaphone Preludes" were canned vaudeville acts or filmed prologues with sound track. In making the track for *The Jazz Singer,* Warners had intended that only the musical numbers be recorded on disk, but Jolson began ad-libbing, surprising even Warners and demonstrating that spoken lines could also be recorded. Sound films permitted not only Warner Bros., which owned neither a distribution system nor a chain of first-run theatres, but also independent theatre owners such as Gumbiner to compete with the downtown movie palaces that could afford live prologues and big-time vaudeville acts. "Canned vaudeville" meant that Warners could capture more impressive performers on film than the other theatres could get live. Their program consisted of a silent feature and a vaudeville act on film, with synchronized sound on disk.[26] In late 1927 the Tower showed both the Warner Bros. program and the Fox Movietone Newsreel. By autumn 1930 virtually all Hollywood studios were producing only talkies.

Gumbiner also requested that both his theatres be air-conditioned and kept at a uniform temperature of seventy degrees at all times. Air-conditioning, invented in 1908 by Willis Carrier, had previously been used only in hospitals and industry to control humidity. In 1921, the Central Park Theatre in Chicago introduced it as a creature comfort, as did Grauman's Metropolitan Theatre in Los Angeles in 1922. Movie theatres used air-conditioning routinely thereafter, the revenues from which allowed the Carrier company to survive the Depression.[27] Painted icicles dripping on a banner hanging from the marquee became as necessary as the marquee itself in theatre vocabulary and an important selling point (fig. 49).[28] Ads for the Tower Theatre in 1927 read:

Leave Your Fan at Home!

Manufactured Weather makes every day a good day at the Tower Theatre. When you enter, you will realize that H. L. Gumbiner has fulfilled one more great obligation to his public. He has included in this theater the marvel of manufactured Weather. This is a Carrier Conditioned Theater providing to the patrons a copious supply of air that is washed and purified, air that is warmed and humidified for ideal comfort in winter, air that is cooled and dehumidified for invigorating comfort in Summer, air that is greatly diffused throughout the theater without the slightest draught.[29]

Eager to promote his investment, Gumbiner had a window installed on the landing between the first floor and the restrooms from which patrons could view the weather machinery.[30] One of the exterior poster cases at the Los Angeles contained a recording apparatus that continuously compared the temperature inside and outside.[31] A plaque over the drinking fountain advertised ice-cold water.

Even though the Tower had introduced talkies to Los Angeles four years earlier, the Los Angeles premiered in 1931 with a silent movie, Charlie Chaplin's *City Lights,* when no other theatre would dare revert to the obsolete type. Only the independent Chaplin would attempt to make a silent movie after talkies were the accepted norm. *City Lights* was not technically silent, because it was accompanied by synchronized music and sound effects, though not by spoken words. The film was released through United Artists, organized as a distributing company for publicizing and renting independent productions of its founders and owners, Mary Pickford, Douglas Fairbanks, Charlie Chaplin, and D. W. Griffith, none of whom was associated with a studio. Previews of the new Chaplin film had not gone well, exhibitors were reluctant to book the film, and the circuit-theatre owners had a wait-and-see attitude. The Los Angeles Theatre, which was unaffiliated with any studio, was a logical choice—perhaps the only choice—for the premiere. The building was completed in time for the premiere; both the movie and the theatre cost nearly $1.5 million.

On 30 January 1931, the opening-night audience paid ten dollars a seat to see the new movie at the new theatre. A crowd of twenty-five thousand also gathered in front of the theatre to get a glimpse of Hollywood glamour in a Depression setting. Police attempted to control the throngs along Broadway as limousines pulled up to the flood-lit theatre to deliver Chaplin and Albert Einstein. Police cars and ambulances maneuvered through the crowds, which had smashed the shop windows next to the theatre. It is unclear whether the violence was caused by the excitement of a Hollywood premiere or by the blatant contrast between the well-dressed attendees and those waiting in a breadline across the street.

Chaplin was understandably concerned about the reception of his latest film. Dreading the evening, he felt a mixture of nausea and nerves. As he described it:

> The proprietor [Gumbiner] had built a beautiful theatre but, like many exhibitors in those days, he knew little about the presentation of films. The picture started. . . . [The audience] began to laugh! . . . I had got them! All my doubts and fears began to evaporate. . . .
>
> Then a most incredible thing happened. Suddenly in the middle of the laughter the picture was turned off! The house lights went up and a voice over a loudspeaker announced: "Before continuing further with this wonderful comedy, we would like to take five minutes of your time and point out to you the merits of this beautiful new theatre." I could not believe my ears. I went mad. I leaped from my seat and raced up the aisle: "Where's that stupid son of a bitch of a manager? I'll kill him!"
>
> The audience were with me and began stamping their feet and applauding as the idiot went on speaking about the beautiful appointments of the theatre. However, he soon stopped when the audience began booing.[32]

Lee's memories of the evening revealed a different emotion:

> The biggest thrill for me was meeting Albert Einstein and Charlie Chaplin at the opening night. It was a gala Hollywood opening, the world premiere. . . . After meeting those two men, anything seemed possible.[33]

From the beginning, the Los Angeles Theatre was plagued with financial problems. According to Lee, Gumbiner thought that studios would be unable to resist public demand for entertainment in such a lavish theatre, thereby enabling Gumbiner to break the studio-chain monopoly.[34] But Gumbiner went broke trying. Unable to book first-run films, he could not complete the funding arrangements to cover construction costs and had to declare bankruptcy.[35] To collect his fee, Lee was forced to file a "friendly" lawsuit against the theatre and Gumbiner.[36] The theatre went into a court-supervised receivership for over eight months and finally closed in December 1931. It remained dark for some time during the Depression and was later reopened by William Fox as a second-run theatre. For a while, it played host to MGM premieres. During World War II, it took in thirty thousand dollars a week, but in the 1950s, the bottom dropped out. In the 1970s, the Los Angeles revived, playing to Hispanic audiences, but by the late 1980s it was again in trouble.[37]

Gumbiner never gave up faith in his palace, however. In 1939 he wrote Lee a letter praising both his theatres and their architect:

> There is no doubt in the mind of anyone who has visited the Los Angeles Theatre, including Mr. Rotheralfel [sic] of the Roxy, also the Radio City, of New York. After reviewing with me the lay-out and beauty of the Los Angeles Theatre he personally acknowledged to me that in his opinion the Los Angeles Theatre was the most outstanding cinema house in this country and also in Europe. . . . Also the Tower Theatre was acclaimed by professional architects to be the most outstanding 1000-seat house in the country [perhaps this statement was actually Lee's, because a sign on the construction fence proclaimed this before the building was completed; see fig. 139]. . . . In my opinion there is no better qualified man than you in the architectural professional [sic] to erect any building that requires new thoughts and new ideas.[38]

The language of this testimonial reveals that Gumbiner was a showman, not a businessman, cut from the same template as Rothafel or Grauman. There is a pattern of naïveté in the letter that characterizes the hyperbole and mythology of Hollywood, where glamour and illusion reigned over common sense and Depression hardships. Gumbiner was insufficiently aware of the underlying economic realities necessary for the success of a consciously designed fantasy environment, whereas successful palace operators knew they were selling make-believe in hard currency.

Movie palace decor was limited only by the architect's imagination, the desired public image, and the client's budget. By the early 1930s, each of these would be stretched to the limit in a fierce competition for the largest, grandest, most unusual, or most beautiful entertainment temple.

This quest led from period revivals to exotic revivals. Concurrently with the discovery of King Tutankhamen's tomb in 1922 came a passion for things Egyptian in the United

States. Cemeteries, banks, and even prisons suddenly sported lotus columns, buttressed walls, and hieroglyphics. Exotic motifs were ideally suited for the escapist architecture of the movie palace. Meyer and Holler's Egyptian Theatre (Hollywood, 1921) was described in the professional journals as a "Temple of Egyptian Art";[39] Meyer and Holler also designed Grauman's Chinese Theatre (Hollywood, 1927). Architects replicated hallways, sculpture, friezes, and choir galleries of specific and generic European ancestry.[40] Penciled notes on the drawings for the Los Angeles refer to specific plates of the Petit Trianon for authenticity in detailing. The Fifth Avenue Theatre (Seattle, 1926) was an exact copy of the throne room at the Imperial Palace in the Forbidden City, and the architect, R. C. Reamer, employed local Chinese artisans to help with the sculpture and decorative effects.[41] Hiring ethnic workers for such tasks, as Lee did for the interior of the Los Angeles, was not unusual and provided useful material attesting to the building's authenticity.

In Southern California, this quest for exoticism often took the form of Spanish Colonial, because it was thought to be historically accurate and geographically appropriate. Examples included the Fox (Bakersfield, 1929–30, Lee; fig. 44), the Fox Florence (Los Angeles, 1931, Lee; fig. 51), and the Fox Arlington (Santa Barbara, 1931, Plunkett and Edwards). These theatres often featured a Spanish courtyard garden as part of the exterior design (figs. 53, 54). Pre-Columbian motifs were utilized in the Mayan Theatre (Los Angeles, 1927, Morgan, Walls and Clements).

Exotic styles not only connoted escape but demonstrated the ambivalence of American attitudes in the 1920s. Having seen much of Europe during the war, American soldiers returned with images of French châteaus and Tudor cottages that over the next decade sprang up in bungalows, apartment buildings, and commercial architecture throughout the United States. However, national disillusion with international commitment and the rejection of a position as a world power shaped the isolationism and laissez-faire policies that characterized the 1920s. Period revival architecture was the cultural expression of that ambivalence. It drew on historical images of a more innocent time, but beneath the thin veneer of these superficial styles were identical American boxlike bungalows and office buildings.

Period revival and exoticism thus constituted design by ornamentation in theatres as well as in residential buildings. The architecture of plan, organization, hierarchy, and the original meanings of these forms became irrelevant. The new purpose was to conjure images of escape and fantasy. Sounding like Lina Lamont in *Singin' in the Rain,* John F. Barry in the 1926 *Paramount Pep Club Yearbook* proclaimed it the theatre manager's duty to help people "seek escape from the humdrum existence of daily life."[42]

Between 1914 and 1922, at least four thousand new theatres opened, most of them palaces, replacing the smaller, passé nickelodeons.[43] Studios were able to parlay large publicity campaigns into box office receipts, first when the film opened and then again when the film was released in suburban theatres. First-run policies and luxurious theatres justified higher admission prices. The studios quickly learned that first-run presentation houses and major feature releases were mutually beneficial economically. This was one of the reasons the studios began to invest in first-run houses.[44]

In the 1920s, the percentage of motion picture theatres owned by independent exhibitors, such as Gumbiner, steadily decreased. Independents were defined as owning fewer than four theatres. Circuit-theatre chains, on the other hand, were operated by exhibitors, who had no financial affiliation with producer-distributors but who banded together or were bought by single-interest owners to accrue the same advantages of strength in numbers as the studios were acquiring.

The third branch of exhibitors were the studios. Most of Lee's movie palaces were built for Fox West Coast Theatres (FWC), a subsidiary of Wesco Corp. controlled by Fox, marking the beginning of a long relationship with that theatre chain. In 1927, Harold Franklin, president of FWC, stated that of the eighteen thousand motion picture theatres in the United States, one thousand were owned and operated by studios. He rationalized this first-run monopoly as "natural and logical . . . [so as] to maintain a contact with the ultimate consumer. . . . At the same time [the system] afford[s] independent theater owners an opportunity to gauge the public reaction to the pictures presented, and serv[es] as a guide to value."[45]

The means of acquisition were not without critics, including the infamous Stanley Company's use of "wrecking crews" and "dynamite gangs" to intimidate theatre owners into selling their enterprises to Adolph Zukor and Paramount. By 1930, Paramount-Publix, Fox-Loew, Warner Bros., and RKO owned between twenty-five hundred and three thousand theatres in the United States and Canada, which included most of the first-run and many of the second-run theatres in those countries.[46] The Federal Trade Commission responded by filing an antitrust suit against Fox and the other studios, which dragged on for a decade.

In the 1920s, theatre-chain operation, whether controlled by the studios or by the circuits, became an industry modeled after other industries, consolidating ownership and adopting a mass-marketing and big-business approach. Ownership shifted from private hands to public stock. Corporate studios applied the chain-store strategy to retailing motion pictures. By the end of the decade, company purchases and mergers resulted in seven firms holding oligopolistic control of film production and first- and second-run exhibition.[47]

In 1926 Adolph Zukor announced that he planned to control all three thousand first-run movie theatres in the United States.[48] Marcus Loew, William Fox, and Carl Laemmle, among others, competed with him in collecting regional theatres, but the most successful operation was Zukor's Paramount-Publix, which began with the Balaban and Katz (B&K) chain.

B&K had perfected the regional chain in Chicago between 1917 and 1923.[49] In 1924 they joined with Zukor, who controlled Famous Players–Lasky. The regional B&K in Chicago was transformed into the national Publix Corporation, the world's largest theatre circuit. Theatres were standardized and efficiently directed by a central authority in New York: Sam Katz. All advertising, promotions, prologues, design changes, architecture, and even the ushers' uniforms were determined by the central office and carried the Publix logo. Many newly acquired theatres were renamed Paramount to develop brand-name recognition and loyalty. They were selling more than movies; they were selling a corporate image. As their ad in *Variety* said, "You don't need to know what's playing at a Publix House. It's bound to be the best show in town."[50] Two

EXTERIOR

FOX WILSHIRE THEATRE, BEVERLY HILLS, CALIFORNIA

S. Charles Lee, Architect

TWENTY-FIVE STORY OFFICE BUILDING FEATURE OF ALTERNATE DESIGNS FOR AN OFFICE BUILDING AND THEATRE PROJECT. PROPERTY IS SIX HUNDRED FEET LONG AND CONTAINS TWO THEATRES—ONE OF ONE THOUSAND SEATS CAPACITY, AND ONE OF THREE THOUSAND SEATS.

S. Charles Lee, Architect.

million customers a day agreed. In 1929 Publix agreed to merge with Warner Bros., but the threat of an antitrust suit prevented the merger.[51] At the same time, studio-sponsored advertising became a major source of income for newspapers. In turn, newspapers began giving more coverage to movies, movie stars, and the publicity campaigns that accompanied new releases. More publicity extended the run at de luxe houses but hurt the independents, who had to wait longer for third-runs.

Like many other industries in the 1920s and 1930s, film exhibition was increasingly administered on a national basis, and regional and local businesses could not compete. Such a system enabled a handful of companies to survive the Depression and the decline in film attendance while many small theatres went bankrupt (see appendix A). Chain operations grew primarily through mergers, takeovers, and the acquisition of existing urban and suburban theatres.

New construction was designed to fit the corporate image as well as popular and regional forms., Examples of theatres reflecting the new ethic were Lee's Spanish Art Deco Fox Wilshire (Beverly Hills), Deco-Spanish Fox Phoenix, atmospheric Fox (Bakersfield), and Spanish Colonial Revival Fox Florence (Los Angeles), all built between 1928 and 1931 (figs. 44, 46, 49, 51). These were all typical movie palaces done for a single chain, but they reflected changes in style and in evolution of the type.

In atmospheric theatres the interior was designed to look like an exotic outdoor space, be it a Persian courtyard, Middle Eastern market, giant aquarium, or Never-Never Land. Three-dimensional gardens, trees with wire and plaster "leaves," windows, balconies, and roofs adorned the walls. Some even included plaster pigeons. Bridges crossed the proscenium, while overhead, sunsets, twinkling stars, and floating clouds on a blue plaster sky were effected through blinking lights.[52] Advertisements for Brenograph machines touted the effect of "a canopy of clouds moving across a field of twinkling stars . . . to complete the illusion that the pictures are being viewed beneath nocturnal skies." The air dome, in a sense, lived on in a controlled environment. Such pre-Disneyland fantasy became the everyday world of theatres as signs such as the one at the Paradise Theatre (Faribault, Minn.) reminded the staff, "Please do not turn on the clouds until the show starts. Be sure the stars are turned off when leaving."[53]

The scenographic auditorium of Lee's Fox Bakersfield resembled a Mediterranean village and skyline (fig. 45). Indirect lighting added mood to the ivy-covered "facades" with their coats of arms, arched windows, and red-tiled roofs. The interior scene harmonized with the Spanish Colonial Revival exterior. A one-hundred-foot office tower, fitted with cathedral glass windows and a four-color revolving lamp on top, rose above an iron marquee outlined in neon. The theatre included backstage facilities and was flanked by eleven income-producing rental shops (fig. 43). The lobby featured massive beams of painted wood and tapestries depicting the Spanish discovery of the New World, but there was little other ornamentation hinting at a modernistic future. As in his earlier theatres, once again patrons could view the air-conditioning equipment from the stairs connecting the lobby and the balcony. The ceiling over the balcony looking down onto the lobby followed the incline of the balcony, echoed in massive beams.

In the auditorium, "the hot glare of the [Bakersfield] desert sun without is smoothed to the soft light of a summer moon by means of indirect lighting enhanced by star effects

42 Fox Wilshire Theatre and alternate versions of the Wurlitzer Building (S. Charles Lee, 1928–30). In his designs for the Wurlitzer Building, which had a theatre on the ground floor, Lee toyed with both a historicist and a modern aesthetic.

Theatre Plans

S. Charles Lee, Architect

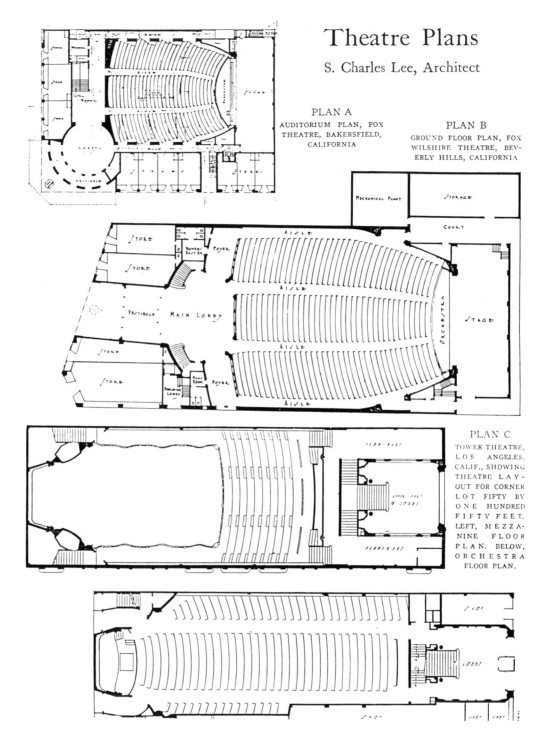

PLAN A
AUDITORIUM PLAN, FOX
THEATRE, BAKERSFIELD,
CALIFORNIA

PLAN B
GROUND FLOOR PLAN, FOX
WILSHIRE THEATRE, BEV-
ERLY HILLS, CALIFORNIA

PLAN C
TOWER THEATRE,
LOS ANGELES,
CALIF., SHOWING
THEATRE LAY-
OUT FOR CORNER
LOT FIFTY BY
ONE HUNDRED
FIFTY FEET.
LEFT, MEZZA-
NINE FLOOR
PLAN. BELOW,
ORCHESTRA
FLOOR PLAN.

43 Fox Theatre, Bakersfield; Fox Wilshire
Theatre, Beverly Hills; and Tower Theatre, Los
Angeles (S. Charles Lee, 1926–30).
Auditorium plans. Note the inclusion of shops
along the facade, intended to attract
customers and to bring the owner
additional rental income.

44 Fox Theatre, Bakersfield, California, 1929 (S. Charles Lee, 1929–30). Early drawing, which was more dramatic than the built version.

45 Fox Theatre, Bakersfield, 1930. Atmospheric auditorium.

in the theatre ceiling."[54] The auditorium walls upon which the summer moon shone were decorated with acoustic plaster to suggest tiled roofs, textured surfaces, grilled windows and balconies, elements of a romantic Spanish horizon. The proscenium in this seventeen-hundred-seat auditorium was extra wide, having been designed for Grandeur Pix, a short-lived wide-screen idea developed by Fox in 1929.[55]

John Eberson, who designed over one hundred atmospherics beginning with the Hoblitzelle Majestic (Houston, 1923), described these romantic locales as the kinds of places "royal nabobs and lords gather to barter everything from fruit to human souls."[56] This level of fantasy and the lure of an environment suggesting escapist intrigue led to competition in exotica as each theatre tried to extend the boundaries of the imagination and suggestion. Eberson turned to this technique, he said, in an effort to "avoid being boring," and to satisfy the public need for variety and newness.[57] More important, it was a means of distinguishing one grand palace from all the others, of trying to give each one a unique sense of place that outdid every other extravaganza. Eberson may have been the best known, but there were predecessors. J. E. O. Pridmore had based the Cort Theatre (Chicago, 1908) on an ancient amphitheatre, complete with painted sky, stars, moon, and hanging vines.[58] Not everyone found the coy fantasy of atmospherics charming. Englishman P. Morton Shand described them as "this nauseating stick-jaw candy, so fulsomely flavoured with the syrupy romanticism of popular novels and the 'See Naples and die' herd-nostalgia."[59]

More telling of Lee's aesthetic direction was the Fox Wilshire (figs. 46, 47, 48). The theatre was located one block inside the border of Beverly Hills, which gave Fox a first-run flagship palace that drew patrons from that city as well as from outlying areas but did not compete with its other flagship theatre in downtown Los Angeles. The twenty-five-hundred-seat palace was "of modern design throughout with decorations in varying shades of silver, coral and black in a magnificent edifice."[60] The abstract classicism of the concrete facade and the elegant stylized interior decoration were the epitome of modernism as depicted in Art Deco set designs of that era.

Movie palaces such as the Fox Wilshire were expensive to build and maintain, especially during the Depression. The entertainment value of period and exotic revival architecture waned with rising disillusion over the old order, and modern design took its place. The forward-looking modernist lines of Art Deco, and later of Streamline Moderne, also reflected the economic hard times in which they were built. "Modernistic" architecture, as it was called, was an optimistic rejection of the pre-Depression boom that had culminated in a bust; the new style reflected the hope of moving forward instead of backward.

In the first third of the twentieth century a battle waged in the architectural press among Revivalism, a holdover from the nineteenth century (actually the style was Neorevivalism, because the buildings represented a reassembly of old elements); Modern, the nonhistorical approach of Frank Lloyd Wright, the Bauhaus, and others; and Modernistic or Moderne (fig. 42). Modernistic was subdivided into, and later christened, Art Deco and Streamline Moderne. Again, it was a decorative, not a substantive, approach. According to an architect of the period, Moderne was suitable for cinema design because it "offers the decorator a fresh and fertile field for the play of imagina-

46 Fox Wilshire Theatre, Beverly Hills, ca. 1930 (S. Charles Lee, 1928–30).

FOX
WILSHIRE
THEATRE
A STRIKING HOUSE IN BLACK AND SILVER
DESIGNED FOR NEIGHBORHOOD PATRONAGE
2500 CAPACITY

S. CHARLES LEE
ARCHITECT
2404 WEST SEVENTH STREET
LOS ANGELES

47 Fox Wilshire Theatre, 1930.
Advertising brochure, probably designed by
Lee's office, featuring a montage of the
Art Deco theatre, described as "a striking
house in black and silver."

48 Fox Wilshire Theatre, 1930. Proscenium.

49 Fox Theatre, Phoenix, 1931 (S. Charles Lee, 1930–31).

tion."[61] Art Deco produced a luxurious quality through the use of rich materials and new decorative motifs. For the movie palace trying to simulate richness and luxury, Deco was an ideal substitute for Louis XIV. As Lee explained, "You couldn't afford to build monuments and we looked for another type of stimulating architecture."[62] The form grew out of French, Italian, and German experimentation with modern lines and was a consciously new and deliberate "style." The style proved a good solution for exterior treatment as well, by allowing for better artistic integration of sign and facade. Modern sign designs with electric lights never sat very comfortably on Italian villas and French châteaus.

Walter Rendell Storey, writing in the *New York Times* in 1929, suggested that such "Modernistic treatment" was a way for the motion picture theatre to develop a style of its own—a declaration of independence from the legitimate tradition. Its stark color contrasts and limited palette were more closely attuned to black-and-white movies than to live drama. Even though it "is at first disconcerting because of its apparent lack of decoration or meaning," Storey determined that Modernistic was following the Modernist manifesto of Form Follows Function.[63]

Hardly devoid of ornament, as advocated by Modernism, modernist Art Deco substituted geometric abstractions for Rococo, covering every inch in the new style and colors (figs. 47, 48, 50). It was still a case of superimposed decoration, however. Marcus Priteca claimed that he chose the style for the Pantages (Hollywood, 1930) as "an original treatment that would best exemplify America of the moment . . . motifs that were

50 Fox Theatre, Phoenix, 1931. Auditorium.

modern, never futuristic—based on time-tested classicism of enduring good taste and beauty."[64] This strand of American modern did not reject history but merely substituted modern decorative motifs for period revival.

The introduction of sound into motion pictures required renovation of existing theatres to accommodate the speakers. In new buildings, it eliminated the need for a stage or orchestra pit. Theatre owners such as Marcus Loew responded quickly to these changes because of the popularity of the talkies and the money to be saved. Lee's Fox Wilshire, however, was designed to incorporate live entertainment. The facilities included a full stage, basement greenroom, dressing rooms, and large proscenium, which made possible its conversion into a live theatre in 1981 (fig. 43).[65] Atop the building was a six-story tower with a rotating "Fox" sign visible for miles (fig. 46). The two top floors of the tower contained an apartment suite for Howard Sheehan, one of the vice-presidents of Fox. This apartment, with its Art Deco built-ins of exotic woods and sleek chrome, resembled a set design right out of *Topper* or *Grand Hotel*. Comparably lavish Art Deco palaces included Stiles Clements and Albert Lansburgh's Wilshire Wiltern (Los Angeles, 1931) and J. R. Miller and Timothy L. Pfleuger's Paramount (Oakland, 1931).

Lee's eighteen-hundred-seat Fox Phoenix combined two popular styles (figs. 49, 50). The exterior was a dramatic Art Deco–stylized Spanish with chevron and circular motifs set against a concrete facade. A Spanish crown adorned the sleek marble base of the box office. The interior was pure Deco, from the lobby furnishings to the wall and ceiling murals and light fixtures. Much of the modernist look derived from the materials and colors used. The organ grilles were silver leaf highlighted with gold. A metallic sunburst spread across the ceiling from radiating acoustic frames of the proscenium arch.[66]

Automobiles profoundly affected all aspects of twentieth-century life, including moviegoing habits. Theatre designers on the West Coast, which ranked highest in cars per capita, were among the first to take into account this trend toward the private automobile. Theatre muralist Anthony Heinsbergen, Sr., blamed the death of the movie palace on "no good pictures and television. But do you know what really killed them? No parking. People started going to suburb theatres so they could park their cars. It's as simple as that."[67]

Before the automobile became popular, people often took the streetcar to the movies after work or shopping. By the 1920s, however, the population had come to rely increasingly on personal transportation; as a result, parking became a problem, and people were reluctant to drive downtown to the movies. As early as 1931, Lee had advocated adding parking underneath Pershing Square, a large park in downtown Los Angeles one block away from his Los Angeles Theatre and other theatres along Broadway, but it was considered too costly.[68]

By the early 1930s, theatre designs were responding to the needs of the automobile. The Fox Florence, which opened 8 April 1932, was a neighborhood palace (figs. 51, 52). The seventeen-hundred-seat theatre embodied many of the characteristics of a downtown palace, but it was located in the Florencita district, a suburb of downtown Los Angeles. The Spanish Colonial Revival building, with shops facing the street, was

51 Fox Florence Theatre, Los Angeles, 1931
(S. Charles Lee, 1931). Note the "Free Auto
Park Entrance" on the far right.

52 Fox Florence Theatre, 1931. Plan. Here
the shops surround the interior patio in
addition to opening onto the street.

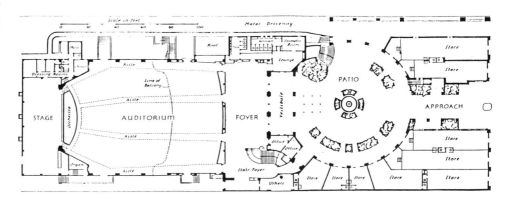

designed around a central courtyard containing a Mexican fountain and tiled stairway (figs. 53, 54). Set at the entrance to the courtyard, between the shops, the box office was sheltered under a lacy marquee. The interior featured heavy wooden beams painted in panels that complemented the arched doors and Spanish baroque furnishings (figs. 55–57). A roof of red tiles carried out the Spanish motif.

One of the arches along the facade covered a porte cochere labeled "Free Auto Park Entrance." Cars went past the courtyard, where passengers could be let off, and on to a parking lot at the rear (figs. 51, 52). Providing convenient access to safe parking encouraged people to go to the movies on impulse and certainly lessened the chance of losing potential customers who could not find a place to park. The automobile became a part of the moviegoing process by physically passing through the facade of the building. The Fox Phoenix was the beginning of Lee's acknowledgment of the role of the automobile in American life, especially in Los Angeles. The theatre now had to be attractive, and accessible, to drivers as well as pedestrians. Lee would continue to perfect this feature, making the automobile increasingly integral to the structure and plan.

53 Fox Florence Theatre, 1931. Patio courtyard.

54 Fox Florence Theatre, 1931.
Fountain in patio courtyard.

55 Fox Florence Theatre, 1931. Interior
lobby, with stairs leading to balcony.

56 Fox Florence Theatre, 1931. Balcony lobby.

57 Fox Florence Theatre, 1931. Auditorium.

The move to the suburbs had begun with the nickelodeon around 1913–14. As one suburban writer lamented: "What has happened to our communities? It is impossible to find in the vicinity of New York any town with a population over five hundred free from the blight of the nickelodeon. . . . What will it take to stop them?"[69] Russell Merritt credits that move from the dirty side streets in questionable big-city neighborhoods to the main streets of bedroom communities with establishing a national audience for the movies and paving the way for the movie palace. Neighborhood palaces such as the Fox Florence marked the transition between the movie palace of the 1920s and the neighborhood house of the 1930s.

Through the 1930s, owing to changes in aesthetic ideas as well as budgetary considerations, theatre design became increasingly restrained and simpler, drawing closer to commercial Art Deco and the strand of Modernism that challenged historical principles. Streamlined design reached its peak during the middle and late 1930s, by which time the movie palace had been replaced by the next phase of movie theatre design, the neighborhood house.

More significant than the change in style and decoration was the economic reorganization of movie theatres in the 1930s, when they came under the control of corporations. The largest and one of the last movie palaces built in the United States, and one of the few still operating as a movie palace in the early 1990s, was the Art Deco Radio City Music Hall (New York, 1932, Donald Deskey). Movie theatres had entered the world of big business, as Will H. Hays demonstrated in his dedication of Radio City: "This is not a dedication of a theatre—it is a reaffirmation of faith in America's indomitableness and fearlessness. [It] rises like a Pharos out of the blinding fogs of irresolution and bewilderment to proclaim that leadership has not failed us. . . . [This is] the bravest declaration of faith in their country's stability that the Rockefellers, father and son, America's most useful citizens—have yet offered. Let us rise and salute them and all their works.[70]

This emphasis on being new-fashioned—seen in the increasingly ornate and exotic palaces—was an integral part of movie theatre design from the days of the storefront, and one reason why each theatre type lasted only a few years. The movie palace expressed its new presentation techniques by clothing them in the newest old—and later new—styles. Historical styles were not unique to theatre design, but in the movie theatre they were carried to an extreme. Although Beaux-Arts-trained architects regularly designed Renaissance Revival banks, churches, office buildings, and legitimate theatres, often using style books as sources, all constraints fell away with the movie palace. The classical vocabulary merged with Art Nouveau lines and overt symbols of wealth, culture, and power in the forms of Greek temples, royal palaces, grand hotels, opera houses, and cathedrals.

Many theatre designers, including Rapp and Rapp and Sexton and Betts, argued that the movie theatre of the 1920s represented the cultural expression of changing American social values.[71] Having risen to prominence following the "war to make the world safe for democracy" and having flourished in multiethnic cities, this most popular of the popular arts provided a place for democratization in a setting of distinct class differences: imperial palaces. The architecture "thrills one class and attracts the other," commented a leading architectural journal in 1927.[72] Immigrants would be acculturated and the masses liberated as they reveled in luxury and beauty unavailable to them anywhere else except the church. The new religion, with its shrines, reliquaries, rituals, and gods, was to operate as a cultural melting pot, in which everyone was treated with equal respect. Factory workers and scrub women would rub shoulders with the Astors and the Vanderbilts. It is unlikely, however, that very many shoulders touched. Balconies were still designed with separate entrances, and lobbies were usually divided by brass railings, both as indicators of where blacks (and not just those in the South) were to stand and sit. Architects, writing in professional journals, referred without apology or embarrassment to "nigger heaven," a racist term for the uppermost balcony.[73]

Movie palace architects of this period claimed that architectural design centered on pleasing the customer. Movie palaces replaced nickelodeons the way talkies replaced silent movies—quickly and irrevocably. Attendance figures verified the popularity of the new forms. The vocabulary of the new theatre carried with it the trappings of the traditional theatre, with its royal boxes, ceiling murals, and stairways. The psychology of entertainment inherent in the architecture began with escape and slowly evolved into glamour, especially as period revival and exotic revival gave way to Modernism characterized by Art Deco motifs. The very form of the movie palace had established an environment of excess, but exotica of place gave way to exotic form and material expressed in sleek lines with no historical references. Modernistic Art Deco palaces were an expression of the New World promised by the twentieth century, hoped for with the end of the Depression, and guaranteed by the technology of make-believe.

5
Feature Presentation
The Movie Theatre Takes Shape

In the latter half of the 1920s, the full vertical integration of production, distribution, and exhibition took place within the studio system. Famous Players–Lasky was the first studio to take this step, in 1919; others followed suit. By 1930, there were five such firms: Famous Players–Lasky (later Paramount); Warner Bros.; Loew's; Fox; and RKO. Thus, the major studios known as the "Big Five" constituted an oligopoly of production and theatre ownership, controlling the structure and conduct of the industry through their numbers. The rest of the theatres were managed by smaller circuits or by a few independents who were unaffiliated with any circuit.

Immediately following this business consolidation, however, the nation entered the devastating economic downturn of the 1930s. The effects of the Depression reverberated throughout the motion picture industry. One by one, the studios entered hard economic times. By 1929, Fox was already in trouble, and after merging with a small independent firm, was reorganized into Twentieth Century–Fox in 1935. Paramount went into receivership in 1933, then into bankruptcy, and reorganized in 1936. Loew's was controlled by Fox when Fox went into receivership. After being put into a trust, Loew's stock went public and the company emerged as MGM. RKO faced bankruptcy in 1934 and was reorganized in 1939. Even Universal, which sold its theatres, went into receivership in 1933 and was reorganized in 1936. Only Warners, Columbia, and United Artists managed to survive—with their theatre empires intact.[1]

Theatres also underwent hard times. Average weekly attendance dropped from ninety million in 1930 to sixty million in 1932, and the number of theatres remaining in operation fell from nearly twenty-two thousand to just over fourteen thousand (see appendix A). Studios and theatre operators responded to the economic crisis with new marketing strategies. The studios produced escapist movies—the well-known screwball comedies, gangster films, and musicals of the era. And theatre owners introduced double features, or "duals," with the intention of giving customers more for their money.

Theatre managers also tried a variety of come-ons and giveaways to stimulate attendance. Such lures as Bank Night, Bingo, and Dish Night promised either free gifts or a chance to win money or large items as an inducement to spend scarce Depression income at the movies. On Dish Night, for example, managers distributed a free dish to each customer. One could thereby accumulate a set of dishes by going to the movies once a week, at a time when most families could not afford real china. The sale of popcorn and candy replaced the once-free service amenities owners could no longer afford.

The studios could ill afford to spend money building or maintaining the movie palaces of the 1920s, which had become passé in style. Subsidized services were the first to go—the nurses, military ushers, and restroom attendants. Male ushers were replaced by lesser-paid women. Managers were advised to place these "pretty girls" in strategic places—near shabby spots in the carpet or draperies, for example—to distract patrons and defray replacement costs. Theatre owners resorted to remodeling instead of new construction as a means of expressing the contemporary attitude. The few theatres that were built were much smaller and simpler in scale than those of the previous decade; such adjustments reflected not only the lack of available capital but also the change in public life-style. Many patrons no longer willing to travel downtown to go the movies went to the neighborhood movie house instead. In spite of unemployment, automobiles were not to be sacrificed, and the new theatres reflected this emphasis on modernity, suburban living, and automobility. These combined efforts were successful, as attendance figures confirmed. In 1934 attendance began to climb.

Regardless of this upturn, exhibitors still resented the studios, who seemed to have suffered less during the Depression and who continued to dictate the terms of the relationship. "Block booking," introduced by Adolph Zukor, was a prime point of contention, along with designated play dates and other exhibition policies. Block booking meant that the exhibitors contracted to buy a whole package of titles rather than being allowed to negotiate each picture individually. They were thus compelled to show films they did not want, and programming was in the hands of the studios. The system thereby prohibited exhibitors from choosing their own programs. Studio-owned theatres also had a monopoly on first-runs. Independent theatre organizations petitioned the government to intervene in the name of antitrust. In 1933, as part of the New Deal, Franklin Roosevelt had instituted the National Recovery Administration (NRA), which urged local businesses and industries to establish their own codes of conduct. In Hollywood, this meant the studios, who already controlled the industry and had a financial stake in the regulation of theatres. As proof of their patriotism and cooperation, theatre lobbies carried the insignia and film logos were followed by the NRA eagle proclaiming "We do our part." The studio-controlled codes endorsed block booking and the elimination of theatre-sponsored lotteries and drawings, which smacked of gambling. Dish Night survived, but only through the efforts of the pottery manufacturers' lobby.[2] In 1935 the Supreme Court declared the NRA unconstitutional, and the battles resumed; independents again pressured the federal government to intervene in the production-distribution-exhibition relationship.

During this decade social and economic forces served as a catalyst in the emergence of the motion picture theatre as a mature architectural type. Independent of its historical roots, it required no references to church, vaudeville, or opera. Moviegoing was a socially acceptable form of behavior and no longer needed an architectural defense. The design of theatres was now based on functional requirements and scientific and technological innovations, and cased in a new modern aesthetic. Gone was the applied ornamentation; decorations grew out of structural and pragmatic elements.

Lee's architectural career reached its peak during this decade. His unique contribution as a motion picture theatre architect emerged: he was able to capture the magic, glamour, and excitement of an entire theatre district in a single building, at a fraction of the cost of the movie palace. The theatres he designed during the 1930s fall into three categories representative of the decade: remodelings, novelty theatres, and neighborhood houses.

On 31 July 1931, only six months after the gala opening of the Los Angeles Theatre, the Studio Theatre had a much quieter opening in Hollywood. If the former illustrated the dramatic economic discrepancies of the Depression, the latter was an example of a more realistic struggle to conquer it. At a cost of twelve thousand dollars, or less than 1 percent that of the Los Angeles, Lee remodeled a storefront on Hollywood Boulevard into a new three-hundred-seat theatre (figs. 58, 59). It was intended to be the first in a chain of innovative and low-cost theatres.

Harold Franklin, after being removed as president of Fox West Coast, formed a syndicate with Howard Hughes to build a chain of four theatres. They commissioned Lee to design a prototype of what they called the "automatic theatre," the first of which was the Studio. The idea was to economize by making the theatre what might be termed a "machine for viewing." Billed as the "World's Most Unique Theatre," the Studio was designed with electronic gadgets and simple machinery. So streamlined was the setup that it required only a cashier and a projectionist to operate the business. The box office, though still on the sidewalk, was now attached to the building. The cashier took in money but no longer issued tickets, which would have required collection by an usher. Instead, patrons passed through a turnstile next to the box office, which led to electronic front doors that opened when approached. A counter next to the turnstile compared the number of tickets sold with the number of customers entering and recorded whether they were adults or children.

Inside the lobby were coin-operated machines selling cigarettes, candy (before most theatres began to allow candy inside), and even photographs. There was also a soda fountain that sold "orange foam," with the promise "What a man you'll be!" This stand, which was accessible from the street, also attracted thirsty pedestrians who were not interested in the movie, thus earning additional profits for the owners. A weather machine for air-conditioning carried the boastful slogan "We manufacture weather better than Mother Nature herself; Fresh Air All Year Round."

The Studio, part of the trend toward efficient design prevalent during the 1930s and the only automatic theatre built, was well published in the professional journals. Although the Hughes-Franklin chain was discontinued, theatres throughout the United States used many of the ideas developed in this experiment.

The growth of theatre chains and the impact of the Depression on movie palaces were directly linked to the development of the so-called neighborhood house. The downtown palace gave birth to the neighborhood palace, which in the 1930s became simpler and utilized more-modern architectural imagery. Even the term indicated a different vision of attendance habits. Since the 1920s cinemas had been moving away from the city toward the suburbs, especially in Chicago and Los Angeles. The first- and second-run system encouraged smaller, independent theatres near housing developments. Theatre-chain acquisitions of these theatres during the 1930s eliminated the competition with first-run houses in the city because the chain ended up owning all the theatres.

58 Studio Theatre, Hollywood, 1931 (S. Charles Lee, 1931). The prototype for a proposed series of "automatic theatres," although no others were ever built.

HOLLYWOOD'S SENSATIONAL AUTOMATIC THEATRE

S
CHARLES
LEE
ARCHITECT
2404 W. 7TH ST.
LOS ANGELES
CALIFORNIA

Stylistically, many neighborhood houses, whether independent or chain-operated, followed the latest trend: Streamline Moderne. The same psychology of design and same economic opulence of previous decades were applied, only on a smaller scale and in the smooth lines of the machine aesthetic. Single-story buildings adorned with flashy marquees, bright lights, vertical signs, and ornate box offices sat next to parking lots and suburban shopping centers. Automobiles had become a primary factor in theatre design, changing the shape of the marquee, the layout, and even the proportions of the building. Although these individual buildings no longer had to compete with large downtown commercial blocks, they nonetheless dominated their surroundings, both physically and psychologically.

In plan, neighborhood houses returned to the simple hall with a box office, sloped floor, screen, and projection booth. Because live entertainment was never a factor, there was no stage (only a narrow apron), no orchestra pit, and fewer rooms and services. The theatres sat between eight and twelve hundred people and focused on comfort and efficiency. The lobbies, which were closer to living rooms than to royal parlors, were furnished to create a homey environment. Small lamps and torchères had replaced dripping chandeliers, perhaps as a reflection of the image of domestic security longed for in the Depression. The screen was smaller and was no longer "masked" or framed in most houses of this period. Plaster swirls replaced the layers of draperies.

Although the focus during this era was on function rather than on fantasy, Lee's Academy Theatre suggested that both could be accommodated. Architects and engineers scientifically studied seating arrangements to optimize the line of sight and comfort—analyzing the best chairs and the number of inches between them—and compared the cost per seat of various construction techniques.[3] Notes on acoustics, sound, air-conditioning and ventilation, projection angles, safety, and lighting suggestions filled their notebooks. The newly emerging field of industrial design had begun to influence theatre design. Even remodeling called for clean lines, modern graphics, and the conversion of eyesores into smart, functional buildings. Thus, by the 1930s the idea of architecture as an escape was redirected into architecture that did not distract from the escape of the movie.

During this period, Lee refined his philosophy concerning the psychology of motion picture theatre architecture as entertainment, eventually creating an architectural signature. Although each theatre had a unique and distinctive appearance, all shared an unmistakably dramatic flair. The composite Lee theatre of the 1930s demonstrates the talent and business acumen of the man. His theatres, now refined and the formula perfected, embodied visibility, seduction, and comfort. Yet in spite of the sleek lines and reduced budgets, Lee still fulfilled his promise that "the show starts on the sidewalk."

For pedestrians, this meant a terrazzo sidewalk of colorful marble swirls that encircled the box office and set the building apart from surrounding structures. Overhead, one was protected by the canopy of the marquee, the soffit of which echoed the terrazzo pattern in neon. On all sides, the pedestrian was surrounded by color, light, and lines that gently lured one toward the box office and through the door (fig. 60). As Lee explained it: "We have attempted to stimulate the escape psychology in the design of our theatre fronts, to throw off the cares of the day and dwell for awhile in the land of make-believe. . . . We

59 Studio Theatre, 1931. Advertising brochure featuring a montage of the Studio Theatre.

have therefore departed from the customary shapes or ornament and functionalism of the office building, home or hotel."[4]

Theatre visibility began long before one neared the doorway, however. Whether in the city or the suburbs, a distant tower, usually outlined in neon, announced the motion picture theatre beneath. Although downtown theatres such as the Los Angeles or Tower used not only the tower but the entire facade as signage, the suburban neighborhood house relied on a solitary streamlined tower to suggest presence and monumentality. During the day, its height drew attention; at night the structure was enhanced with neon stripes and glowing balls of light. The Tower Theatre (Fresno), which contained 5 miles of neon tubing, featured an 8-foot ball of colored light atop the tower (fig. 69).[5] So prominent was the tower that the theatre and the entire neighborhood thereafter became known as the Tower District, the home of such businesses as Tower Home Appliances, Tower Cake, Tower Music, and Tower Beauty Shops. The 130-foot tower of the Academy Theatre featured a neon spiral, described by Lee as a "traveling lightning bolt," that could be seen 10 miles away (fig. 77).[6] Neon block letters spelled out "Academy" on one side and "Preview" on the other. These alternating messages were visible only at night, as descending streams of white, green, and red neon light repeatedly unveiled the words on the tower and then led to the marquee. The spiral motif was quoted a few feet away in the neon sign announcing the parking lot entrance.

60 Fremont Theatre, San Luis Obispo, 1987 (S. Charles Lee, 1941–42). All the lines of the lobby, from the box office and the marble terrazzo to the undulating side walls containing the poster cases, coordinate to pull the customer toward the entry. The design motif is echoed even overhead in the soffit lighting.

The automobile gave rise to changes in theatre architecture, from the shape and size of the marquee to parking lot accommodations. Pylons grew taller so that one could see the theatre name from several blocks away in a moving vehicle. It is noteworthy that as automobiles brought about an increase in the size of individual elements in proportion to the building, economic constraints also dictated a building that was smaller and simpler. The marquee grew larger, and the tower slimmer but more dominant. Much of the lot was frequently devoted to parking, which had the effect of setting off the building physically. The Tower (Fresno) even had a parking attendant to guard the 150 cars in the free lot.

After sundown, exterior lighting defined the building against the skyline, frequently changing its silhouette. The marquee of the Tower Theatre (Compton, 1935–36) redefined the building at night through light and shadow instead of through mass and volume (figs. 61, 62). Day and night reversed solid and void. Lights flashed the name of the theatre in every direction—vertically, horizontally, and at an angle to the street (figs. 63, 67). Light patterns, color, and design integrated the marquee and the facade.

The marquee was always the most important and distinctive feature of a movie theatre. A marquee typical of the period proclaimed to the public: "This is a movie theatre; this is the Tower Theatre; and we are currently showing 'Woman Wanted' and 'The 39 Steps.' We're also giving away $1,100" (fig. 62). The marquee created a visual landmark, extending from the facade so that the building stood out physically and aesthetically from all others on the street. In the 1910s and 1920s, marquees were dark, flat, delicately decorated sources of detailed information as in the Tower Theatre (fig. 29), but during the 1930s, they were transformed into what Ben Hall has called "electric tiaras."[7] Bold and bright, the later marquees were outlined in moving lights, known as "flashers" and "chasers," that danced in the reflections of windshields (figs. 67, 69).

To make the marquee more readable to automobile traffic, the size and shape changed from a small rectangle to a large trapezoid that projected obtusely from the facade. During this evolution, the amount of information decreased while the graphics became larger. What started as a simple sign announcing a film eventually enveloped the entire facade. The marquee of the Academy, for example, was a seventy-foot semicircle. At the Bruin Theatre (Los Angeles, 1937) the horizontal band of light wrapped around the corner and could be seen from all directions (figs. 65, 66). Located in a busy theatre district, the Bruin was distinguished from its competition by a thousand square feet of coordinated colored lights that blinked in harmony. The message constituted the architecture; the walls had virtually disappeared. Lee capitalized on the value of this huge billboard as an advertising medium, realizing that it outdid newspapers in attracting customers.[8]

The outer lobby was usually "soft" instead of square, that is, it had no hard edges. Undulating lines and rhythms pulled customers toward the door, guiding and entertaining them, without their necessarily being aware of the seduction. All the lines of this space, from the terrazzo to the walls to the soffit lighting, embraced the patrons in geometrics, florals, or sunbursts of light and color. Lee noted perceptively that the color should be "flattering to women patrons."[9] Well-lit and carefully placed poster cases, framed in lights, chrome, or aluminum, lined the curved front of the theatre. At the

61 Tower Theatre, Compton, California,
1936 (S. Charles Lee, 1935–36). The
tower can be seen for miles around and acts
as a beacon to attract patrons and to mark
the location of the theatre in the cityscape.

62 Tower Theatre, Compton, 1936. At
night, positive and negative spaces are
reversed.

63 La Reina Theatre, Sherman Oaks, California, 1938 (S. Charles Lee, 1937–38). Lights extend in every direction, and the name of the theatre can be read from five angles.

64 La Reina Theatre, 1937. The back wall of the auditorium was covered with waffled acoustic panels that absorbed noise.

65 Bruin Theatre, Los Angeles, 1988 (S. Charles Lee, 1937). The marquee wraps around the corner and can be seen by traffic approaching from four directions.

66 Bruin Theatre, 1988. At night, the lighted marquee and the entry lobby are all that can be seen of the structure.

67 State Theatre, San Diego, 1941
(S. Charles Lee, 1939–40). In addition to
attracting customers, the lighted beacon
outlines the streetscape.

Tower Theatre (Santa Rosa, Calif., 1939) concealed neon tubes in the poster cases combined with mirror-backed lamps recessed in the ceiling to illuminate the Vitrolite-paneled outer lobby.[10] At the Academy, the free-standing cases were fitted with fluorescent illumination inside and colored neon light at the back, creating the illusion at night that the poster cases were floating in a luminous rose-colored background.[11]

In the center of the entrance was an island box office, designed, according to Lee, to be "attractive in appearance and flattering the attendant."[12] Many of his box offices were architectural marvels in themselves, repeating the theme of the building (figs. 68, 70, 79, 86). Rippling plaster "lids" resembling the caricatured marcelled hair of leading men sat atop glass walls, which were etched with flowers, the name of the theatre, or the pattern of the terrazzo. The base was polished aluminum, stainless steel, bronze, or marble. The entry doors echoed these motifs with circular windows, etched glass, or polished bronze.

The whole interior had a set-design quality, beginning with the lobby. Built-in sofas for lounging, small signs announcing restrooms and exits, and overhead cove lighting catered to the physical and psychological comfort of the customers. Lee believed that the lobby should be modern but not severe; ornamentation should be well-placed and "lean to the unusual."[13] Mirrored-glass trim around the doors expressed a modern feeling, as did the use of exotic materials. The Tower (Fresno), for example, showcased "rare woods from the tropics, gold [leaf] beaten to the thinness of a hair, and silver [foil] flattened into paper thickness" (fig. 71).[14]

For the first time, movie theatres introduced candy, heretofore prohibited for sanitary reasons as well as for protection of the expensive interior furnishings. Popcorn appeared first, followed by candy and soft drinks.[15] The new candy counter, subtly and attractively lighted, was gradually allotted an increasing amount of floor space and a more central location. Owners found that refrigeration, first used to keep the air comfortable, could also be used to preserve candy and to keep drinking water ice-cold. Lee designed one of the first candy counters, a portable unit that could be folded up at night.[16] It was entirely self-contained, with an air-conditioning unit that kept the air at a constant temperature so that chocolates would not turn color. This design soon became standard and led to large candy counters that included popcorn-making machines. As yet another innovation, Lee invented a popcorn machine that kept the popcorn warm.[17]

The plans of Lee's Depression-era theatres were carefully thought out for a conve-

68 Vogue Theatre, Oxnard, California, 1986 (S. Charles Lee, 1941). Box office.

69 Tower Theatre, Fresno, California, 1939
(S. Charles Lee, 1938–39).

70 Tower Theatre, Fresno, 1987. Box office.

71 Tower Theatre, Fresno, 1939. Light trap.

nience and economy that complemented their visual strengths. Lee designed primarily in plan, and only secondarily in terms of style. The plan was based on, and in turn dictated, the circulation and comfort quotient of the space. Toilet facilities should be easy to find without directions. Amenities such as smoking or cry rooms—what Lee called "monkey rooms"—were provided for adults and children who required immediate gratification so as not to disturb others. These rooms, now found on the same floor as the auditorium, were streamlined heirs of the plush basement lounges and nurseries, but without the extras. Speakers and windows connected these spaces to the auditorium. To provide security, the manager's office was placed in the corner of the building, with a view of the box office, lobby, and parking lot.

Separating the auditorium from the lobby, usually on axis with the entry, was what Lee termed a "light trap," which he patented (figs. 71, 80).[18] It was his solution to the problem of light in a dark auditorium. If the auditorium doors were parallel to the screen, light leaked in every time the door was opened, creating a distraction and a glare on the screen. Latecomers who could not adjust their eyes to the darkness blocked the aisles, which became congested, noisy, and dangerous. To correct these problems, the auditorium was turned at a right angle to the entry when possible, and the doors leading to the auditorium were set back from the lobby or placed at either end, creating a short hall that separated the lobby from the auditorium. This hall, decorated in the theme of the theatre, was dimly lighted. Concealed illumination projected from all around a three-quarter-inch plate-glass panel, creating a molded effect at the edges. People could wait in this hallway as their eyes adjusted to the semidarkness. This space not only created a passage into the auditorium but blocked the noise coming from the lobby.

The auditorium was designed so as not to distract from the movies or break the mood when the houselights went up. Wall treatments, which might be murals (a holdover from the movie palace) or plaster ornamentation or just swooping lines, tied the interior together visually (figs. 74, 82, 87). The proscenium arch also underwent changes. Gone were the organ grilles, but their space was still reserved for decorative treatments, such as plaster feathers over exit doors. Together with the light pattern on the ceiling, the walls blended the interior in shape, color, and harmony, translated as great swirling patterns that led the eye to the screen. Movie palace chandeliers had given way to decorative lamps and recessed neon tubes. Indirect lighting, controlled by dimmer switches, provided subtle distinctions of light, and the arrangement of fixtures complemented the interior motif. Additional house lights were installed for the giveaway advertising gimmicks common during the Depression, so that both the emcee and audience members could read the ticket numbers.

Lee began to experiment with "black" light to create decorative effects in the auditorium. This was the popular term given to the phenomenon of luminescence, or the "conversion of invisible near-ultraviolet energy to radiation in the visible portion of the spectrum by means of fluorescent or phosphorescent materials."[19] Fluorescent light picks up any surface upon which fluorescent material has been applied. The technique had been used for years in stage productions to create special effects or to mark locations for people and props. New lamps and materials now made possible its use in decorating the front of the house. Fluorescent fibers were woven into the carpets and fluorescent

72 Tower Theatre, Fresno, 1939. Auditorium with house lights on.

73 Tower Theatre, Fresno, 1939. When the house lights are turned down, the fluorescent lights pick up the different patterns painted on the side panels as well as patterns on the carpet.

74 Carlos Theatre, San Carlos, California, 1940 (S. Charles Lee, 1939–40). In the auditorium, bold lines, large-scale graphics, and recessed outlines all guide the eye toward the proscenium and frame the curtained screen. These features were frequently destroyed in the 1950s, when wide screens were installed.

paint applied to the walls and murals. When the lights dimmed and the decorative ceiling fixtures—fluorescent lights controlled from the projection room—were lighted, new patterns emerged in the darkness, highlighting or completely changing the decoration seen under the houselights (figs. 72, 73).

Lee was the first architect to use black light as a decorative element, and the Academy (1939) was the first theatre in the United States to feature it. The second was the Tower (Fresno); during construction, the owners spent fifteen hundred dollars redoing the auditorium to accommodate the new technique. The auditorium of the State Theatre (San Diego; 1939–40) was the first to be completely illuminated by black light.

Neighborhood houses were generally limited to one floor, with no balcony or mezzanine, although the floor sloped up toward the back of the house to maximize the view the screen. Designers paid great attention to comfort and luxury—or at least the illusion of it. Seats were carefully planned so as to maximize sight lines and allow appropriate legroom and personal space. Self-folding and retractable seats, which had names like Bodiform or E-Z-Pas, were upholstered in napped fabrics, usually red. The manufacturer of Bodiform chairs claimed they were "constructed on a scientific principle of posture control . . . [and] to eliminate clothes soiling and tearing hazards."[20] The Tower (Fresno) boasted of its "backache proof" chairs, which were designed to adjust to the weight of the user. Although the Tower could have crowded more seats into the space, this was a short-term method of increasing revenue. Customers would come back only if the environment were comfortable. Air ventilation was distributed throughout the building with separate controls to take care of the lower and higher portions of the auditorium.

Technical innovations centered on acoustics and projection. The rear walls of the La Reina (Los Angeles, 1937–38), Tower (Santa Rosa, 1939), and State (San Diego, 1939–40), for example, were waffled with angular panels and treated with acoustic plaster to minimize distortion (fig. 64). These panels were incorporated into the design and could be painted to harmonize or contrast with the side walls.[21] At the State, "The auditorium walls are treated with a specially prepared mineral that, together with the Lee patented system of wall construction, creates a perfect hearing at all tone levels, and every instance . . . is clearly heard in any part of the auditorium."[22] All of these innovations came about in the midst of the Depression, while studios were facing bankruptcy. Lee's emphasis on the pragmatic and efficient paid off. And he proved one did not need to sacrifice aesthetics.

Lee went so far as to consider the different needs of theatres on the East or the West Coast, or the differences between summer and winter, when the overcoats people carried absorbed sound.[23] Screen materials were improving, which also improved the quality of the acoustics. When Walt Disney commissioned Lee to design the Disney Theatre (1939–41), used for previewing Disney movies and cartoons at the studio in Burbank, Disney requested an advanced sound and projection system. Anticipating stereo-type sound for cartoon effects, Disney, together with Lee, created a sound system that surrounded the viewers and became "a forerunner of what was to come twenty years later."[24] In the theatrical tradition of ballyhoo, these technical innovations were exploited for publicity. For example, an article in the local newspaper described how the auditorium of the Tower (Santa Rosa) "was constructed with only one thought in view—the showing of motion pictures . . . [although] the auditorium is completely wired for 'television,' 'if and when' this latest marvel becomes practical."[25]

Each of Lee's theatres was given a theme (sometimes in the form of a gimmick), which was revealed in the stylistic motif and sometimes in the name. The Tumbleweed Theatre in Five Points (El Monte, Calif., 1939), for example, was built for a client with limited capital and a location as isolated as the name implied. The client said he needed the theatre for film-buying purposes and told Lee he would accept a barn, as long as it had a projection room. That's exactly what he got: a barn and farmyard (fig. 75). The exterior tower was a wooden structure with a simulated windmill and wishing well. The farmyard contained a small pond with ducks and geese and other barnyard objects such as wagon wheels. Inside, the building was kept plain. The lobby contained Early American furnishings such as farmers might have, and the auditorium was decorated with wagon-wheel light fixtures and murals of mules and cactus. The open-beamed ceiling captured

75 Tumbleweed Theatre, Five Points (El Monte), California, 1939 (S. Charles Lee, 1939).

the mood yet was inexpensive to construct. The entire theatre, including neon, cost thirty-five thousand dollars, a low in theatre construction cost.[26] At a time when most theatres cost $200–225 per seat, the Tumbleweed cost only $75 per seat.[27] The decorative creativity used in this theatre kept costs down, gave the client a unique structure, and capitalized on the imaginative environment motion picture theatres encouraged. But the Tumbleweed still had all the requisite elements: tower, light, marquee, interior comfort, and recognizability as a type.

The Academy Theatre, at $125–150 per seat, on the other hand, was to be the epitome of sophistication (figs. 76–79). In keeping with plans to use the theatre for the Academy Awards, the etched-glass figure of a woman holding an Oscar adorned the light-trap wall (figs. 80, 81). The theatre was never used for that purpose, however.[28] Streamlined styling was evidence of the theatre's modernity. Machine-made industrial materials such as glass block, polished aluminum, and chrome tubing—all hard, shiny, and slick—accented the novelty and luxury of the building.

Streamlining, which permeated the Depression decade, was an ethic borrowed from industrial design. Engineers had developed the concept for automobiles and other transportation machines, including ocean liners, trains, and airplanes. In 1933 Lee received his pilot's license, which enabled him to impress his clients by flying them to building sites in his streamlined Beechcraft (fig. 83). His interest in aerodynamics fed his search for new and original architectural images, leading him to experiment with streamlined architecture. Wind-tunnel studies showed that a parabolic curve offered the least resistance to a solid moving through air or water, thereby increasing its speed and efficiency. In the 1930s the principle was applied by industrial designers to every product imaginable. Many items, such as pencil sharpeners, toasters, and radios, had no need for

76 Academy Theatre, Inglewood, California,
1939 (S. Charles Lee, 1939). The ultimate
Streamlined Moderne theatre.

77 Academy Theatre, 1939.

78 Academy Theatre, 1939.

79 Academy Theatre, 1939. Streamlined box office and lobby.

80 Academy Theatre, 1939. Light trap.

wind-tunnel resistance, but the status associated with speed, efficiency, and modernism was a strong selling point.

Streamlining was the style of the future, as seen in World's Fair buildings, science fiction comic books, and Flash Gordon movies. The visually dynamic quality of this new aesthetic attracted the attention of passersby, especially motorists. Interestingly, the Chrysler Airflow, the first streamlined car, introduced in 1934, was less successful than the streamlined theatre, which had no practical use for speed. Automobile designers and historians have suggested that the styling of the Airflow was too extreme to be popular.[29] It violated a basic principle of industrial designer Raymond Loewy: MAYA—give the public the Most Advanced Yet Acceptable. Chrysler had heedlessly projected people into the future instead of previewing the future at a level of acceptable risk. But at the movie theatre, one could borrow from the future and escape for an afternoon without making an embarrassing, permanent investment.

Streamlining was applied liberally to every conceivable building type. Its swooping lines, horizontal emphasis, and smooth veneer projected an image of modernism, the promise of the twentieth century. This was a new concept of integrated design in which the architect incorporated all parts of the outer shell into a sleek, deliberately designed object. The ornament was an integral part of the structure—indeed, the structure was the ornament (fig. 85). This unified approach to design contrasted with the functional approach of earlier decades, in which the accidental shape of a building was the sum of necessary parts attached where needed, then decorated with applied ornament.

Gone were the hard edges and corners. Rounded surfaces let the wind and the eye slide effortlessly around the facade (figs. 77, 78). "Speed lines," the horizontal bands of

81 Academy Theatre, 1939. Detail of light trap. A ten-foot-high carved-glass panel depicts the Academy of Motion Picture Arts and Sciences. The Muse is holding an Oscar because this theatre was intended to house the Academy Awards, although they never took place there.

82 Academy Theatre, 1939. Auditorium with cove lighting.

83 Charles Lee next to his airplane. Lee, who taught himself to fly, used to impress clients by flying his Beechcraft to job sites.

thin parallel lines resembling the trail left by a speeding object in comic strips, seen on the De Anza Theatre, added to the illusion of movement (fig. 84). Porthole windows made reference to sleek ocean liners (figs. 85, 86). The building in its entirety was of a single piece and resembled the machine, particularly a state-of-the-art transportation machine (fig. 95).

The revolutionary impact of the 1930s on architecture and design can be seen by comparing the design of buildings and automobiles between 1931 and 1939. Both the theatres and the cars parked in front of them were marked by a change from boxy and static forms with delicate detailing to horizontal configurations with broad sweeping lines (figs. 34, 84).

Given the financial constraints on new construction imposed by the economic realities of the Depression, many theatre owners could not afford to build these futuristic theatres yet needed a contemporary image. Existing storefronts or older theatres were often remodeled to accomplish the same goal. On several occasions, Lee convinced clients that remodeling their old theatres into modern showcases would increase their

118
Feature
Presentation

84 De Anza Theatre, Riverside, California, 1939 (S. Charles Lee, 1937–39).

85 Vern Theatre, Los Angeles, ca. 1941 (S. Charles Lee, 1939–41). The ribbed portion of the upper facade was created by casting concrete against corrugated iron forms.

profits and thus pay for itself.[30] After Lee's remodeling in 1935–36, the Lyceum Theatre (San Francisco, ca. 1920) appeared to have an entirely new, modern facade (figs. 88, 89). In fact, the only things new were the box office, poster cases, and marquee.

Some remodelings were more substantial. In 1940, the owners of the Alexander Theatre (Glendale, 1925) commissioned Lee to remodel their Greco-Egyptian theatre. Designed by Arthur Lindley and Charles Selkirk for the Orpheum circuit, the building was set back from the street and remained almost invisible to passersby (fig. 90). Lee left the auditorium virtually unchanged but added a one-hundred-foot neon tower with a spiked starburst at the top, bringing the glamour of the theatre out to the sidewalk. A three-dimensional marquee aimed at the street targeted the passing motorist and pedestrian. The theatre, renamed the Alex, suggesting its more modern and accessible nature, now dominated the street (fig. 91). The walk from the streamlined box office to the front door was paved with terrazzo and lined with aluminum-framed poster cases and swirling waves of plaster. Recessed lighting made the stroll mystical.

Lee performed similar services for dozens of other theatres, including the Fox Long Beach (1931), Westlake (Los Angeles, 1935), Beverly (Beverly Hills, 1936), and Grand

86 Right, Vern Theatre, 1941. The porthole windows on the facade and in the doors are reinforced by the wavelike patterns etched on the box office.

87 Below, Vern Theatre, 1941. Auditorium.

88 Opposite top, Lyceum Theatre, San Francisco. Before Lee's remodeling.

89 Opposite bottom, Lyceum Theatre, 1937 (S. Charles Lee, 1935–36). Lee modernized the theatre simply by enlarging the marquee and increasing the scale of the graphics and by removing the canvas awnings and installing a new box office in the lobby.

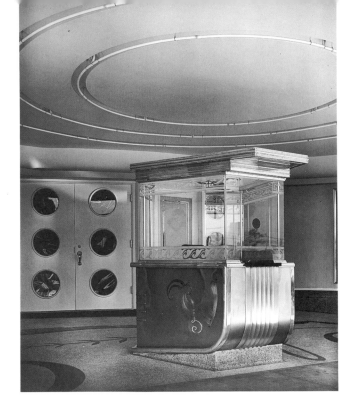

90 Alexander Theatre, Glendale, California, 1940 (Arthur G. Lindley and Charles L. Selkirk, 1925). Before Lee's remodeling.

91 Alex Theatre, Glendale, California, 1942 (S. Charles Lee, 1940). The theatre, which is set back from the street, is brought out to the street by the use of a canopy. A new tower and box office make the theatre more visible. The name was shortened to match the jazzy new facade.

Lake (Oakland, 1936). Remodeling ranged from new marquees, box offices, and lobbies to complete overhauls of the auditoriums.

Lee's Depression-era commissions were by no means limited to theatres, however, and his success with this genre led him to apply the same theatricality of style and showmanship to his nontheatre buildings. His attention to detail and emphasis on innovation also remained trademarks. His Municipal Light Water and Power stations throughout Los Angeles County resembled giant jukeboxes that utilized light to advertise their product—like the movie marquee (fig. 92). The sleek glass-and-metal facade Lee designed for the Carv-Arts Studio (1937), the firm that produced several of the stylized, etched-glass light-trap murals, contrasted with the pedestrian brick of the side and rear walls.

Like theatre owners, store owners also wished to lure customers. When Highland Avenue, in the heart of Hollywood, was widened in the 1930s, several owners of buildings along the way commissioned Lee to remodel their storefronts. One of these owners was cosmetics manufacturer Max Factor, whose existing facility was nothing more than a warehouse and garage (fig. 93). Lee's experience with motion picture theatre design and his attitude about flattering women patrons through the use of light, color, and backdrop made him the ideal architect for Max Factor's new showroom, which was intended to boost sales. The new plans also called for improved manufacturing facilities and an efficient laboratory for testing materials. Lee submitted two designs: the French-

92 Municipal Light Water and Power office, Los Angeles, 1984 (S. Charles Lee, ca. 1935). Facade identifies the building and "sells" the product: light.

93 Max Factor offices and factory,
Hollywood, ca. 1930.
Before Lee's remodeling.

94 Max Factor offices, showroom, and
factory, ca. 1935 (S. Charles Lee, ca.
1935). As remodeled by Lee.

Deco facade that was accepted (fig. 94), and a Streamline Moderne high rise that the company rejected as being too modern and too costly in renovations (fig. 95).[31] The new Max Factor Building (Hollywood, ca. 1933) was a movie set that promised movie-star beauty both inside and out (figs. 94, 96). Rooms designated for blondes, brunettes, or redheads were designed according to the colors and lighting most flattering for applying and selling makeup. Even the owner got a new office, one worthy of a film mogul (fig. 97).[32]

Lee's own office on Wilshire Boulevard is another example of his approach to Depression-era remodeling. Lee had lost his home early in the Depression, and business had become so poor that the office rent was becoming a burden. He decided to find his own building as soon as he could collect a substantial fee. He looked for the cheapest lot he could find on Wilshire and found an old two-story house at 1648. Wilshire had just been widened, requiring the setback of the Victorian house on the lot.[33] The Lee family would live in the back, maintain an office in the front, and rent out any remaining space. Lee redesigned only the facade of the house, changing the style to modern Deco. From the back, however, the house was still early twentieth century in design. The front presented a public image; behind that facade was private space.

The de facto building restrictions forced by Depression conditions revealed one of Lee's most significant contributions: the modern, economical theatre that captured the

95 Max Factor Building. Model of proposed streamlined building.

96 Max Factor showroom.
Interior lobby.

97 Max Factor Building.
Max Factor's office.

allure of the movie palace on a smaller scale. With less attention given to lavish ornamentation, the integrity of the architecture and the manipulation of space came to the forefront. Because he saw himself first as a businessman, he was always conscious of budgetary restraints. This awareness gave him an advantage when working on small projects for financially strapped studios or nonaffiliated clients. He was able to design small theatres that combined the psychology of movie palace splendor and the glamour of the urban theatre district in a single building.

The theatres and movies of this period were well matched. Each provided an escape that was grounded in the strengths of the American character. The movies dealt with American situations, not European operettas, and the heroes, such as Everyman Jimmy Stewart, hoofer Fred Astaire, and chorine Ginger Rogers, represented average, wholesome Americans whose naïveté, Yankee ingenuity, and luck paid off. The theatres were sets in which these characters would have been comfortable. They further made this fantasy world accessible to the moviegoer, who then perpetuated the romance and escape of the screen by taking it from the auditorium through the lobby and out onto the terrazzo sidewalk.

The psychology of entertainment during the 1930s translated into comfort, security, and optimism. In a decade when the country doubted the present, streamlined styling provided an optimistic expression of faith in the future. Flashy, jazzy, and full of confidence, Streamline Moderne "moved" forward in sleek, aerodynamic lines. Theatres symbolized Hollywood to the rest of the country. This was the land of orange groves and dreams and movie stars waiting to be discovered and romance waiting to be filmed. The name Hollywood Theatre was given to motion picture houses all over the country. Lee's theatres, including the Hollywood (Hollywood, 1936), were modern in their stylistic trappings but consciously provided a secure, familiar, and welcoming environment. "Theatres," Lee said, "should be attractive showplaces for the product, but not distract or interfere with the illusion."[34] By that standard, he succeeded.

6

Newsreel

The Impact of World War II

When S. Charles Lee's Fremont Theatre opened on Memorial Day of 1942, in San Luis Obispo, California, it was billed as "The Theatre of Tomorrow" (fig. 98).[1] But it was very much a theatre of its day—reflecting the events at Pearl Harbor six months earlier. On opening night, admission prices were fifty-five cents for adults; fifteen cents for children; and thirty-five cents for men in uniform. The feature was *This Above All:* "When HELL breaks loose . . . they desire Love above all." In the film, Tyrone Power, an embittered soldier, finds courage and love through Joan Fontaine, a British patriot. All proceeds from the first night went to the local USO. Jackie Cooper, Constance Bennett, and Laurel and Hardy sold over $1 million worth of war bonds and defense stamps at a bond rally that night at the theatre.[2] Throughout the war, the messages "Buy War Bonds" and "Latest News from All Fronts" ran on the Fremont's marquee.[3]

After being seated by uniformed usherettes, the opening-night audience was on its feet for "The Star-Spangled Banner" and the Pledge of Allegiance. Manager Lou Rosenberg remarked that although the building was "built of steel and stone it has a heart and soul" and promised that he would strive to provide entertainment for all who entered.[4] The theatre, constructed in ten months and named for General John C. Fremont, was to be the last Fox theatre built until the end of the war, when building restrictions would be lifted.[5] In the interim, most architectural materials were being diverted to the war effort. Theatre remodeling, as well as the new design that came after the war, reflected these shortages and substitutes.

World War II would eventually lead the United States out of the Depression and refocus American priorities on preparation for war. Movies were a welcome escape from private deprivation, but in addition the theatres became community centers for war-bond drives and newsreel presentations.

Except for a small number deemed necessary to keep morale high on the home front, no motion picture theatres were built in the United States during the war years.[6] The war reduced available labor, claimed strategic materials priorities, and imposed gasoline rationing and other regulations on the civilian population. Even production of popcorn machines was limited.[7] In 1942, the War Production Board (WPB) curtailed theatre construction and earmarked all sound and projection equipment for military use. Civilian use was authorized only after army and navy orders had been filled. The Armed Forces and Medical Corps required a great deal of projection and sound equipment for training films. In 1941, of the nearly four thousand 35-mm. projectors produced, only a small percentage were designated for civilian purposes or as replacements for worn-out equipment.[8] In the early stages of the war, the WPB, as a conservation measure, prohibited even the production of repair parts.

But the motion picture industry fought back, dedicated as it was "to a defense of the Nation's Morale through a constant vigilance to adequately maintain our Physical Theatres and their equipment . . . so that the Entertainment, Instruction, and Mental Relaxation produced by the Studios and by Our Government may be portrayed to the Public with a maximum of effectiveness . . . FOR THE DURATION!"[9] It helped that John Eberson, a prolific motion picture theatre architect and industry propagandist, had been appointed to the WPB. He, in turn, promoted industry support for voluntary cooperation as well as for officially imposed directives. President Franklin Roosevelt issued a public statement in which he recognized the necessity of keeping motion picture theatres operative to maintain the morale of the public and to present various propaganda films. A blanket priority classification of "AA" was issued, covering all repairs and replacement of equipment for theatre sound systems but not new theatre construction.[10]

On 15 February 1942, Walter Winchell, "himself a Navy man," broadcast this announcement:

ATTENTION MR. AND MRS. UNITED STATES: The Government has certified the motion picture industry as a necessary war industry. This is not the creation of a special privilege. It is an honest recognition of the importance of the movies—the American Way of Life. . . . Almost as a unit, the men and women of the screen have volunteered to stand behind a gun. The finding that their work is an essential service means that a movie camera is as much an instrument of war as a machine-gun and that an actor's work can be as helpful as a riveter's. In their assigned post of duty, their daily work, they are more than accepting the government's direction. They are obeying orders. The world of movie stars and the starlets is proud to appear in support of the Army, Navy, Marines and Coast Guard. Every facility of the American Theatre of Art—is at the command of their fellow Americans now fighting in the far flung theatres of war. Hollywood values an Academy Award. But it thinks more of the Congressional Medal of Honor.[11]

A survey conducted in 1943 by a House Naval Affairs Subcommittee verified that a lack of theatres contributed to "high labor turn-over resulting from, and breeding, moral delinquency and conditions harmful to the morale of war workers."[12] The committee recommended that $25 million in materials and equipment be allocated for theatres and other recreational buildings. This finding encouraged architects and theatre owners to begin planning new theatres once again.

The motion picture industry appeared to take its patriotic duty seriously. In addition to enlistees, the industry offered Selective Service recruitment films and organized the War Activities Committee of the Motion Picture Industry (known before Pearl Harbor as the Motion Picture Committee Cooperating for National Defense). Motion picture theatres played a role in boosting morale, keeping the public informed, selling war bonds, and showing propaganda films. They also served as collection points for hundreds of thousands of tons of scrap metal, rubber, and rags. Theatre managers applied the art of selling tickets to the areas of nationalism and patriotism. In 1942 a war message appeared on movie screens every thirty minutes during operating hours.[13] Walter T. Brown, director of publicity and associate coordinator of the War Activities Committee, estimated that the industry's contribution totaled $200–300 million. Some of the efforts included war-bond campaigns at home, film production for the Office of War Information, personal appearances by movie stars, and the shipment of Hollywood films to troops overseas. The industry also offered 30,661 free movie days, on which admission to the theatre was by bond; the theatre took no profits and the distributor received no rental. Brown estimated that this drive brought in at least $100 million.[14]

Such self-sacrifice paid off at the box office in terms of admissions and public relations. Between 1941 and 1945 theatre attendance averaged eighty-five million per week, as compared to sixty-nine million a decade earlier (and forty-nine million a decade later; see appendix A). On 4 December 1945, the government presented the War Activities Committee with a one-hundred-pound bronze plaque in recognition and appreciation of its services during the war. It read:

98 Fremont Theatre, San Luis Obispo, California, 1941 (S. Charles Lee, 1941–42).

For the plea of conservation and watchfulness. . . . Thanks to the unselfish and sincere assistance of everyone, no theatre went out of business—and mighty few had to close for any length of time at all—because of mechanical breakdown.[15]

S. Charles Lee's Lakewood Theatre (Lakewood, Calif., 1944–45) was a prime example of the ad hoc attitude fostered by such regulation. Architects, builders, and theatre owners learned to make do, substituting whatever materials were available for traditional but rationed or outlawed ones. With the restrictions on building materials and the labor shortage, it was unclear how Fox would be able to complete the theatre as scheduled for the Lakeville Corporation. Lee, however, engineered a solution. In 1935–36 he had designed a combination theatre and city hall in Quincy, California. Called the Town Hall, it was built of wood, because in the 1930s that was the most abundant material in the mountains around Quincy. Because there were no wartime restrictions on moving a building, Lee negotiated with the owner to buy the theatre and have it moved to Lakewood. Lee described the process: "They took the building apart, marking all parts of it like a child's block set, and used it as the base for starting the Lakewood Theatre. Before we were through with modifications, it was a modern theatre built with modern materials. That's how the permit was issued."[16] "Modifications" meant changing a $25,000, 400-seat building of wood and stucco into a $92,000, 1,000-seat theatre of brick, steel, and wood.[17] Shortages could greatly stretch the creative abilities of designers and clients.

The Tower Bowl (1941), a bowling alley in the heart of downtown San Diego, represented another of Lee's signature buildings, this one conceived in a "theatre de Luxe style" (fig. 99).[18] The front facade featured an eighty-foot curved steel tower, similar to the highly visible tower on top of the Fremont Theatre. The tower was made up of revolving bowling balls five feet in diameter that spelled out "BOWLING" on one side and "TOWER BOWL" on the other, illuminated in neon (fig. 100). The steel for the tower as well as for the rest of the structure had been ordered and was on its way to San Diego when the government banned the use of steel in nonessential buildings. Lee convinced the authorities, however, that steel already en route before the order was announced should be exempt. "After a great deal of effort and wire-pulling we were given permission to use this much steel and no more—no more was needed."[19]

With thirty-two lanes, Tower Bowl was one of the largest bowling alleys in the United States at the time. And as a center of entertainment and relaxation, it served much the same purpose as the wartime movie theatre: that is, the enhancement of morale. The building covered a narrow fifty-foot lot in the front as well as a wider one at the rear. On Broadway—the street serving as a traffic lane for disembarking sailors—a marquee beneath the twirling tower advertised "Bowling, Billiards, Cocktails, and Entertainment." Terrazzo flooring worthy of a movie theatre led from the Broadway entrance past the bar and cocktail lounge, which could be seen through porthole windows, to the bowling lanes at the rear. The ceiling and walls of the lounge were illuminated by a color reel that splayed varying colors across the space. The back entrance was adjacent to the parking lot.

The area containing the lanes had a distinctly different feeling than the bar or cocktail

99 Tower Bowl, San Diego, 1941
(S. Charles Lee, 1941).

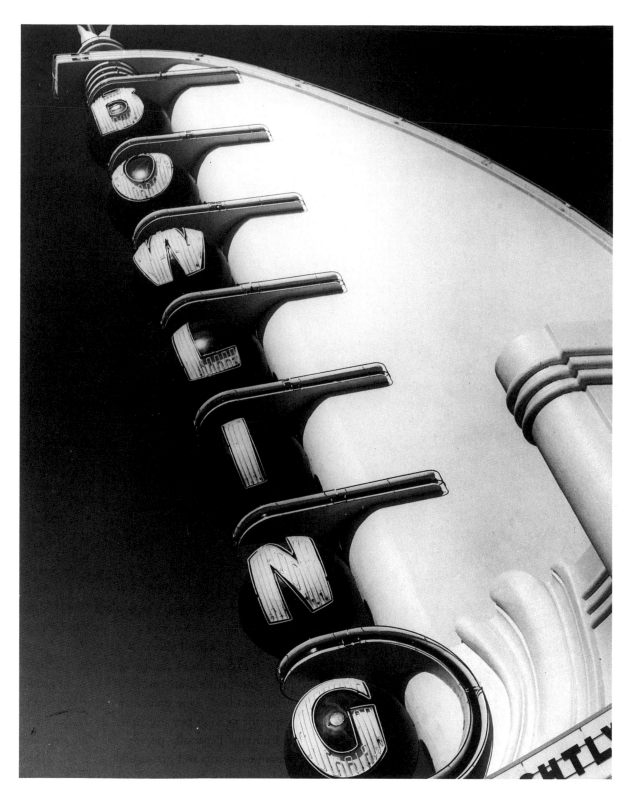

100 Tower Bowl, 1941. Vertical sign with
rotating bowling balls that spell out
"BOWLING" on one side and "The TOWER
Bowl" on the other.

lounge, because it was oriented toward family entertainment. It was a large room, with a twenty-two-foot ceiling painted in blue, gray, and sienna. The walls, decorated with murals that might have graced a theatre auditorium, were treated with acoustical material to control the noise. A bowler's bench, designed and patented by Lee, had a locking device for reserved balls. Special lighting effects were used throughout the building. The enclosure behind and over the pins was carefully lighted, thus eliminating shadows and making the ball visible at the end of the alley. The enterprise proved very successful, although it became difficult to obtain maple bowling pins owing to war conditions.

What little construction did take place during the war was generally limited to either remodeling or war-industry buildings. Lee kept his business alive primarily by remodeling theatres, particularly newsreel theatres, but also by designing a chain of movie theatres in politically neutral Mexico and building housing for war workers in Inglewood. The latter, known as Del Air, was a development of four hundred 2- and 3-bedroom houses that sold for $100 down and $50 a month. According to Lee, all were sold within two weeks.[20]

Because of building restrictions that limited new construction, the only way theatre owners could keep their facilities up-to-date was to remodel. The solution to economic limitations in the 1930s became the solution to political realities in the 1940s. Once again, remodeling, though little more than an inexpensive face-lift, gave theatres the appearance of being new and modern. In 1941 Lee renovated several neighborhood theatres, including the Capitol, California, and Glendale theatres in Glendale, as well as the Florencita in Los Angeles. They were refurbished with new entrances, modern poster cases and box offices, new terrazzo floors and carpeting, and a new marquee. The structural glass Lee chose for the California and Capitol opened up the front of the building visually.

NEWSREEL THEATRES

The hunger for news from the front gave rise to a new type of theatre: the newsreel theatre (fig. 101). Newsreels, introduced from France in 1909, were shown in American theatres from the 1910s until the 1950s, when television news took over.[21] Usually about ten minutes long, they were shown before or between feature films and consisted of footage of recent events (recent meaning from a few hours up to two days old), as well as "soft" news such as sports, fashion, comedy, and human-interest stories. Two types of news events were reported: scheduled events (which were covered both before and after they occurred) and unexpected events; and both were dramatically narrated with an anchorman's urgency. In the days when the radio or newspaper was the main source of news, such live action was indeed a novelty. Especially popular prior to and during World War II, newsreels made international events and personalities come alive for the viewers. The soft news was presented with equal drama.

By the late 1920s newsreels were a regular part of the bill in 90 percent of American theatres. Fox, who introduced sound specifically for Fox Movietone News, was the largest producer of newsreels. As early as 1930, Fox predicted the development of a chain

Theatre Row at Night, Dallas, Texas

101 Theatre row, Dallas, ca. 1942. Theatre district on Elm Street includes four theatres. The marquee of the newsreel theatre (on the far left) works as a headline to the stories shown inside.

of theatres devoted exclusively to newsreels.[22] The Trans Lux Corporation in New York City experimented with a chain of "daylight" newsreel theatres, which used rear-screen projection, thereby eliminating darkened auditoriums and the related expense of ushers. As a further economy, the ceiling in such theatres could be lower because there was no projection beam to clear. Trans Lux theatres, many of which were designed by Thomas Lamb, were noted for their "ultra modern designs," often carried out in silver and black.[23]

For about a quarter, one could drop in and watch an hour of newsreels, which ran continuously. The experience was much like watching an hour of television news in later decades. Lee designed newsreel theatres in Oakland, Beverly Hills, Los Angeles, and Arizona. Some were new or additions to existing theatres; more often they were remodelings. The Morosco (Los Angeles) became the Globe (fig. 102). The Oakland Newsreel, a remodeled storefront, had formerly housed Tinn's Chicken and Steak House. In 1941 a newsreel addition to the California Theatre in San Diego was planned but not built, apparently because of war restrictions.

The theatres had names that proclaimed their function, such as Newsview, and facades typically featured symbols of news and world events (figs. 102–104). A giant globe over the marquee, for example, identified a newsreel theatre. Most had only a few hundred seats, creating a more intimate atmosphere than the imposing first-run theatres. Audiences could cheer and boo the men and women on screen as though these real-life heroes and villains were actors. Such partisanship extended to the producers of the newsreels and the management. In response to public criticism of William Randolph Hearst's policies, theatre managers began cutting titles that included the Hearst name from Hearst Metrotone News and inserting their own subtitles. The company responded officially by deleting the Hearst name entirely and changing the name to "News of the Day"; it even hired a new narrator so that the voice would not be recognized.[24]

102 Globe Theatre, Los Angeles (S. Charles Lee, ca. 1945). Sketch.

Following the war, some neighborhood theatres began to feature "local newsreels"—16-mm. films of community events, produced by theatre managers and owners at a moderate cost or using film supplied by the participants. They proved to be great money-makers. Theatre owners figured that at seven scenes per one-hundred-foot reel (featuring close-ups, of course) and seven people per scene, one reel translated into 49 people who would pay to see themselves on the silver screen. Multiply 49 "movie stars" times five friends and relatives, each paying an average of 30 cents for admission, and the owners raked in an additional $73.50 per evening for a minimal outlay.[25] As an added advantage, the theatre became even more of a community center in the mind of the public.[26]

Television news began in 1953, and within a few years the newsreel and newsreel theatre had disappeared. The only remnants of the once-popular form were a few marquees balancing huge globes, even when the theatre had been turned into another business. The Globe Theatre in Los Angeles, for example, became the Globe Swap Meet. In 1989, one newsreel theatre remained in the United States, part of a permanent exhibit of the McKissick Museum at the University of South Carolina, in Columbia. It operated seven days a week all year, showing clips from a collection of vintage newsreels.[27] As its legacy, the newsreel theatre demonstrated the potential of film in bringing world events to the viewer, culminating in live television coverage.

103 Proposed "Town" newsreel theatre (S. Charles Lee). According to Lee, "It is meant to speak up to the people to come in and see what is inside, and is planned for a locality where the newsreel has become an important attraction."

104 Proposed "Diana" newsreel theatre
(S. Charles Lee). The facade was to be built
in plastic, making it transparent.

Newsreel remodelings helped keep Lee's Los Angeles office in business during the war. In 1942, he also opened an office in Mexico City, which had no war-related building restrictions. Harold Franklin, former president of Fox West Coast and co-owner of the Studio Theatre in Hollywood, had moved to Mexico, where he organized a joint venture between Fox and a Mexican syndicate to build a chain of theatres. The syndicate was to build the theatres, and Fox agreed to operate them—with the stipulation that Lee be the designer. Lee subsequently built nine theatres and a moving picture studio for this group.[28]

The theatres in Mexico City contained the physical characteristics of a modern movie theatre and were built of concrete, brick, stone, and steel. Regional touches included handmade Mexican tiles on the roofs and domes and hand-carved stone trim on the exteriors. Although bricks still had to be carried by donkey to the site of the Teatro Linda Vista in Mexico City, the completed building effectively combined modernism and regionalism in design and ambiance (figs. 105–108). The facade resembled a church, with Churrigueresque detailing and colorful trim of Mexican ceramic tile. Behind the box office and adjacent to the theatre was a restaurant, whose Mediterranean atmosphere enclosed four dining rooms, offering English, Russian, Dutch, or Spanish cuisine.

The auditorium of the Linda Vista contained twenty-five hundred seats and was decorated with murals done by American and Mexican craftsmen. Each panel depicted a dance native to a particular Mexican province (fig. 109). Fluorescent materials outlined the murals, making them visible during performances. Fluorescent lighting was also used in the aisles. The light trap featured a stylized carved wooden figure on a leather background, flanked by walls and a ceiling paneled in walnut.

The 1400-seat Teatro Lido, located at the intersection of two busy streets, utilized a circular marquee similar to that of the Bruin Theatre in Los Angeles (figs. 66, 110). Atop the marquee was a 120-foot tower with a revolving flashlight. The building included fifteen storefronts along the two streets. These two theatres showed both Mexican and American movies. In the lobby of the Chapultepec Theatre, located in a Moderne office building, Lee used sleek lines, mirrors, and light, in contrast to the traditional decorative elements in his other Mexican theatres (fig. 111).

As with his design for the Tower Theatre in Los Angeles, Lee's Mexican plans tested local building ordinances, which were changed as a result. The plans that he submitted to the Mexico City building department were rejected because the aisles led to exits that emptied onto a large lot adjacent to the building. The existing building ordinance had been written at the time the Teatro Nacional, patterned after the Paris Opera, was built. This nationally renowned live theatre featured a central auditorium surrounded by a large corridor. All aisles and exits led to the corridor, which eventually led to the street. The building department insisted that Lee add such a corridor to his theatres. Lee recalled the rationale that the chief of the building department offered: "Let us assume there's a fire in the auditorium. In my plan, the people would run directly to the outside and catch pneumonia; in their plan they would cool off on their way to the outside! In order to offset this complex arrangement, I was able to get the Minister of Health to issue

105 Linda Vista Theatre, Mexico City, 1942
(S. Charles Lee, 1942).

106 Linda Vista Theatre, 1942.

107 Linda Vista Theatre, 1942. Box office.

108 Linda Vista Theatre, 1942.
Lobby and light trap.

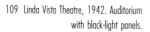

109 Linda Vista Theatre, 1942. Auditorium
with black-light panels.

110 Lido Theatre, Mexico City, 1942
(S. Charles Lee, 1942). The exterior is
similar to the Bruin, with the addition of a
120-foot tower.

111 Chapultepec Theatre, Mexico City, ca.
1944 (S. Charles Lee, 1943–44). The
ultramodern lobby is right out of set designer
Van Nest Polglase's drawing book.

an edict to the building department stating that my plan would not cause more deaths than theirs, and eventually they asked me to rewrite their ordinance."[29]

POSTWAR THEATRES

Like other motion picture theatre architects during the war, Lee spent time at the drawing board making postwar plans, while restrictions were still in effect. The year-end summary of projects in *Southwest Builder and Contractor* for 1944 listed sixteen commissions for new or remodeled theatres in Lee's office, estimated to cost $1.5 million.[30] Although all the projects were planned for construction immediately following the war, they reflected wartime thinking as well as more-optimistic projections based on existing restrictions, the promise of new products, and the emphasis on recovery. All these factors, plus gasoline and rubber rationing, helped to promote the suburban neighborhood house.

Aesthetic considerations were dictated to some extent by the practical matter of available materials and labor. Nearly all materials required to design a theatre were restricted during the war: steel, copper, bronze, aluminum, lumber, and chrome, including nuts and bolts. Other materials, such as silk and cotton, were difficult to obtain, as was labor. In response, architects and decorators were forced to rethink their attitudes and use new materials. Wartime technology had introduced newly developed fabrics, including synthetics, and new plastics such as Vermiculite and Formica. Professional journals suggested substituting fabrics such as velon or saran and protein fabrics made of soybeans and peanuts for traditional materials.[31] Writers lauded the versatility of lead, magnesium, Plexiglas, Fiberglas, and aluminum.[32]

Even after the restrictions on materials and equipment were relaxed, it took time for limited supplies to meet the backlog in demand. By 1947, there were still government restrictions on construction; the focus was on affordable civilian housing for returning soldiers and their new families. Although theatre attendance reached its peak in the postwar years, averaging ninety million per week between 1946 and 1948, new construction and maintenance lagged.

Concrete and glass, two materials not restricted, became crucial architectural elements not only during but also after the war. Another important component of architecture was also unrestricted: light. Architects made great strides in the application of light to motion picture theatre design; this new element in combination with glass fronts served to open up the facade and create striking visual effects. These readily available materials, as well as the many synthetic products developed during the war, created a new structural and ornamental aesthetic, suggesting that the emerging architectural forms were dictated as much by pragmatism as by modernist ideology.

As early as 1942, motion picture theatre architects had been discussing plans for the postwar theatre in such journals as *Film Daily Year Book* or *Theatre Catalog*.[33] The stated purpose of the latter, published as a yearly edition of *Motion Picture Herald*, was "(1) To record the design and construction trends of each year, and (2) To forecast future developments that have physical theatre possibilities."[34] *Theatre Catalog* did not publish editions in 1943 or 1944, as there was no building going on, but in 1945 published ninety-six pages of sketches and plans, since there were still no photographs of completed buildings to show. Typically, the sketches showed dramatic facades of bold lines, whereas the plans stressed economy and flexibility. Gone were the flamboyant curves and excessive ornament that spoke of conspicuous consumption and exorbitant expenditures. Vertical signs were disappearing, having been integrated into the marquee sign. The facade, featuring structural glass and light, hosted Moderne curves and squares, often angled or skewed.

The *Theatre Catalog* of 1945 devoted three pages to postwar sketches Lee had done for theatres on the West Coast. The mild climate of the region permitted the use of lightweight structural materials, including porcelain, glass, and plastics. Other materials Lee chose were plaster, terra cotta, and concrete. A proposed newsreel theatre was designed to be built in plastic (fig. 104). In another proposal, a glass facade revealed an interior lobby in the fashion of an enormous billboard (fig. 112). The sketches displayed huge sweeping curves with towers, marquees, and signs that grew organically out of the facade (figs. 113–115). Oversized lettering spelling out the theatre name emphasized the building's visibility and presence on the street. Glass also kept construction costs down and exploited light to give the theatre a dramatic appearance at night. Lighting effects in combination with the glass and plastic facades were designed to make the theatre its own advertisement in "a blaze of color." As the writer observed, "Certainly no passer-by could observe any of these spectacular fronts without being conscious of the theatre."[35]

As built, Lee's theatres were somewhat tamer than his proposals: the sketch for the Bay Theatre, for example, is far less reserved than the final incarnation in Pacific Palisades (1948–49; figs. 116, 117). Economic and social factors tempered the flamboyance, but his buildings were still theatrical, even if set in sedate suburban commercial districts. Postwar theatres were serviced primarily by automobile traffic, with very little foot traffic. Although Lee continued to experiment with new forms and technology and to respond to new developments and changing needs, he retained the uniqueness as well as the sense of place and identity associated with his work.

One of these experiments was the Quonset hut, developed during the war, when speed of construction was paramount. The Quonset hut was a prefabricated shelter made of corrugated metal, shaped like a half-cylinder. Not only was it inexpensive to build and operate (it could be heated and cooled easily), but the acoustics were excellent.

Similar to the Quonset hut in form, but predating it, was the lamella roof, which Lee utilized in several postwar theatres. This was a trussless roof made up of a series of short wooden sections arranged in a diamond pattern (fig. 118). Short timbers, beveled and bored at the ends, were bolted together at an angle in a network of mutually braced and self-supporting pieces that formed a continuous arch, eliminating or minimizing side walls.

The idea originated in Europe in 1908 and was introduced to the United States in 1923, but it was not commonly used until the 1940s and 1950s. Most were built on the West Coast, where building codes were more flexible owing to the accommodating climate. The waffled ceiling was particularly popular because it required no steel and relatively short segments of wood, which was an unrestricted material. Yet it provided a

112 Theatre design (S. Charles Lee, 1947).
The glass front was designed to be especially
spectacular at night.

113 La Tijera Theatre, Los Angeles, 1947 (S. Charles Lee, 1948–49). After World War II, Lee's sketches show an exaggerated perspective; curved lines have given way to angles, and the drive-through marquee appears in almost every drawing.

wide, unobstructed span with no supporting columns. Other advantages included its strength, acoustics, and resistance to wind and earthquakes. The Helix (La Mesa, 1947– 48), Avo (Vista, 1948), Puente (Puente, 1947–48), Visalia (Visalia, 1946–49), and Garmar (Montebello, 1949–50), all in California, used lamella roof construction, leaving the structural system exposed on the interior (figs. 119, 120). A flat facade containing signs, a marquee, and the exterior and interior lobbies fronted one end of the barrel-vault-shaped building, creating a Western "false front" effect.

The typical Lee theatre of the 1940s postwar era had a distinctive look that had evolved from his signature of the 1930s yet reflected changing times. The buildings were squarer, sparer, and less streamlined in appearance, but not without glamour. Bold replaced sleek. The scale and proportions were larger and designed more with the highway and automobile in mind, as witnessed by the parking facilities and the drive-through marquee (fig. 113). The entire building, not just the marquee, was now readable from a car. The pedestrian ground level was less assertive and more discreet, with a quieter box office. The space above the marquee featured a huge decorative motif; above that, at the top, the name of the theatre was often spelled out in enormous letters, which now grew out of the building rather than being attached to it (fig. 116).

Even the graphics were designed for motorists. Theatre names were generally short

114 Theatre sketch, ca. 1945–47
(S. Charles Lee).

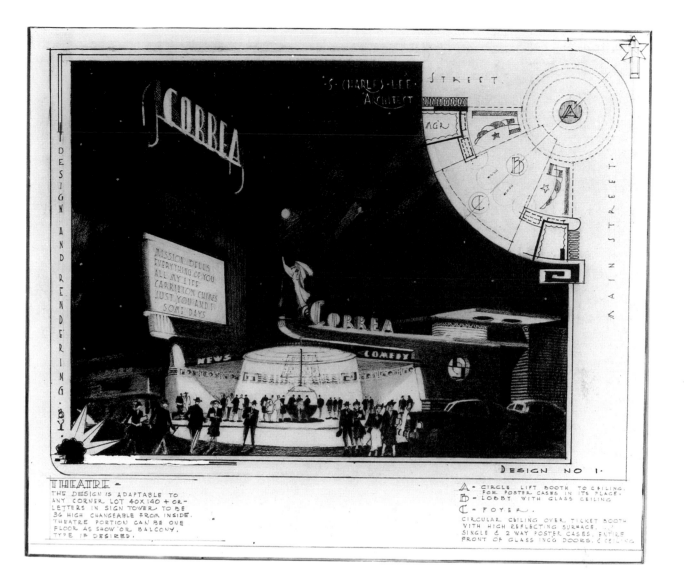

115 Theatre sketch, ca. 1945—47
(S. Charles Lee). Plan and rendering for a
theatre "adaptable to any corner lot,"
with glass facade, two-way poster cases,
and thirty-six-inch letters changeable
from the inside.

116 Bay Theatre, Pacific Palisades,
California, 1947 (S. Charles Lee). Sketch.

117 Bay Theatre, 1949 (S. Charles Lee, 1948–49). As built.

118 Example of lamella construction.

119 Puente Theatre, Puente, California, 1947 (S. Charles Lee, 1947–48). Under construction.

120 Puente Theatre, 1948. Auditorium with exposed lamella roof.

and easy to grasp, even at high speeds. They often conveyed the location of the building, such as the Miami (Florida, 1946–47), La Tijera (a boulevard in Los Angeles, 1948–49), or Picwood (at Pico and Westwood boulevards in Los Angeles, 1946). Picture frames with pie-crust edges outlined the lobby entrances on the otherwise square facades of the Avo (Vista, 1948), Harper (Fontana, 1948), and Visalia (Visalia, 1946–49) theatres (figs. 121, 122).

The steel tower had become little more than a strip of neon light that suggested the tower element, as seen in the Picwood. Vertical signs had evolved from metal attachments to steel towers, and now to pylons of neon, stucco, or Vitrolite that flowed "naturally," if obtrusively, out of the lines of the building. They were especially prominent at night (figs. 123, 126).

Parking availability was advertised in lights, along with the names of the theatre and the featured film. The layout of the Helix Theatre was planned in such a way that the desk in the manager's office overlooked both the lobby and the forty-five-thousand-square-foot parking lot.

Beginning in the 1930s with the porte cochere at the Fox Florence, Lee had toyed with the idea of adapting the design of the building to the automobile (see fig. 51). He now integrated it perfectly and functionally into the marquee. At the Arden and La Tijera theatres, the drive-through marquee literally drew the automobile into the theatre (figs. 124–127). The marquee extended over the automobile entry so that the parking entrance was a part of the facade. Lee placed the box office along the driveway under the marquee so that drivers could purchase tickets from the car window, deposit passengers in the lobby, and drive to a free, well-lighted parking lot, which was frequently attended. It was no coincidence that these theatres were in southern California. Lee recognized, and designed to accommodate, an essential truth of the twentieth century: the automobile was an extension of the driver, not merely a means of transportation. Like the drive-in, the drive-through acknowledged the importance of the motoring experience as pleasure and allowed for the smooth transfer of amusement without having to reject one for the other.

In contrast to the exterior square facade, the lobby area was increasingly baroque. Plaster forms resembling kidney-shaped swimming pools framed recessed coves in the ceiling and behind the candy counter. Lobbies of the 1940s predicted the amoeba-like and boomerang shapes used by industrial designers in the 1950s.

The light trap was becoming smaller and less important as the demand for additional merchandise space in the foyer grew. "Eventually, we had to design the entrances around the merchandising, as this source of income was of great importance to the exhibitor," Lee explained.[36] In designing the candy counter, he used fluorescent lighting that spilled over the space, creating an eerie effect. A plaster hood shielded the display and directed the circulation of cool air over the candy. The effects of war were felt at the refreshment stand, too. Because of sugar rationing, popcorn replaced candy. Buttered popcorn was preferred to plain, but butter, also rationed, added to the cost, so alternatives were sought.[37] Until the war interrupted the supply, coconut oil with butter flavoring was used. The balance between concession sales and film-related income continued to

121 Avo Theatre, Vista, California, 1989 (S. Charles Lee, 1948). Typically, in postwar theatres the exterior lobby has shrunk to allow more interior space for the concession stand, but the architectural trim still extends over and onto the sidewalk, making the theatre stand out on the street.

122 Main (Visalia) Theatre, Visalia, California, 1949 (S. Charles Lee, 1946–49). Drawing.

123 Picwood Theatre, Los Angeles, 1948 (S. Charles Lee, 1946). The lighting pattern makes the facade appear to float. Each stripe and letter was timed to flash first in succession and then in unison, thus animating the building.

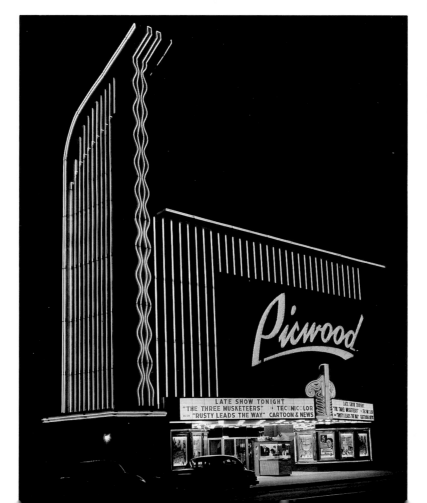

124 Opposite top, Arden Theatre, Lynwood,
California, ca. 1947 (S. Charles Lee, 1942–
47). The planning was begun during the
war, but the theatre was not built until after
the war.

125 Opposite bottom, La Tijera Theatre, Los
Angeles, 1949 (S. Charles Lee, 1948–49).

126 Above, La Tijera Theatre, 1949.

127 La Tijera Theatre, 1949.
Drive-through marquee.

128 Lido Theatre, Mexico City, 1942
(S. Charles Lee, 1942). Auditorium walls are
treated with Acoustipulp, the ceiling with
neon, and the carpet with black light.

change in favor of the former, until motion picture theatres were really only popcorn, candy, and soda booths that showed movies on the side.

Auditoriums in the 1940s featured bold lines and a proscenium framed in large graphics (distinctive design features that were often destroyed in the 1950s, when wide screens were installed). The decor included recessed lighting, neon, and black-light effects in continuous coves (fig. 128).

By the late 1940s black lighting, which Lee had introduced a decade earlier, was standard in theatres. Seasonal decorations, such as flags for the Fourth of July, could be painted on either side of the proscenium and then painted over for the next holiday promotion. Some companies offered prefabricated fluorescent murals. To some degree, the use of black light accomplished the same purpose as the light trap: it helped people find their seats in the dark or locate objects dropped on the carpet. Furthermore, the amount of light given off was sufficient to highlight the escapist environment without distracting from the screen. The result was more aesthetically intriguing than the light trap, however, and it was also a great, though costly, strategy for attracting patrons. A promoter explained its publicity potential:

> Now is the time to delight and mystify your community with the colorful spectacle of fluorescence in black light. There are tens of millions of Americans who have yet to see their first black-light mural. Where an unparalleled job of decoration, no matter how lavish and costly, will command only perfunctory attention in the newspapers, black light will get headlines and feature stories. Every patron will tell the neighbors. The movies will be exciting again.
>
> What would not Phineas T. Barnum or Flo Ziegfeld have given for black light? It is yours—now![38]

DRIVE-IN THEATRES

Immediately following the war, the limited availability of materials in the face of an increasing market demand contributed to yet another phenomenon in the motion picture theatre: the drive-in. This new theatre type, which required only a minimal investment in materials and labor, serviced the burgeoning suburbs.

Entrepreneur Richard Hollingshead patented the idea and built the first drive-in, which opened 3 June 1933, in Camden, New Jersey. He predicted that the last two things Americans would give up were the car and the movies. With that idea in mind, he developed ramps, studied angles, and perfected sight lines and traffic patterns to accommodate four hundred cars arranged in a field with a screen situated so that it was clearly visible through the windshield of every car. Architect Howard Hall designed the wooden screen and civil engineer S. Herbert Taylor laid out the ramps. Six hundred cars showed up the first night and paid an admission of twenty-five cents per person or one dollar per car. The following week, he added a concession stand.[39]

Hollingshead patented the ramp and entrance-exit system, selling franchises for one thousand dollars plus 5 percent of the gross.[40] The second drive-in was built in Los

Angeles in 1934. Ten more were built in the 1930s; by 1945 there were 102. After the war, however, they grew exponentially. In 1944, *Motion Picture Herald,* a trade magazine for theatre owners, accurately predicted a drive-in construction boom, having anticipated the following postwar conditions:

1. The joy of being released from gasoline rationing.
2. The availability of all-beef hot dogs.
3. Resumption of normal restrictions upon the amorous impulses of youth.
4. Need for fresh air after years of propaganda. . . .

The drive-in will grow, some—but as a social phenomenon reflecting the average American's inability to decide which he likes better, the movies or automobile riding. A drive-in theatre permits him, at one and the same time, to get a little of each.[41]

These reasons reflect an attitude shaped by wartime conditions rather than by the postwar perspective of building families and suburban neighborhoods, but the magazine was right about the growth of drive-ins. They multiplied in the United States, from 548 in 1947 to over 4,000 less than a decade later (see appendix A). This rapid growth can be explained not only by their popularity but by the reasonable cost of constructing them. Drive-ins tended to be located on the edge of town, where land was cheaper. The amount of landscaping and decoration varied widely.

Lee designed several drive-ins, including the Edwards (fig. 129). The screen formed a windswept parallelogram, angled away from the street, making it easy to read as a signboard, and the marquee formed an acute angle toward the street, reaching out to passing traffic. Both gave the illusion of speed and movement. The Rancho Drive-In (San Diego, 1948) featured a neon mural of a Mexican scene. These two theatres,

129 Edwards Drive-In Theatre, Arcadia, California, 1948 (S. Charles Lee, 1948). The marquee is a free-standing element in the drive-in.

designed the same year, were early examples of the genre; in 1948, there were only 820 drive-ins in the United States.

At the drive-in, the architectural show started at the driveway. The drive-in theatre was the ultimate automobile architecture. Motorists no longer needed to leave their cars; the parking lot had replaced the building in importance. The cars themselves became the form, providing the shape, color, line, and structure of the space. Indeed, automobiles were the only physical elements in the theatre other than the screen, box office, concession stand and projection booth, and exterior fence. Traditional architectural ornamentation was limited to the back of the screen and the box office. Its primary purpose, however, was still to pull customers in from the highway and give the theatre definition, recognizability, and distinction.

The drive-in was a social phenomenon as well as a business. It successfully combined public and private life during a period in which Americans were trying to strengthen both. The family could go out together without paying a baby-sitter or worrying about the behavior of family members. Families could watch movies together but also talk, fight, sleep, or kiss without disturbing others. It was also healthier; children were less likely to be exposed to communicable diseases at a time when polio was still a threat. At the same time, patrons were interacting with other people in their cars. The drive-in provided an opportunity for people and their new cars to be seen.

Theatre buildings of the postwar era, including drive-ins, were shaped by wartime attitudes and postwar thinking, which emphasized suburban living and an aesthetic shaped by nonstrategic construction substitutes and newly developed products. The political, social, and economic events of the 1940s had changed motion picture theatre architecture, attendance, and management policies. One of the greatest changes was the priority given to the automobile, which had to be accommodated for a theatre to be successful. The car changed the theatre in terms of location, lot coverage, style, and graphics.

After years of deprivation—accompanied, ironically, by record attendance—exhibitors were eager for a return to stability. Hoping for the advantages of both war and peace, they foresaw an end to government restrictions and expected an even larger audience than before. The technology of wartime could now be adapted to private enterprise. In 1945, in a discussion of postwar projections, the editors of *Theatre Catalog* crassly gave a hindsight view of the role of war: "War, however it may be condemned on moral, ethical, and spiritual grounds, can at least be condoned—if not indeed be justified—for purely materialistic reasons."[42]

By the time theatre construction resumed in the late 1940s, the buildings were simpler and cleaner in line and form. These aesthetic changes were the result not only of substitutions, experimentation, and wartime inventions but also of the acceptance of the "less is more" philosophy of architecture. While all but a handful of contemporary housing and office projects in the United States were still utilizing traditional, historic images, the motion picture theatre was boldly embracing postwar Modernist tenets.

During the 1940s, the psychological escape provided by movies had also undergone a change. At the beginning of the decade, the motion picture theatre had thrust people into reality—a controlled, optimistic, yet threatened reality. Newsreels, bond drives, and scrap metal collections made the war real; escape came in the form of patriotism, community, and cause. After 1945, there was an attempt to relegate the war to the past as quickly as possible. The theatre captured the emphasis on economic and psychological recovery. It promoted suburban living and the optimism of a future made possible by a physical, moral, and technological victory. The imagery of the motion picture theatre of this period was no longer of the distant past, nor of the space-age future. It was of the immediate future.

In 1948 the Supreme Court voted unanimously that Paramount, the defendant named in the lawsuit brought by the Justice Department, and the four other major studios constituted an illegal trust. Vertical combinations gave them control of production, distribution, and exhibition, resulting, the court ruled, in price-fixing and the restriction of competition. In the so-called "consent decree" or "divorce decree," the Big Five (Paramount, RKO, Loew's, Twentieth Century–Fox, and Warner Bros.) agreed to divest themselves of their theatres under court order. Theatre ownership and management now came into the hands of independent owners and theatre circuits not connected to the studios. This change limited the opportunity to monopolize first-run exclusives and encouraged smaller theatres. It also resulted in higher ticket prices. Theatre builders no longer had the financial resources of the studios to absorb the costs of leasing movies, advertising, or commissioning lavish new theatres. As ticket prices rose, movie attendance dropped precipitously.

The other event of 1948 that affected movie attendance and theatre operations was the commercial expansion of television. Between 1947 and 1957, weekly movie attendance fell by one-half, as 90 percent of American households acquired a television set—a novelty that offered free entertainment.[1] The effects of these trends would fundamentally alter the design and operation of theatres in the following decades.

Motion picture theatres responded by capitalizing on their strengths and offering things television could not. Studios introduced technical innovations, such as wide screens and stereo, and stressed the absence of commercial interruptions. At the same time, producers tried to improve the perceived quality of their movies in an attempt to counteract the appeal of television, with some initial success. Business at the drive-in theatre boomed, however, because it offered the excitement of the theatre and the comfort of the living room. In spite of these attempts, motion picture theatre attendance never equaled that of previous decades.

S. Charles Lee's response to the upheaval was to retire from the practice of architecture at about the age of fifty. He foresaw that the changes in film exhibition techniques brought on by the consent decree and television would change the nature of motion picture theatre architecture. No longer could the studios finance the construction or maintenance of theatres, and the independents could not afford to do so on the previous level. Lee's investments required his full attention, so he turned his energies to his business projects. Motion picture theatre construction changed in the wake of the "divorce," as did Lee's attitude toward architecture from his new perspective as a developer.

Producers and exhibitors had long and bitterly feuded over the economic and legal

7
Intermission
From
Architecture
to Business

obligations between them. When booking films, independent theatre owners were at the mercy of the studios that also owned their own theatres. Managers were still forced to agree to block booking, thus limiting their control over which pictures they could show in their theatres. The Justice Department sided with the independents and, after a thirty-six-year investigation, granted a divorce to the exhibitors. As a result, Paramount divested itself of its theatres in 1949, followed by RKO in 1950, MGM and Fox in 1952, and Warners in 1953.[2] The studio organization still constituted an oligopoly, but the Big Five firms were no longer fully integrated.

With the divorce decree, exhibitors were freed from block-booking requirements but also lost the advantages of subsidized film leasing, advertising, and construction and maintenance costs. Films were now distributed according to competitive rates, which rose quickly. Ironically, the breakup probably helped the studios more than it did the exhibitors, who argued that the relief granted the complainant was working exclusively in favor of the defendant.[3] The two trade organizations of exhibitors, Allied States and Theatre Owners of America, Inc., still felt themselves the victim of a conspiracy, convinced that the movie industry was the only one in which the wholesaler sat up nights figuring ways to drive the retailer out of business.[4] Debate now focused on the pros and cons of federal regulation of the industry and distribution practices. By 1955, $400 million in lawsuits was still pending against film companies on miscellaneous antitrust charges as exhibitors continued to look to the courts for relief.[5]

Studios were producing fewer (and, the exhibitors argued, poorer-quality) pictures each year, while requiring the exhibitors to pay higher fees in the midst of a decreasing market. Higher admission prices (between 1948, the year of the divorce, and 1952 they had increased by 50 percent) combined with the competition offered by television kept people away in droves (see appendix A). Although independent theatre owners had always felt at a disadvantage vis-à-vis the studio-owned theatres, now all theatres were owned by independents. Not only did they have to maintain their theatres without any financial assistance from the studios, but the Korean War further threatened their ability to do so.

On 16 October 1950, the National Production Authority (NPA) issued Order M-4, again limiting both new construction and remodeling by imposing restrictions on materials.[6] This time, however, the industry did not respond with the patriotism and self-sacrifice it had shown during World War II. Korea was a United Nations–ordered police action, not an American-declared war for democracy. The movie industry, which had not yet fully enjoyed its hard-earned postwar recovery, fought back. Editorials in the trade publications explained, "The industry would be glad to make the same sacrifices that it did during World War II, but it cannot afford to stand idly by while its security is undermined."[7] The NPA eventually rescinded its order.

But the greater threat to theatre owners was television, which was growing exponentially. In 1945, there were nine stations operating in five cities; by 1950, eighty stations served three million home sets; and by 1952, two thousand stations were scattered across the country.[8] Families who did not own a television watched their neighbors'. Theatre operators reassured themselves that once the novelty wore off, home television, with all its commercial interruptions, would be no competition for the public theatre. Movies and television were different media with different formats. As the quality of television broadcasting improved, however, with the promise of color and movies in one's home, exhibitors felt the threat more keenly. Industry commentator Fred C. Matthews tried to allay their fears, assuring theatre owners that color television could not compare with the quality of color movies and was "still off in the distance. . . . The greatest menace may well prove to be the much despised phonevision. . . . When a family can invite a dozen of the neighbors into its living room to watch a recent movie at a total cost of $1, we have a situation which may well cause the theatre plenty of trouble."[9] Matthews proved to be half right, albeit unwittingly. The home video market would cut into theatre attendance heavily in the 1980s. When cable television first loomed on the horizon in the 1960s, theatre owners responded with an organized if unsuccessful campaign urging people to reject "Pay TV."

All these factors, plus higher taxes and the rising cost of living, combined to lower theatre attendance dramatically, beginning in 1949. The first year, attendance dropped by 20 million a week, and the following year, by another 10 million. By 1953, theatre attendance was down to 45.9 million per week, a drop of nearly 50 percent from its peak of 90 million per week in 1946–48. "Like the Communist menace," Matthews warned in an editorial in *Theatre Catalog,* "it [declining attendance] is here."[10] In a twofold response, the industry attempted to accommodate television while at the same time introducing innovative technologies, including stereoscopic and stereophonic devices and gimmicks aimed at strengthening its competitive advantage.

First called "theatre television," closed-circuit programming was intended to include television broadcasts in the motion picture theatre. These supplemental programs— presented before the feature film began, between shows at a double feature, or as special events—were offered to patrons as an inducement to go to the movies. Beginning in 1950, theatre designs typically included television-viewing lounges with large screens. Theatre owners assumed at the time that theatre television would replace newsreels and that theatres devoted only to televised events might emerge, similar to newsreel theatres. But there were problems. Installation of projection equipment was expensive, and the audience was limited, in spite of the advantages of the large screen. The fifteen-by-twenty-foot screens were three hundred times the size of home viewing equipment.[11] By 1952, more than seventy-five theatres in thirty-seven cities offered large-screen television equipment.[12] Even drive-in theatres began to offer television in the lounge adjoining the concession stand. In 1953, for example, the S-3 Drive-In, in Rutherford, New Jersey, offered the heavyweight title fight for ten dollars a car.[13]

Theatres continued to experiment with television lounges, but by the mid-1950s, the majority of homes had television, which offered new programs seven nights a week, including movies and news broadcasts. By 1958, there were 27 million television sets in private homes; that same year, theatre attendance reached an all-time low of 39.6 million.[14] The success of theatre television was limited to sporting events, probably because television had not yet begun to carry such major sports events such as the World Series or prizefights. Lee built several Quonset-hut television theatres in Mexico— cantinas with television—providing theatres for workers who could not afford televisions of their own.[15]

As a more effective means of competition, theatre owners hoped to offer something that television could not, in a setting unavailable at home. Several schemes were tried, including wide-screen projection, simulated three-dimensional effects, and stereophonic sound. The first of these, Cinerama, was unveiled on 30 September 1952, at the Broadway Theatre in New York.[16] The process, developed by Fred Waller to help train gunners during World War II, consisted of a three-camera and seven-track-microphone system. When projected onto the screen, the sights encompassed viewers in a curve 146 degrees wide and 55 degrees high, thus filling in their peripheral vision and giving a more three-dimensional effect.

Cinerama, however, was expensive to film as well as to exhibit. Theatres had to have three coordinated projectors, seven speakers, and an unreasonably wide screen. The Broadway Theatre, which was remodeled for the premiere of *This Is Cinerama,* gave up orchestra seats to make room for the additional projection booths. Prosceniums, curtains, and even box seats had to be removed to accommodate the screen and speaker system. Floors had to be strengthened, and electrical power increased. Even though it had been shown in only thirteen theatres, by 1955 *This Is Cinerama,* a travelogue that featured a stomach-churning roller coaster ride, had grossed more than $20 million (fig. 130).[17] Although business boomed as people flocked to see the new technique, the expense was prohibitive for most theatre owners and the number of films shot for Cinerama was limited. In addition, the process was not suitable for all types of filming. Wide-angle action scenes, for example, worked better than intimate close-ups. Most of the movies filmed in Cinerama were generally shot in a conventional manner as well. In fact, the Cinerama Dome Theatre in Hollywood, designed and built in 1963 especially for the technique, showed a Cinerama film for the first time in 1988, on the twenty-fifth anniversary of its opening.[18]

In 1953, one year after the introduction of Cinerama, CinemaScope appeared. Developed by Henri Chretien, and purchased and marketed by Spyros Skouras, president of Twentieth Century–Fox, it was a more practical way of achieving the same experiential effect, but with less distortion. This system involved the use of an anamorphic lens that horizontally compressed a large picture onto ordinary 35-mm. film; when the film was projected, with the help of a compensating lens that spread the light beams out horizontally, the original shape of the image was restored and filled the wide screen. Although CinemaScope did require a triple-sized curved screen and additional speakers, an ordinary projector fitted with an additional lens could be used. Regular film, cameras, and projectors produced an image with a screen ratio of 8:3 instead of the standard 4:3. Burned by the Cinerama experience, some theatre owners were reluctant to invest in a wide screen if there was no guarantee that the new film type would be available. To reassure them, Fox announced that all their movies would be filmed with this process, as it cost no more to shoot or project than traditional film. *The Robe* introduced the new process to the public on 16 September 1953 at the Roxy Theatre in New York City; the premiere was followed by a successful run in one hundred cities.[19] By the end of 1953, between two and three thousand theatres were showing CinemaScope.[20] Darryl F. Zanuck, vice president of Fox, described it with traditional hyperbole: "The exhibitor may now show his patrons things the eye has never before witnessed in a

"The biggest new entertainment event of the year." - LIFE

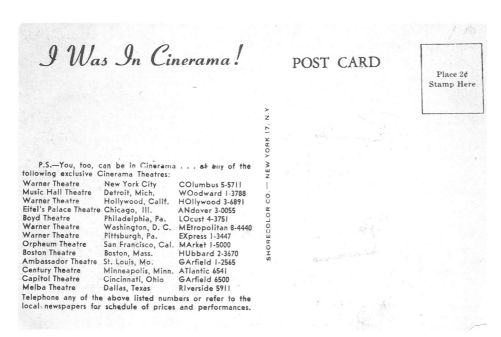

I Was In Cinerama!   POST CARD

Place 2¢
Stamp Here

P.S.—You, too, can be in Cinerama . . . at any of the
following exclusive Cinerama Theatres:

Warner Theatre	New York City	COlumbus 5-5711
Music Hall Theatre	Detroit, Mich.	WOodward 1-3788
Warner Theatre	Hollywood, Calif.	HOllywood 3-6891
Eitel's Palace Theatre	Chicago, Ill.	ANdover 3-0055
Boyd Theatre	Philadelphia, Pa.	LOcust 4-3751
Warner Theatre	Washington, D. C.	MEtropolitan 8-4440
Warner Theatre	Pittsburgh, Pa.	EXpress 1-3447
Orpheum Theatre	San Francisco, Cal.	MArket 1-5000
Boston Theatre	Boston, Mass.	HUbbard 2-3670
Ambassador Theatre	St. Louis, Mo.	GArfield 1-2565
Century Theatre	Minneapolis, Minn.	ATlantic 6541
Capitol Theatre	Cincinnati, Ohio	GArfield 6500
Melba Theatre	Dallas, Texas	RIverside 5911

Telephone any of the above listed numbers or refer to the
local newspapers for schedule of prices and performances.

SHORECOLOR CO. — NEW YORK 17, N.Y.

130 "I Was in Cinerama," postcard, 1955.
The emphasis in Cinerama was on
making the viewer feel involved
in the action on screen.

theater. Spectacle has always been one of the greatest, if not the greatest, magnets for an
audience. Now we have a potential unequaled in all the long centuries of theatrical
history."[21]

But it was equaled—by Paramount's VistaVision and by Todd A-O. The former,
introduced in 1954 in the film *White Christmas,* was achieved by running the 35-mm.
negative horizontally instead of vertically, thus widening the picture and increasing the

depth-of-field focus. Paramount announced it would make all its feature pictures in VistaVision and offered the technique free to all other producers.[22] Todd A-O, named for showman Michael Todd and the American Optical Company, premiered in 1955 with *Oklahoma!* Nicknamed "seamless Cinerama," Todd A-O accomplished an effect similar to Cinerama with a single camera and projector. Ultimately, CinemaScope, with a projected ratio of 2:66:1, became the most widely used process. It necessitated the fewest changes in projection systems: new lenses, some minor alterations in the projectors, and a new screen. Installation of the new screens, however, resulted in the destruction of the small proscenium openings in many older theatres. Panavision, manufacturer of anamorphic lenses, developed Ultra-Panavision, a wide-screen system with no discernible distortion that was compatible with other processes. The Ultra-Panavision process produced a negative from which any size format could be printed, thus giving exhibitors a choice that matched their screen size.[23]

Other novelties included 3-D, introduced in 1953 in the film *Bwana Devil.* This technique gave the illusion of a layered three-dimensionality that the other techniques could not approach. The human eye perceives depth through two methods. The first is depth perception, wherein the brain interprets the overlapping images, the shadows, and the relative size of objects seen by the eyes. Cinerama and CinemaScope depended on this technique as well as on peripheral vision to trick the brain. The other method, stereopsis, refers to the ability of the brain to put back together the two distinct images sent from slightly different angles by the right and the left eye. This was the basis of 3-D; the artificial creation of this effect. Anaglyphic lenses produced a picture in which the right component (red) of the composite image was superimposed upon the left component (green), resulting in a three-dimensional effect when viewed through correspondingly colored filters. Two cameras were used to separate the images, which were then reunited by two perfectly synchronized projectors along with plastic polarized glasses issued to the viewers with their admission tickets. Objects appeared to come off the screen and go over the audience's heads. But the combination of awkward glasses and the fuzzy B pictures released in 3-D doomed it to failure. Some movies, such as *Kiss Me, Kate,* were filmed both ways.

All these wide-screen and directional-sound techniques meant financial investment—in projectors, speakers, and screens. In addition to the purchase of equipment, wider screens meant remodeling. Many of the prosceniums built or remodeled during the 1930s and 1940s were destroyed, as were the floral motifs and side murals that framed them. But the investments paid off as the public began to respond; by the mid-1950s movie attendance had leveled off to about half of what it had been a decade earlier.

Not only had the new techniques of the 1950s aroused public curiosity, but in 1954 the federal tax on admissions was reduced from 20 to 10 percent, while ticket prices remained constant. As a result, in August 1954 theatre attendance reached 80.1 million per week.[24] Movie industry stocks rose; Hollywood was making a comeback, although it would never equal its glory days of the 1940s.

In spite of increased attendance, however, competition was stiff, especially for the entrepreneur who owned a single theatre. In addition to the capital investment required, the studios were releasing fewer pictures, averaging only twenty to twenty-five per year instead of fifty. Thousands of small, traditional theatres—that is, the ones that still had narrow screens and monophonic systems—were driven out of business. As Cole Porter decreed in "Stereophonic Sound," from *Silk Stockings* of 1955:

> Today to get the public to attend a picture show,
> It's not enough to advertise a famous star they know.
> If you want to get the crowds to come around
> You've got to have glorious Technicolor,
> Breathtaking Cinemascope and
> Stereophonic sound.
>
> . . . .
>
> The customers don't like to see the groom embrace the bride
> Unless her lips are scarlet and her bosom's five feet wide.
> You've got to have glorious Technicolor,
> Breathtaking Cinemascope or
> Cinerama, VistaVision, Superscope or Todd-A-O
>
> . . . .
>
> Cinecolor or
> Warnercolor or
> Pathécolor or
> Eastmancolor or
> Kodacolor or
> Any color and . . .
> As an extra tonic,
> Stereophonic sound.[25]

The number of theatres during this period remained relatively constant. Although four thousand of the eighteen thousand theatres in America closed, they were replaced by an equal number of drive-in theatres, which accounted for half of summer movie attendance in the 1950s.[26] The "cow pasture" theatres, as the originals were called, disappeared, replaced by busy, sophisticated enterprises, nicknamed "ozoners."[27] There were several reason for this prosperity: building restrictions and shortages had less impact on drive-ins; the land, usually located on the outskirts of growing suburbs, was cheaper; and construction and maintenance costs were lower than for indoor theatres. In addition, the quality of projection and sound was improving; in-car speakers were replacing archaic systems such as centralized-sound, underground, overhead, and bi-car speakers.

Owners cleverly capitalized on the convenience factor and the family orientation of the drive-in. Recreational facilities included fully equipped playgrounds, sometimes with a "trained matron" in attendance, miniature golf, swimming pools, pony rides, and miniature trains that conveniently stopped at the concession stand. Customer services included gas and service stations, windshield cleaning, bottle warming, and in-car heaters and bug killers. Walk-in business was accommodated in lounges that sat between 150 and 600 additional people in air-conditioned or heated comfort near the profitable concession stand.

Drive-in operators knew how to create and then exploit uniqueness.[28] Some provided parked cars for those who did not own an automobile and arrived by bus. Another provided stalls for horses. The Fly-In Drive-In Theatre in Belmar, New Jersey, designed by Claude Birdsall, had space for five hundred cars as well as fifteen airplanes.[29] Although only eight to ten planes dropped by per week, the real boost the aerial operation gave the owner was in the form of publicity and ballyhoo.

It seemed the only problem ozoners could not solve easily was segregation. In a paper titled "Drive-In Theatres of Today and Tomorrow," delivered at a convention of theatre owners on 18 September 1949, drive-in theatre consultant and designer George M. Peterson said:

> Many exhibitors request information as to segregation of the patrons in the Drive-In Theatre of Tomorrow. Most indoor exhibitors know the answer to this problem, but to others it presents a real difficulty. The Supreme Court of the United States has twice ruled that the Federal Segregation Law was unconstitutional, as the racial question was one for the States to decide. . . .
>
> One method used to segregate the whites and the colored, when state laws permit, is to provide one or two ramps at the rear of the drive-in theatre for colored only, and to provide a small concession and rest rooms for the use of the colored patrons. There is little objection, on the part of the whites, to the colored parking on the ramps, but a large percentage of the whites do object to using the same concession and rest rooms with them. We all realize that this is really a tough problem to solve, so all that can be done is to work out the best solution possible and keep within the law.[30]

Although postwar Americans appeared to make the drive-in theatre a part of their lives, the generation following did not. As the automobile became an accepted part of daily life, the thrill of sitting in one's car at night to watch a movie seemed less inviting. In addition, relaxed social mores decreased the importance of the drive-in as an opportunity for unsupervised privacy. By 1989, only fifteen hundred were still in operation.[31] The suburbs had grown beyond their 1950 borders, and the lots that used to be on the edge of town were now valuable as potential sites for shopping centers, industrial parks, or self-storage facilities. Drive-ins could generally stay in business only by finding supplemental sources of income during the day, such as weekend swap meets.

Nostalgia in the 1980s for the good old days of the drive-in produced an assortment of enterprises inspired by the original notion. The American Classics Drive-In, a converted warehouse in Manhattan, was probably the world's first walk-in drive-in. Customers arrived on foot or by cab, paid $5.00 per person ($7.50 on weekends), and parked themselves in 36 vintage convertibles to watch movies from the 1950s.[32] A hotel in California offered, as one of its rooms with a theme, a "50s Drive-In," where one slept in a Cadillac convertible and watched *Rebel without a Cause* projected onto a wall.[33] Raging Waters in San Dimas, California, introduced the Dive-In. There, customers floating in inner tubes in a huge pool watched such period classics as *Creature from the Black Lagoon* projected on a screen next to the pool.[34]

A survey of new theatre construction in the 1950s indicates that although construction costs per seat indoors and per car outdoors were comparable, drive-ins grossed more because they averaged more than two customers per car. They also did much greater business at the concession stand. For every dollar of admission at the drive-in, another forty cents was spent on refreshments.[35] By 1955, the forty-one hundred drive-in theatres grossed more in concessions than all the fifteen hundred indoor theatres, selling four times as many soft drinks alone.[36]

According to industry statistics, despite a drop of 22 percent in attendance between 1948 and 1949, concession sales at all theatres increased more than eight times.[37] By 1956 attendance was half of what it had been in 1948, but concession sales had increased more than forty times.[38] According to *Film Daily Year Book* and *Motion Picture Almanac,* in the early 1950s attendance figures continued to be inversely proportional to concession sales. This continued rise in food sales was due not only to the end of sugar restrictions but also to concentrated merchandising efforts to maximize concession profits. Commenting on the resulting changes in design of the ever-increasing concession area, Samuel L. Lowe, president of Theatre Candy Company and consultant to a company appropriately named Extra Profits, advised the theatre owner: "The location of the sales equipment is obviously most important. . . . Best results are obtained by a 'head-on' shot to the main patron traffic flow, and after the box office has been patronized (particularly if the box office is instructed to make small change whenever possible)."[39] Some theatres removed from eight to twenty seats to have the concession stand in a more desirable location.[40]

To boost sales, a smiling attendant would be instructed to avoid "the negative 'May I help you?'" and instead take the initiative with the inviting suggestion of "hot popcorn" and "ice cold Coca Cola"; she was also told to "'trade-up' her merchandise by pushing items with top profit and suggesting additional purchases."[41] "Will that be a large?" proved a better response to a drink or popcorn order than "Right away." Professional journals debated boxed versus bagged, "wet pop" versus "dry pop" (the stage at which seasoning is added to popcorn), fresh versus prepopped corn, vending machine soft drinks versus counter-poured, cups versus bottles, gum versus Life Savers, and extra profits versus extra maintenance.

At the turn of the century, horse-drawn peanut and popcorn wagons served their wares at parks and circuses and in front of nickelodeons, and later to people standing in line waiting to buy theatre tickets. Candies, nuts, and tobacco products were also sold by "butchers" who roamed the aisles of vaudeville houses and nickelodeons. Lee had earned money selling candy this way when he was a child. During the 1920s, a few of the larger motion picture theatres introduced the sale of candy through coin-operated devices attached to the backs of the seats, but "after the 1929 Crash, confectionery in theatres, like many types of businesses, went into temporary oblivion."[42] Greek-immigrant candy makers opened shops adjacent to the theatres and sold premovie snacks. During the mid-1930s, theatre owners, tired of cleaning up the debris of people who brought these and other foodstuffs inside, went into the confectionery business to offset cleaning costs.

171
**From
Architecture
to Business**

Candy counters, including Lee's self-contained air-conditioned unit, replaced the earlier machines. Candy sales kept many theatre owners in the black during the Depression, returning a profit of 45 percent on gross sales.[43]

In 1945, one theatre had experimented with selling frozen foods from vending machines in the lobby, so that the busy housewife could do her shopping after the matinee.[44] From time to time theatres had attempted selling a variety of merchandise, including sheet music, records, and toys.[45] As early as 1931, Lee had gone so far as to include soda fountains and full-scale restaurants, such as those in the Los Angeles Theatre. Generally, these proved less than successful in the United States, although the restaurant at the Linda Vista Theatre (1942) in Mexico City was very successful.

Although in-theatre restaurants solved the problem of waiting in line, the clientele was limited to people who had purchased tickets; no one was going to pay just to get into the restaurant. At the Miami Theatre (1946–47), which included a Huyler's Restaurant, Lee solved that problem by placing the restaurant in a storefront that was visible from both inside and outside the building (figs. 131–133). Customers could enter the restau-

131 *Miami Theatre, Miami, 1947*
(S. Charles Lee, 1946–47).

132 Miami Theatre, 1947. Box office and lobby.

133 Miami Theatre, 1947. Huyler's Sweet Shop Restaurant.

rant from the foyer, the lobby, or the street; this ease of access increased the potential market for both the eatery and the auditorium. Lee ingeniously designed the kitchen in the basement, complete with dumb waiter, in order to leave the main space above open for aesthetic treatments. The interior lobby of the Miami also featured a soft drink bar and a regular snack bar (fig. 134). Built shortly after the war, the Miami was one of the last theatres designed around customer amenities. In addition to the restaurant and soda fountain, Lee included a series of grand lobby spaces done in a tropical motif to match the Florida locale. In fact, the lobby spaces and auditorium were translated into an overscaled aquarium through which moviegoers moved and "swam," as though they were fish (figs. 135, 136). Some seats even had hearing aids, reflecting the increased social awareness surrounding design issues, which had been brought about by the large number of disabled veterans returning from the war (fig. 137). Another feature, aimed at wooing back families, was a cry room with a view of the screen.

By 1953, movie theatres accounted for more than one-fourth of candy bar sales in the United States, although popcorn was always the best revenue producer for the theatre.[46] Movies and popcorn had become indivisible, and theatre managers took advantage of the tendency of popcorn to sell itself:

> The fragrant aroma of popping corn, the intriguing sizzle of a kettle about to flip its lid, and the sight of the white and golden balls of fluff bouncing around a spanking-clean machine add up to perfect merchandising, and do most of the selling necessary where popcorn is concerned. For this reason, it is extremely good business to have the

134 Miami Theatre, 1947. Lobby with drink bar.

135 Miami Theatre, Miami, 1946
(S. Charles Lee, 1946—47). Because this
theatre was located in a tropical locale, Lee
used an aquarium theme, giving moviegoers
the perspective of fish in a tank.

136 Miami Theatre, 1946.

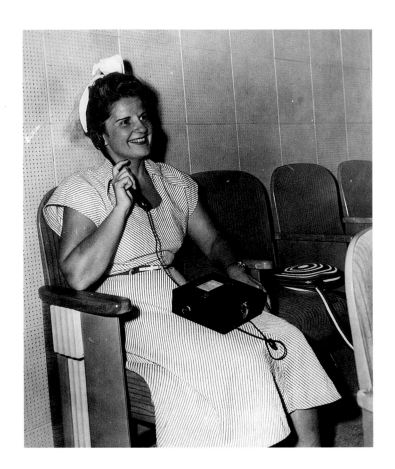

137 Miami Theatre, 1947. Hearing aid device built into seat.

popcorn machine where it is readily visible to all parts of the lobby to serve as a beacon to attract attention to the rest of the stand.

It is equally good merchandising to place beverage dispensers close by the popcorn machine.[47]

Salting the popcorn heavily helped push soft drink sales.

Given the post–World War II boom in candy sales and the attending slump in attendance, the business of the motion picture theatre was rapidly becoming the business of selling popcorn, candy, and soda. Movies were virtually a sideline, an activity that accompanied chewing. The profits were in the "second box office," as the concession stand was referred to in an industry publication.[48] In 1951, the candy counter represented 20 percent of the revenue for a theatre.[49] By 1989, it was the main source of income for theatre operators, accounting for 80 percent of the profits.[50] Even video rental stores began selling theatre-type candies and popcorn for their customers to take home.

Theatre designers recognized the new reality of concession income. Instead of providing plush seating and luxurious surroundings to entice the customer inside, the architect focused on efficient traffic around the candy counter. The atmosphere that had once pampered the customer was now given over to brightly colored candy boxes. Theatre facades were plainer, and the interiors less exotic and mysterious. Several auditoriums could be served by one centrally located concession stand or a series of candy sellers. Lobbies were frequently larger than auditoriums.

Lee, however, was not interested in designing fancy candy counters or buildings whose purpose was to get people out of them. He had specialized in creating inviting places that people were willing to pay to come back to on a routine basis. Design focused on "brand-name loyalty"—choosing the Fox over any other theatre showing the same movie because it was a better environment. As the snack bar began to prove more profitable than the box office, the focus on design changed to one that discouraged lingering. Once customers bought their quota of food and drink, they were to be replaced with new customers as quickly as possible.

The demand for flagship theatres was gone, and the demand for theatres in general was decreasing. Although these trends had an impact on his business, he had no desire to adapt or diversify. His real estate investments over the years had produced a substantial portfolio that demanded an increasing amount of attention. Around 1950 he changed professional directions to pursue his business and property interests, at first combining real estate development and architecture, though finally eliminating his architectural practice entirely.

While Lee was exploring various avenues, his accountant introduced him to another of his clients, Samuel Hayden. Hayden had been considering the purchase of one hundred acres on Century Boulevard near Los Angeles International Airport but felt the project was too large for one person. Around 1948 Hayden and Lee bought the land in partnership, forming the Hayden-Lee Company, and planned an industrial subdivision. They offered the lots for sale, but after several months still had no buyers. The partners then changed their approach and developed what they call an industrial FHA.

The Federal Housing Authority, set up as part of the New Deal in 1934 under the National Housing Act, was designed to strengthen the private housing market by insuring loans made by private lending institutions for moderate-cost homes. The purpose of the program was to aid homeowners—at a time when homes were being foreclosed at a rate of one thousand per week—and to "prime the pump" by getting more money into circulation. When the program began, Lee drew up a dozen designs, floor plans, and elevations of proposed houses that fit the agenda of the FHA and conformed to its conservative architectural guidelines. He presented the idea to the Bank of America for financial support, but the bank officers rejected the idea because they did not want to encourage federal involvement in the private housing market.[51] Lee abandoned the idea at the time but returned to it in the 1950s, after the FHA program had proved a success. As a developer, he built thousands of homes and factories under the FHA umbrella.

Hayden-Lee planned to build factories on the project site, known as International Airport Industrial District, and sell them directly to the users rather than on speculation. The terms, within FHA guidelines, were a down payment of 10–20 percent, with the balance paid over 111 months at 6 percent interest; Hayden-Lee financed the project by borrowing money from the bank at 4 percent, with the loan guaranteed by the federal government. Lee moved his principal office to the site, where he had designed and built several demonstration buildings. The system worked; the factories began to sell, and the government issued a monograph on the project as a successful approach to industrial development.[52]

The entire development adhered to an overall plan that dictated consistency in building design, setbacks, and parking arrangements. The factory buildings were modular units that utilized tilt-up construction techniques. Most of the tenants were small manufacturers involved in the production of such commodities as plastics, food products, and sheet metal. The feature that distinguished one building from another was the facade, which was designed to promote the tenant's name and product. Using a modern aesthetic and boldly scaled geometries, Lee integrated trademark signatures and logos into the facade. Thus, the building identified the company while serving as a billboard for the product (fig. 138). "The show starts on the sidewalk" proved adaptable to commercial-industrial buildings as well as to theatres.

Lee gradually gave up his architectural practice altogether. He explained, "When I was designing theatres, my time belonged to my clients. . . . You can't serve two masters . . . [and] financially it's not too rewarding. It costs too much to sell architecture."[53] He took the view that if his career in development proved unsuccessful, he would return to the practice of architecture, "providing I had not jeopardized my reputation by giving inferior service."[54]

Hayden-Lee built approximately 150 factories on the original parcel. Hughes Aircraft was one of their largest clients, occupying as many as seventeen of the buildings at one time. Hayden's plan was to liquidate as much as possible as quickly as possible at the best margin of profit. Lee's idea was to rent or lease the buildings, retaining ownership of

138 Mellos Factory, Los Angeles (S. Charles Lee, ca. 1951). Food-processing plant.

what he thought would be increasingly valuable property. Hayden was fifteen years Lee's senior and, at age seventy, ready to retire. Around 1955 they dissolved the partnership on friendly terms, dividing the assets equally. After that, Lee decided he would merely lease rather than sell property, maintaining ownership of Southern California real estate that was escalating exponentially in value.[55] In 1985, for example, he arranged a 65-year lease to Stouffer's to build a 750-room hotel near the airport. The property, which Hayden-Lee bought at approximately 15 cents a square foot, was appraised in 1986 at $70 a square foot—a profit of over 46,000 percent in less than 40 years. To complete the lot necessary for the project, Lee paid over $100 per square foot to buy back one of the parcels.[56]

Hayden-Lee engaged in other FHA-sponsored building programs in the 1950s, including large housing developments in California, Idaho, North Dakota, and Arkansas. As a developer, Lee was more interested in the economics than in the aesthetics. One of their projects, Los Prados, in San Mateo, California, was a complex of four hundred houses, an equal number of apartments, a convalescent hospital, and a shopping center It was under construction in 1959 when Soviet Premier Nikita Khrushchev visited Southern California, following the famous "kitchen debates." Lee recalled erecting a sign printed in Russian that said, "Mr. Khrushchev, turn right here and see how the American worker lives." The motorcade stopped while Khrushchev read the sign and then moved on. The incident received attention in the press, creating free publicity for the project and demonstrating Lee's sense of theatrics even in the business of development.

Lee the architect had always been primarily Lee the businessman; architecture just happened to be the business. And he was always alert to business opportunities that might attract new clients, expand his practice, and build up a portfolio of real estate investments. Early in his practice, his "Ask the Architect" column in the *Los Angeles Times* provided a public service while it gave his work exposure and led to new contacts and potential clients. His FHA proposal to the Bank of America was another example of seizing an opportunity to develop his practice. In the 1930s, Lee and Leonard S. Hammel, a realtor, wrote and published the *Los Angeles Blue Book of Land Values,* a guide to construction costs in the city. It included information on property values, census figures, traffic statistics, and depreciation tables, illustrated by photographs of Lee's own work. The preface to the illustrations demonstrates his promotional attitude:

> The building information contained in this volume has been compiled for the Los Angeles Blue Book of Land Values by
>
> S. CHARLES LEE,
> Architect
>
> of outstanding reputation who has designed all of the buildings shown herein and whose experience has covered practically all types of buildings. By a special arrangement with Mr. Lee, the Land Value Book Publishing Company offers to the subscribers of the Blue Book the privilege of having Mr. Lee answer, without obligation, any specific questions, relative to Southern California building.[57]

He cites himself as an authority "of outstanding reputation," thereby implying a privilege to the buyer. Like everything else in his professional career, such tactics were carefully calculated to promote his business; and it was all directed to the world of business and theatre owners, not to fellow architects.

Although still deeply involved with architecture and architectural issues, Lee claimed to have no regrets about giving up his practice. Never one to live in the past, he did not cling nostalgically to his youth. This attitude of always focusing on the current project kept him active even in his eighties. At some point, a person hired to clean out Lee's office discarded his files, correspondence, and the bulk of his architectural drawings and plans, assuming them to be worthless—a decision that architectural historians have regretted. Fortunately, hidden in the attic were some photographs and tightly rolled drawings and plans that survived and were discovered in the 1980s. During that decade, when, to his enjoyment, he was rediscovered as the grand old man of theatre architecture, he was forced to rely on his memory and apocryphal stories to impart his wisdom.

His experience as an architect gave him insight as a developer, although his perspective, and to some degree his attitudes, changed. By the 1980s, he sounded as conservative and pragmatic as he had accused banks of being about the new directions in architecture in the 1920s. He admitted liking nothing in contemporary architecture and was critical of "sterile Modernism," claiming that the cities and streets were filled with monotonous glass box skyscrapers. Post-Modernism, however, had "not defined itself."[58] Lee dismissed this hybrid altogether, admiring neither late Modern nor its progeny. He named Gin Wong as one of his favorite contemporary architects and selected Wong's firm to design the Stouffer's Hotel and other projects. Wong's reputation was stronger in the business community than it was among architecture critics. "I won't be the architect [of the $800,000 hotel]," Lee said in 1984. "Insurance even as a consultant requires a $10,000 deposit. I can't afford it."[59] Nor did he appear to mind.

Not all of his business ventures were strictly for financial profit. He devoted considerable time and expertise to public service projects, including the Braille Institute for the Blind and the International Executive Service Corps, and to administering the S. Charles Lee Foundation. Lee and his first wife, Miriam (Midge) Aisenstein, married in 1927, while he was working on the Tower Theatre. Because several members of her family suffered from nystagmus, an involuntary movement of the eye from side to side, Lee developed an interest in ophthalmology. He funded an eye clinic at Cedars of Lebanon Hospital in Los Angeles and in 1958 joined the Board of Directors of the Braille Institute, serving as both treasurer and vice-president of real estate and building. As such, he was responsible for new building programs and for determining the disposition of all properties acquired.

In 1986 he established the S. Charles Lee Chair in the Graduate School of Architecture and Urban Planning at the University of California, Los Angeles. The grant stipulated that the funds be used to promote the commercial and business aspects of architecture, not just design. These projects allowed Lee to channel his money to his interests—which did not include paying what he considered exorbitant taxes.

His own home, which he designed in 1948, was much more conservative aesthetically than one might expect from the architect of the Los Angeles and Academy theatres, although his continuing attraction to innovative ideas was occasionally evident. Neither a period revival house typical of Beverly Hills nor an outlandish theatrical structure, his was a modest, albeit large, building overlooking the city. Set into the landscape as a low shelter, with open, flowing interior spaces, the house had a Japanese feeling. The shallow-pitched roof that extended beyond the walls reinforced the horizontality of the house. The building was set at an angle on the hillside lot to take advantage of the terrain. Innovations were manifest in the engineering, not in the aesthetics, in keeping with his background as a developer and client as well as with his role as an architect motivated by functional concerns. As examples of Lee's advanced engineering, the house was heated and cooled by forcing air through a plenum in the foundation, and interior walls were plastered with pumice for insulation and sound proofing. The windows in the bedroom were stationary, but the wall beneath the windows opened behind screens and louvers to allow for fresh air without letting in morning light. The swimming pool in the backyard was converted into a lake engineered with electric boats and a pier for his grandchildren and later became home to his koi collection, a species of exotic fish that are shown in competition. In January 1990, at the age of ninety, Lee died in his sleep in this home.

S. Charles Lee's divorce from architectural practice lasted the rest of his life. But the divorce between the studios and theatres lasted less than forty years. By the mid-1980s, encouraged by the laissez-faire attitude of the Reagan administration toward antitrust, studios again began acquiring theatres, and a new round of battle raged between studio-operated theatres and the independents, who were forced into debt trying to compete.[60] According to Morgan Stanley and Company, by 1989 the six largest theatre chains— many of which were owned by producer-distributors—controlled nearly 40 percent of the screens, up from 24 percent in 1986.[61] The six were: UA Communications, Inc., owned by Telecommunications, Inc.; Cineplex Odeon Corp., owned by MCA Inc.; AMC Entertainment, Inc.; General Cinema Corp.; Loew's Theatres Management Co., a subsidiary of Columbia; and Carmike Cinemas, Inc. In spite of static attendance since the late 1960s, most of these companies were involved in a building boom. It was estimated that by the early 1990s, there would be twenty-six thousand screens, a projected increase of 13 percent over 1989.[62]

More screens meant more competition for the same audience, and once again the independent owner found it difficult to compete with the corporation. This time theatre attendance was further threatened by the home video market, which benefited the studio but not the independent theatre owner. In the 1980s studios were demanding a greater percentage of the box office—43 percent, up from 37 percent.[63] Even as second-run theatres tried to woo back the audience with one-dollar admissions, Paramount began taking 35 percent of the ticket price or $1.10 per ticket, whichever was higher, thus forcing the theatres to increase their ticket price.[64]

While the divestiture was in effect, theatre design had undergone drastic changes in response to economic realities. Not only did theatres cost more to build, operate, and maintain, but the studios no longer subsidized owners for such expenses. The profits were in popcorn, not in auditoriums, and the architecture was in the concession stands. Eventually, all amenities that encouraged lingering were removed or limited to money-making operations, such as coin-operated video games.

The trend toward theatres subdivided into multiple spaces began in 1962, with two-

and three-screen houses.[65] AMC gave birth to the "multiplex" with a four-screen theatre in 1966 and a six-screen theatre in 1969. A single theatre housing six to eighteen screens soon became standard; the facilities were created either by divvying up single-screen entities or by commissioning new construction. Stark and efficient auditoriums serviced by a brightly decorated lobby or a series of candy concessions became the norm, increasing the box office and the efficiency of theatre operations. Drive-ins were also turned into multiplexes. The number of theatres in the United States came to be measured not in buildings but in the number of screens, housed in fewer buildings and concentrated in the hands of fewer businesses.

Gone were the glamorous names—the Palace, the Tower, the Academy. Theatres were now being named for the shopping mall that had swallowed them up or for the number of screens they boasted, such as the Cineplex Beverly Center or the Century 14. Or they had no names at all. A small marquee hidden in the protective corridor of a Santa Fe, New Mexico, shopping mall reads simply "The Movies."

The facade was reduced to a back-lit plastic sign—one could hardly call it a marquee—listing the names of the dozen movies inside, along with their ratings by the Motion Picture Association of America. The box office was no longer an island, having been moved against the facade, where it dispensed computer-generated tickets for several auditoriums. The lobby was bright and easy to find; in fact, one had to maneuver to get past it and into the auditorium that matched the ticket. Signs indicating the name of the movie playing in a given auditorium were smaller than the menus at the candy counter. Concessionaires once again began selling popcorn and drinks to people waiting in line to get into the smaller auditoriums. Each screen was set in the center of a blank wall, embellished by neither proscenium curtains nor decorative walls nor seductive lighting. The hard-backed, cushionless seats of plastic (still usually red) were practical and easy to clean. Seldom were the floors carpeted; instead one's feet stuck to concrete sticky with soft drinks. The show no longer started on the sidewalk, but selling popcorn did.

In the late 1980s, theatre owners and moviegoers began to recognize what had been lost in the shopping mall–shoe box approach to theatre design. Successful programs such as "The Last Remaining Seats" series of the Los Angeles Conservancy, a local preservation group, proved that the public was yearning for the old days. These programs showed old movies in period theatres, including Lee's Los Angeles Theatre, accompanied by live entertainment, reminding seasoned viewers of the movie theatre experience and introducing young viewers to it for the first time. When Cineplex Odeon acquired the Gordon Theatre in Hollywood, rather than split it into several auditoriums, the owners restored it as the Showplace Theatre. In 1987 the same company built the eighteen-screen, $12-million Universal City 18 Cinemas, with illusions of glamour and allusions to theatres past. Architect David Mesbur included a seventy-foot-wide, forty-six-foot-high lobby with floors of gray-and-pink marble and a grand, if sterile, staircase. A European-style café served espresso and pastry. Ten of the auditoriums were equipped with the Lucasfilm THX sound system. The Alhambra Theatre in San Francisco was left as one theatre, and its 1926 Moorish detail restored. As more screens served an audience that remained constant, owners rediscovered customer service and amenities. By the end of the 1980s Dolby sound and a high-resolution screen-projection system were usually found in at least one auditorium per multiplex.

Theatre managers realized that to compete with the home video market and cable television, they had to offer the amenities they had spent years eliminating. In the 1970s, the market audience was between fourteen and twenty-four years old, but in the 1980s, theatre owners began pursuing the over-forty audience by offering "a total moviegoing experience" that included iced cappuccino, yogurt, and low-fat popcorn at the concession stand and better projection and sound quality in the auditorium.[1] Filmed shorts demonstrated the promise of Dolby sound and huge speakers. Rocker-type seats featured arms designed to hold paper cups of designer water. Courtesy, cleanliness, and better seats and sight lines began to reemerge as the focus of competition. The announcement in 1989 of the grand opening of Cineplex Odeon's Broadway Cinemas in Santa Monica, California, echoed the philosophy of previous decades, promising:

- four completely new state-of-the-art, wide-screened cinemas
- striking interior design with luxurious plush seating
- Dolby stereo sound systems in all auditoriums
- completely handicapped accessible
- hearing impaired listening systems
- advance tickets for same day film presentations

- plentiful free parking, and . . .
- real butter served on fresh, hot popcorn
- American Express cards welcome.[2]

The theatre business was beginning to rediscover showbiz.

One of the most important qualities provided by the motion picture theatre, but missing in the multiplex or in home video rental, was the sense of community. Theatres provided the "lobby experience": everyone there was sharing the moment. They were watching the same movie at the same time and breaking for intermission at the same point. Even in the lobby, surrounded by friends or strangers, moviegoers shared the emotion, excitement, inspiration, or heartbreak just witnessed. This sharing of joy and sorrow added to and was reinforced by the grandeur of the space.

The real lesson of the movie theatre is that space matters. *Where* something happens affects how it happens. The family-room VCR is cheaper and more convenient than the theatre, but the film is different in that format and that environment. Architecture and design shape our experience and memories, our values and attitudes, and influence our sense of style in other matters. They can enhance or destroy the activities housed therein. Going to the movies is different from renting a video. Going to the mall shoe box is not the same as going to the show. Architecture matters.

In many ways, the movie theatre represented a tangible experience of the American Dream. It was a palpable expression of material success made democratic—everyone who attended was a part of the performance. The industry, too, exemplified the American ethos. Americans had mastered a European discovery and soon led the world in its production and consumption. The movie business was a twentieth-century phenomenon that grew out of changes in life-style made possible by increasing amounts of leisure time and Yankee ingenuity. Being discovered by a movie mogul was an American fantasy that meant instant stardom, fame, and wealth, based on talent, hard work, and luck. The influence of the movies—and of the motion picture theatre—lasted long after the heyday of these two forces. Witness the sales of motion picture posters and memorabilia, the escalating auction prices for the "ruby slippers," and the camera-laden tourists searching for Hollywood and Vine. Americans are still looking for an authentic experience of the American promise, one they used to find at the movies.

Movies, by their very nature, are artificial and impossible. They demand illusion on the part of the viewer. The audience wants to be fooled and tricked and entertained. At Universal Studios in Southern California and in Florida, one of the leading attractions is a tour that demonstrates the falseness of movie making while the tourists participate in the process. At the Disney MGM theme park in Florida, the effect is doubly false, because tourists see a back lot that was never a back lot but was constructed for purposes of the tour. The tour is an illusion of illusion making. Furthermore, the buildings that set the stage are Disneyized copies (that is, built to between three-quarter and seven-eighths scale) of Streamlined Moderne examples in Los Angeles, including Lee's Hollywood Theatre.

The popularity of these tourist spots shows how the public devours the illusory quality provided by behind-the-scene tours. The old movie theatres addressed this need for illusion and what is now seen as nostalgia for the glamorous days of the studio system. The characteristic features of the motion picture theatre type that satisfied these needs, whether by Lee or others, developed from contemporary architectural ideas, political and economic ideology and events, social customs, and the evolution of the industry and its technology. The type reached its apex at mid-century, epitomized by Lee's work, but even after the theatres had lost much of their flamboyance, cultural reference to their features, or vestiges of them, and to their significance continued. These characteristics reveal much about the history of motion picture exhibition and about American life in the twentieth century. They also provide insight into the nature of architectural experience that can be applied to the other building types.

Stylistically, the motion picture theatre evolved from Ecole to eclectic to exotic and back to business. The first movie houses represented attempts to blend into the community, but the owners soon learned the value of distinguishing the buildings on the street. The movie theatre became a distinct type, declaring its independence from other building types. Harold W. Rambusch, decorator of the original Roxy, accurately described the role of the motion picture theatre architect as interpreting the "vocabulary of the past . . . in the vernacular of the day."[3] At the beginning of the century, the Neoclassical facades of both vaudeville and legitimate theatres, common to public buildings of the period, were an appropriated sign of good breeding and education. The Neobaroque palaces of World War I through the 1920s paralleled the period revival styles of other building types, especially housing. Theatre architects exaggerated and mixed the historical references, using them eclectically rather than archaeologically. Exotic architecture of the 1920s and 1930s, rooted in the nickelodeon, reflected the new social freedoms of the period and the release from Victorian inhibitions.[4] Moderne and, later, modern styles revealed the twentieth-century machine aesthetic, captured in the motion picture and its theatres, by then completely independent of live entertainment. Motion picture theatres were recognizable yet not monotonous; the most successful ones exploited the vocabulary of the type.

The nomenclature of each period revealed contemporary attitudes. At first the terms focused on the uniqueness of the form or on borrowed cultural legitimacy. The Kinetoscope, Biograph, and Cinématographe *parlor* indicated the novelty of popular entertainment in a Main Street setting. *Nickelodeon* and *air dome* also sounded gimmicky, whereas *palace* and *cathedral* connoted class and culture. *House, cinema* and *drive-in* were neighborhood terms, and *twin* and *multiplex* communicated, appropriately, an accounting attitude. There had developed a whole catalog of movie theatre names that reflected place, as in Uptown, Fifth Avenue, or Chicago; fantasy, as in Bijou Dream; building features, as in Tower, Grand, and Majestic; or references to excitement and movie tradition, as in Tivoli, Paradise, Capitol, State, Roxy, and Rialto. Less exciting, though indicative of convenience, choice, and a false promise of the communal experience, were the Plaza 10 and the Century 14.

The exterior of the motion picture theatre was designed to attract attention through the use of unusual elements—lights, physical size, ornamentation, or shape. The architect used design to reinforce the glamour, escape, adventure, or romance of the film by extending those qualities to the building, thereby involving the patrons in the experience. The boundaries of the building stretched in all directions, enhanced by dazzling effects. The marquee extended over the sidewalk and its swirling terrazzo patterns. Tall lighted elements projected into the sky. Even the glass-fronted multiplex featured poster cases, red carpets, and signs outlined in blinking bulbs.

The facade had its roots in the storefront or nickelodeon, but designers quickly moved toward fluid elements that created rhythm and movement. Arched forms called to mind the high-class architecture of Neoclassical legitimate theatres and the triumphal arches of movie palaces. Colored lights articulated the facade, spelled out the name of the theatre, and directed the eye to the box office. The animated marquee, introduced in the early moving picture theatres, was unique to the movies.[5] The nickelodeon was the first to experiment with electric lights to highlight the building and advertise the product, a device that had its culmination in the movie palace facade, which typically featured between four and five thousand bulbs.[6] Each new building type took the art a step further, until light patterns known as tracers and chasers twinkled and flickered, drawing the patron to the entry. Marquees were often designed not by the architect of the theatre or building but by a company specializing in marquees. By the 1930s the enormous signs found in vaudeville houses and palaces had evolved into pylons, which, though still large, were more in scale with the building and better integrated into the architecture. Decades later, multiplexes still used lighting to attract moviegoers, though by this time the display was frequently limited to a single strand of white lights.

In a movie theatre, the vestibule provided an unobstructed, recessed exterior lobby that combined the open front of a penny arcade and the enclosed front of a vaudeville theatre or store.[7] Legitimate theatres used only poster boards as advertising, but nickelodeons added banners and signs, in the tradition of the circus. This nebulous lobby space, part indoors and part outdoors, psychologically drew people into the theatre, making them part of the experience even before entering the auditorium.

In the center of the vestibule stood the box office, which combined the ticket window of the legitimate theatre with the ticket booth of the circus or fair in a new architectural expression. By the time of the nickelodeon, it had become a separate structure that was either attached to the rear wall of the outside lobby and flanked by entrance and exit doors, or set toward the street in the center of the vestibule. As early as 1913, *Motion Picture News* noted that the round box office "was as essential to the motion picture theatre as the mortar in front of a drug store or the striped pole in front of a barber shop."[8] Gradually the box office moved away from the facade to its position on the property line, then back to the facade as the lobby (that is, the concession stand) expanded, often to the lot line.

In the mature movie theatre, three considerations determined interior design: safety, comfort, and luxury. Local building codes governed safety, but comfort and luxury were the elements of competition among theatre owners. The prevailing style of interiors moved from the simplicity of the storefront and nickelodeon to the opulence of the movie palace and then back again. Monumentality and elaborate interior design, rooted in legitimate theatre design, began with small-time vaudeville. Eclectic designs were created in plaster relief and marble, made more visible through bright colors. Materials swung from improvisational to grandiose and back to simple, but with continued references to older traditions.

Although indoor lobbies did not exist in nickelodeons, they were soon recognized as an important draw, both as a waiting area and as a source of income. These spaces became increasingly elaborate and then dwindled in purpose and size until they housed only the candy counter and restrooms. Plaster and paint may have echoed a former grandeur, but the majestic staircases, accessory rooms, and promenades had died with the palace.

Lighting was an example of technology applied to movie theatre design. In the auditorium, lighting enhanced or falsified architectural motifs. The Uptown Theatre (Chicago, 1925), for example, incorporated seventeen thousand electric lights.[9] Lamps were used in theatres to bounce, echo, and mix light and color throughout the auditorium. Dimmer boards enabled the house technician to create special effects. The fluorescent lighting introduced by Lee produced changes in pattern with a flick of a switch. Indirect lighting evoked mood.

Beginning with the moving picture theatre and the small-time vaudeville house, architects and engineers studied sight lines, ventilation, and lighting to create the most comfortable viewing experience. The straight-back kitchen chairs used in storefronts and nickelodeons were abandoned for the plush red-velvet seats of the vaudeville and legitimate theatre. Thereafter, almost all motion picture theatres provided padded seats upholstered in royal shades.

The tiny muslin screen of the nickelodeon grew into a huge screen of silver reflective material. Originally framed by black cloth because of the weak light of early projectors, it was later draped and curtained with several layers of royal fabrics. As color film and better projectors were developed, the masking was removed in that it fought with the film. Owing to ideas of modernism and economics, as well as to unusual screen shapes and sizes, the material surrounding the screen eventually disappeared. Sound and the end of live entertainment eliminated the need for organ screens and orchestra pits, which were initially reduced to an apron and finally to a flat wall. In the 1910s the flat floor of the nickelodeon was changed to a sloped floor as a result of studying sight lines. The walls around the auditorium were decorated with murals, feathers, waves, and draperies.

Interior design was determined by engineering as much as by art or architecture. The relationship among the architect, the engineer, and the interior designer was a flexible one, especially if the theatre was part of a large office building. Laymen designed the first theatres to suit practical needs, without giving much thought to a formal plan—until it was discovered that design increased the box office take. Architects were introduced to the design process in the 1910s, and by the 1920s firms specializing in movie theatre architecture began to emerge. The large firms usually had their own engineers and designers on staff or worked with other large firms on joint ventures. As interior design became less ornate, architectural offices handled most of the design as a comprehensive unit, consulting specialists in auditorium design, seating, and acoustics when necessary.

Going to the movies was a complete sensory experience. It was, of course, visually stimulating. In addition, acousticians made it as aurally exciting and modern as the technology of the day would allow. In the era of the nickelodeons and palaces ushers sprayed perfume in the aisles; later, the smell of popcorn would permeate the theatre. The taste of popcorn and Jujubes became inextricably associated with going to the movies. Sumptuous materials—from the marble statues to the napped fabric of the seats—delighted the sense of touch. Motion picture theatre architecture was meant to delight the senses, provide escape, create a mood, and alter one's perceptions for a few hours.

Entertainment is one way of dealing with the fears and fantasies of real life. The motion picture theatre blurred the distinction between the fantasy and reality. Lee understood that. His theatres were part of an urban experience that provided a communal and personal experience at the same time.

In the late 1970s, theatres were being counted not in number of buildings but in number of screens—so that the statistics are sometimes misleading. In fact, many theatre buildings have been lost, many seats have been lost in the course of subdividing theatres, and the community experience has been lost. The lobby is no longer a focal point of shared emotion, like a church, but a transitional point, like an airport, where people are continually arriving and leaving, each with a different agenda.

The concentration of the movie industry in the hands of a few corporations resulted in a monotonous, fast-food approach to cinemas. Unlike the entrepreneurs of the 1920s, who focused on brand-name identification and spent money to make their theatres stand out, the corporate giants have a franchise mentality, with the result that most multiplexes look alike and have standardized formats.

S. Charles Lee's success and his lasting contribution as an architect lie in how his work served the client, the customer, and the city. In so doing, the work also served the architect. In addition to creating a rich physical legacy of buildings that captured time and place, he set an example for the successful practice of architecture. That meant understanding not only the art, the science, and the business of architecture but also the business of business. After identifying the market he wanted to pursue, he developed an expertise in all aspects of the architecture and the industry he was designing for, drawing on an education well grounded in art, architecture, and engineering. He developed a modern aesthetic by applying the Beaux-Arts principles of harmony, rhythm, ornament, and the primacy of the plan to changing ideas about the relationship between form and function. This balance between nineteenth- and twentieth-century attitudes resulted in work that had the strength of each tempered by the challenge of the other. In his theatres, the sequence of spaces was easily grasped, entrances were clearly marked, and traffic patterns were orderly. At the same time, they were the avant-garde of popular taste and represented modernism for the masses.

Lee understood the business of motion picture exhibition. Once he had decided to specialize in motion picture theatres, he learned all he could about the industry and his clients' needs. Instead of publishing his work for other architects to admire, he wrote for journals in the field of exhibition. His clients cared about economics first and art second and testified to his reputation for finishing on time and within budget. Yet within those constraints, he gave the client the flashiest, most modern theatre he could.

Lee also appreciated that a large part of the theatre business was salesmanship, known in the industry as ballyhoo. The business of selling through publicity began during the construction phase, as an article from the late 1940s entitled "The Exploitation of Theatre Construction" pointed out.[10] Illustrated by a photograph of three young women dressed in shorts nailing up a construction sign that announced, "Making way for Wometco's new Miami Theatre . . . to be erected on this site," the article, probably written by someone in Lee's office, used the Miami Theatre (Miami, 1946–47, with Robert E. Collins) as the sole example. The caption read, "The first announcement of the Miami Theatre is publicized by a typical trio of Florida pulchritude. The sign assures public interest and the girls make the picture worthwhile printing."

The show started on the sidewalk, and continued over it and beyond it, even before the building was completed. In turn the theatre and its publicity sold the architect. On the construction signs, the name of S. Charles Lee was almost equal in size to the name of the theatre (figs. 139, 140). The sign at the site of the Tower Theatre (Los Angeles, 1926–27) not only sold the architect, the future theatre, "the finest thousand seat theatre in America," and the Minneapolis Steel and Machinery Co. but also promoted the Cameo Theatre, "cream of the high class photo plays" down the street, "now playing 'The Romantic Age,' all seats 15 cents."

Ballyhoo was more than gimmicks, however. It was a means to secure and maintain clients by understanding and serving their needs. Lee had the ability to draw upside

139 Tower Theatre, Los Angeles, 1927
(S. Charles Lee, 1926–27).
Construction photo.

140 Fox Florence Theatre, Los Angeles, 1931 (S. Charles Lee, 1931). Construction photo.

down, so he could sit across the table from clients and sketch out an idea that matched their perspective. He would use a sketch done for a previous job, change the name, and make necessary adjustments for the new client, giving him or her the image of what the building might be like (figs. 141, 142). After he had the job, of course, he worked out the program and came up with a truly personalized design.

For Lee, architecture was always a means, not an end. The end was to do work he enjoyed, to create buildings he could be proud of, and to make money. He was not a struggling artist but a businessman with a pragmatic emphasis when designing or running the office. He used the establishment of the S. Charles Lee Chair at UCLA to

141 Huntridge Theatre
(S. Charles Lee, 1943). Sketch.

142 Lakewood Theatre (S. Charles Lee, 1944–45). The name "Lakewood" was pasted over a drawing proposed for the "Huntridge."

remind architects and architecture students of the importance of the business aspects of architecture.

"To be a successful architect," he said, "you have to be one-third businessman, one-third contractor, and one-third architect."[11] This practical philosophy was the key to his staying in business in two industries noted for their instability—movies and architecture. He was a good engineer, a good artist, and a good businessman; instead of seeing those categories as limits, however, he used each to strengthen the other two, pushing himself to his limit in all three areas. He offered workable solutions that combined feasibility with creativity.

To satisfy the client, Lee knew he had serve the customer—the moviegoer. The purpose of motion picture theatre architecture was to entice people to return, to pay repeatedly to see and use the space. He created comfortable spaces that were nurturing and stimulating at the same time. Each client wanted a unique building that gave customers a reason to select it from among all its competitors. Product loyalty came from the affiliated studio and the consistent quality of movies shown there, but also from the architecture itself. Lee's best theatres, such as the Los Angeles, Academy, La Reina, and Fremont, followed a building type but were unique, providing an imagery appropriate to time and place.

Lee carved a niche for himself with his signature designs and innovations and through his ability for self-promotion. He advertised his terrazzo sidewalks and exotic box offices the way exhibitors advertised coming attractions. Many of his ideas definitively altered theatre design. One example was the use of light as an architectural element, which by 1950 had become a standard for the type and was being applied to other building types as well. The best of his theatres created a sense of wonder and exploration that embraced users who were willing to pay repeatedly for the experience. There was an accessible monumentality to a Lee building; it was theatrical and imposing but inviting nonetheless. The manipulation of space created a nurturing environment that imparted to the ticket buyer a sense of power and elegance. These theatres were urban and suburban stage sets that included the user as a part of the architectural experience.

The theatres that Lee designed reflected a personality shaped by a midwestern business ethic and West Coast boosterism. They were quietly flamboyant but always in good taste; conservative in their public presentation yet imposing. Like his attitudes, the buildings focused on the present; even when he drew on history, there was no sense of nostalgia. The drawings of unbuilt projects and his preliminary design sketches reveal a great artistic flair, which was tempered by reality when the buildings were executed.

In the 1990s, the effects of time on Lee's theatres are evident, though in varying degrees. The Fremont (San Luis Obispo), for example, is still a wonderful experience. Some buildings are nominally intact and still operating as movie theatres, though bringing back the magic usually requires some imagination. The experience is often diminished owing to lack of maintenance, as indicated by threadbare carpets and deteriorated plaster casts. The cherubs and figures in the Los Angeles Theatre (designated as a Historic-Cultural Monument and listed on the National Register of Historic Places) are hidden under thick layers of dirt. Paint is peeling off the ceiling, and the carpeting is now gaudy in color and badly patched. Moviegoers must negotiate rows of video arcade machines to reach the auditorium. Other theatres have suffered the removal of the box office and the lobby furniture and the replacement of once-charming light fixtures. Instead of ornate etched-glass front doors one now finds utilitarian aluminum doors. The wide screens of the 1950s and the subsequent addition of Dolby sound have desecrated proscenium arches and side walls, or at least have caused the murals to be hidden under fabric stapled to the walls.

Some theatres are still standing but are being used in different ways. In the 1970s the Academy (Inglewood, Calif.) was transfigured into the Academy Cathedral. On the site of the former box office is a plaque that credits God as architect of the church. The dual-purpose American (Newhall, Calif.) no longer operates as a theatre but still serves as the American Legion meeting hall.

Some theatre buildings have been restored and adapted for use as performing arts centers. The Fox Wilshire (Beverly Hills) was renovated in 1981 as a concert hall, and the Tower (Fresno) reopened for live performances in 1989. Renovation of the Alex (Glendale) as a performing arts center for the city began in 1993. To bring the theatre back to its original condition of 1925, however, this renovation includes the removal of the forecourt canopy added by Lee in 1940.

Several theatres have been converted for nontheatrical uses, which has entailed retaining the general form of the building but modifying its appearance. The Vern (Los Angeles) became the Don Quixote Disco Club. The auditorium seats of the Tower (another building both cited as a Historic-Cultural Monument in Los Angeles and listed on the National Register of Historic Places) were removed in preparation for its transformation into a disco club that never materialized—though the current owner is considering restoring it as a theatre. Behind the stalls of the Globe Swap Meet in downtown Los Angeles one can still see the remnants of the box seats and the top of the proscenium. The Gentry (Compton) became a plumbing supply house. Others have been remodeled beyond recognition, though the structure itself remains. The Bay (Pacific Palisades) is now Bay Drugs, while the La Tijera (Los Angeles) was reincarnated as an office building.

In 1987, when the owner decided to demolish the La Reina (Sherman Oaks) and build a shopping mall, neighbors applied to the City of Los Angeles for landmark designation. The city granted their request and thereby imposed a one-year demolition delay intended to provide time to seek alternatives that would preserve the historic building. Tenacious in pursuit of his goal, the owner waited the prescribed period and then set about demolishing everything behind the entrance, restoring what remained as entrance statements for the La Reina Mini-Mall. The box office now serves as a detached display case for a clothing store, and the red snap-on letters of the marquee have been replaced by a black-and-white electronic message board.

Many of Lee's most significant theatres have been demolished. Gone are the Arden and its drive-through marquee, the Fox Phoenix and its Art Deco murals, the Fox Florence and its landscaped courtyard, the Garmar and its postwar modern facade, the Miami and its aquarium motif, the Tumbleweed and its barnyard forecourt, as well as the Picwood and its soaring neon swirls. They have been replaced with fast-food restaurants, parking lots, shopping galleries, mini-malls, and vacant lots overgrown with weeds.

The lesson to be learned from the work of S. Charles Lee is that good architecture is not judged by glossy photographs that please other architects and journal editors. Good architecture makes places where people want to be, where the client is satisfied and the users are served; places that people with no vested interest find wonderful and exciting; places they choose to return to. Lee's stage-set approach achieved an equilibrium among investors' needs, exhibition requirements, and the audience's sense of discovery and awe. The theatres provided what Kevin Lynch has termed "a sense of unfolding" about the architecture, the experience and, by extension, the city.

The idea of architecture as stage set continues to form a significant part of the built environment. Contemporary architects are again searching for imagery and meaning. Current architectural criticism suggests that architecture has become deliberately uncomfortable and disconcerting, reflecting chaos rather than well-organized space. The building has become an art object rather than a usable product. Lee's architecture fostered a comfortable but stimulating environment that continues to evoke powerful memories on both a national and personal level. Perhaps S. Charles Lee's enduring contribution was to demonstrate how important it is that the show start on the sidewalk.

APPENDIX A
Movie Theatre Statistics, 1922–1992

Year	No. of Theatres		Weekly Attendance (millions)	Average Admission	Box Office Gross (millions)
	All Types[a]	Drive-Ins[b]			
1922	—		40.0	—	—
1923	—		43.0	—	—
1924	—		46.0	—	—
1925	19,489		48.0	—	—
1926	21,644		50.0	$.28–.35	$ 750[c]
1927	22,304		57.0	—	750[c]
1928	23,344		65.0	.40–.50	—
1929	23,000		80.0	.35–.55	720
1930	21,993		90.0	—	732
1931	14,126		75.0	—	719
1932	12,480		60.0	—	527
1933	12,574	1	60.0	.23	482
1934	13,386	2	70.0	.23	518
1935	14,161	—	80.0	.24	556
1936	16,055	—	88.0	.25	626
1937	16,251	—	88.0	.23	676
1938	15,701	—	85.0	.23	663
1939	17,003	—	85.0	.23	659
1940	17,541	—	80.0	.24	735
1941	17,919	95	85.0	.25	809
1942	17,728	99	85.0	.27	1,022
1943	17,919	97	85.0	.29	1,275
1944	18,076	96	85.0	.32	1,341
1945	19,198	102	85.0	.35	1,450
1946	18,765	300	90.0	.40	1,692
1947	18,351	548	90.0	.40	1,594
1948	19,323	820	90.0	.40	1,506
1949	18,570	1,203	70.0	.46	1,431
1950	19,106	2,202	60.0	.53	1,376
1951	18,980	2,830	54.0	.53	1,310
1952	18,623	3,276	51.4	.60	1,246
1953	17,965	3,791	45.9	.60	1,187
1954	19,101	4,062	49.2	.45	1,228
1955	19,200	4,587	45.8	.50	1,326
1956	19,003	4,494	46.5	.50	1,394
1957	19,003	4,494	45.0	.51	1,126

continued

Year	No. of Theatres		Weekly Attendance (millions)	Average Admission	Box Office Gross (millions)
	All Types[a]	Drive-Ins[b]			
1958	16,000	4,700	39.6	.51	992
1959	16,103	4,768	41.9	.51	958
1960	16,999	4,700	40.4	.69	951
1961	21,000[c]	6,000[c]	41.6	.69	921
1962	21,000[c]	6,000[c]	—	.70	903
1963	12,800	3,550	—	.74	904
1964	13,750	4,100	—	.76	913
1965	14,000	4,150	—	.85	927
1966	14,350	4,200	—	.87	964
1967	14,500	4,900	—	1.22	989
1968	14,325	4,975	—	1.30	1,045
1969	14,500	4,500	—	—	1,099
1970	14,300	4,600	17.7	—	1,162
1971	—	3,770	15.8	1.65	1,170
1972	11,670	3,790	18.0	—	1,644
1973	—	3,800	16.6	—	1,524
1974	—	3,772	19.4	1.89	1,909
1975	—	3,801	19.9	2.03	2,115
1976	—	3,414	18.4	2.13	2,036
1977	12,275	3,564	20.4	2.23	2,372
1978	12,692	3,626	21.8	2.34	2,643
1979	17,095	3,656	21.5	2.47	2,821
1980	17,675	3,504	19.6	2.70	2,749
1981	18,144	3,354	20.5	2.75	2,960
1982	18,295	3,178	22.6	2.90	3,445
1983	18,884	2,852	23.0	3.15	3,766
1984	19,589	2,840	23.0	3.40	4,031
1985	21,097	2,770	20.3	3.55	3,749
1986	22,665	2,718	19.5	3.65	3,778
1987	23,555	2,507	20.9	3.90	4,252
1988	23,129	1,497	20.8	4.11	4,458
1989	22,921	1,014	21.7	4.45	5,033
1990	23,814	910	20.3	4.75	5,021
1991	24,639	899	18.9	4.89	4,803
1992	—	—	—	5.05	4,871

Sources: Film Daily Year Book, Motion Picture Association of America, National Association of Theater Owners, and U.S. Census of Business. Statistics vary widely; they are hard to find and harder yet to trust before 1918, when the federal government imposed a war tax on tickets. Even then, the numbers are extrapolated from all taxable forms of entertainment until 1922. For consistency and accuracy, I have chosen to use the figures in *Film Daily Year Book* and *Motion Picture Almanac* (as updated) when possible. Figures are not available for all years, as indicated by a dash.

[a] Refers to number of theatres operating that year. Beginning in 1979, refers to number of screens, not to number of theatres.

[b] Drive-in theatres did not exist prior to 1933.

[c] Probably overestimated.

Movie Theatres by S. Charles Lee, 1926–1950

Year	Theatre or Project[a]	Location Client	Remarks[b]
1926–27	Tower	Los Angeles, Calif. H. L. Gumbiner	906 seats Opened 12 Oct. 1927 Closed 1988
1928	Wurlitzer*	Cincinnati, Ohio H. Wurlitzer	1,000 seats
1929	Theatre*	Los Angeles, Calif.	2,500 seats
1928–30	Fox Wilshire	Beverly Hills, Calif. Pacific Amusements	2,500 seats Opened 19 Sept. 1930 Renovated to live theatre 1981
1929–30	Fox	Bakersfield, Calif. Bakersfield Auto Supply	1,675 seats Opened 25 Dec. 1930
1930–31	Fox	Phoenix, Ariz. Fox West Coast	1,800 seats Demolished 1975
1930	*Coliseum*	San Francisco, Calif.	2,400 seats Unknown whether executed according to Lee's design Still in operation
1930	*Verdi*	San Francisco, Calif.	1,000 seats Unknown whether executed according to Lee's design
1930	Chotiner*	Pasadena, Calif. A. H. Chotiner	2,500 seats
1930	Merced	Merced, Calif.	Unknown whether executed according to Lee's design
1931	Baywood	San Mateo, Calif. W. S. Leadley	1,000 seats
1931	Sunkist	Pomona, Calif. Walter Booth	888 seats Opened 4 Nov. 1931 Closed Jan. 1956 Demolished late 1950s
1931	Fox Florence	Los Angeles, Calif. Fox West Coast	1,721 seats Opened 8 Apr. 1932 Demolished 1950s
1931	Fox	Long Beach, Calif. Fox West Coast	2,038 seats Demolished 1980s

continued

Year	Theatre or Project[a]	Location Client	Remarks[b]
1931	*Studio*	Hollywood, Calif. Hughes and Franklin	303 seats Opened 31 July 1931 Store converted into theatre; closed and reconverted into store
1930–31	Los Angeles	Los Angeles, Calif. H. L. Gumbiner	2,190 seats Opened 30 Jan. 1931 Still in operation
1931	Theatre and apartment/ hotel*	Redlands, Calif. R. W. Brown	900 seats
1933	*Kinema*	Los Angeles, Calif.	Original bldg. 1917 Demolished 1941
1933	Theatre	Redwood City, Calif. P. A. Fease	Unknown whether executed according to Lee's design
1934	Modesto	Modesto, Calif. Redwood Theatres	850 seats Still in operation
1934–35	Vogue	Hollywood, Calif. Sheehan and Sinks	800 seats
1935	*Westlake*	Los Angeles, Calif. Fox West Coast	1,949 seats Still in operation
1935	Carmel	Carmel, Calif. Monterey Theatre Co.	650 seats Unknown whether executed according to Lee's design
1935–36	Tower	Compton, Calif. Fox West Coast	1,000 seats Stores added 1940 Demolished
1935–36	*Vogue*	Alameda, Calif. L and O Theatres	864 seats Opened 1936
1935–36	*Lyceum*	San Francisco, Calif.	1,400 seats
1935	Theatre	Visalia, Calif. Golden State Theatre Co.	404 seats Unknown whether executed according to Lee's design
1935–36	Town Hall	Quincy, Calif.	240 seats Dismantled 1945 for Lakewood Theatre
1936	*Beverly*	Beverly Hills, Calif. Fox West Coast	1,270 seats Original theatre 1925 Converted into store
1936	Hermosa	Hermosa Beach, Calif. Fox West Coast	888 seats Unknown whether executed according to Lee's design
1936	State	Stockton, Calif. Fox West Coast	1,510 seats Unknown whether executed according to Lee's design

continued

Year	Theatre or Project[a]	Location Client	Remarks[b]
1936	*Senator*	Oakland, Calif. Fox West Coast	1,642 seats Unknown whether executed according to Lee's design
1936	*Grand Lake*	Oakland, Calif. Fox West Coast	1,700 seats Still in operation
1936	*Anaheim*	Anaheim, Calif. Fox West Coast	Unknown whether executed according to Lee's design
1936	Newman	Newman, Calif. Harvey Amusement Co.	500 seats Still in operation
1936	Theatre*	Los Angeles, Calif.	
1936	*Grand*	Clarkdale, Ariz. United Verde Copper	250 seats
1936	*El Capitan*	San Francisco, Calif. Fox West Coast	2,578 seats Original by Thomas Lamb Unknown whether executed according to Lee's design
1936	*Alvarado*	Los Angeles, Calif.	750 seats Still in operation
1936	Porter	Woodland, Calif. Redwood Theatres, Inc.	550 seats Unknown whether executed according to Lee's design
1936	Theatre	Mitchel, S. D. Baron Bros.	Walter J. Dixon, archt. Lee, consult. archt. Unknown whether executed according to Lee's design
1936	State	Woodland, Calif. Redwood Theatres, Inc., and Fox West Coast	999 seats Replaced theatre destroyed by fire
1936	*Theatre addition*	Hollywood, Calif. Jewel Theatre Corp. and Mr. Yanow	496 seats Unknown whether executed according to Lee's design
1936	*Colony*	Hollywood, Calif.	475 seats Opened Dec. 1936
1936	Eureka*	Eureka, Calif. Redwood Theatres, Inc.	1,638 seats
1936	*Hollywood*	Hollywood, Calif.	717 seats Original 1919 Previous remodel 1927 Closed 1992; converted into a museum
1936	Oroville	Oroville, Calif.	Unknown whether executed according to Lee's design

continued

Year	Theatre or Project[a]	Location Client	Remarks[b]
1936	Rafael	San Rafael, Calif.	1,100 seats Still in operation
1936	San Marino*	San Marino, Calif.	
1936	Sonora	Sonora, Calif.	562 seats Unknown whether executed according to Lee's design
1936	Strand	San Francisco, Calif.	700 seats Unknown whether executed according to Lee's design Still in operation
1936	*Studio*	Hollywood, Calif.	1,000 seats Now the Huntington Hartford Theatre Unknown whether executed according to Lee's design
1936	Ventura Drive-In	Ventura, Calif.	With Clarence J. Smale Unknown whether executed according to Lee's design
1936	*Egyptian*	Hollywood, Calif., or Long Beach, Calif.	Unknown whether executed according to Lee's design
1936–37	Tamalpais	San Anselmo, Calif.	900 seats
1936–38	Nile	Bakersfield, Calif.	Still in operation
1937	*Berkeley*	Berkeley, Calif. Albert Moore	780 seats Still in operation
1937–38	Vogue	South Gate, Calif. Fox West Coast and South Gate theatres	1,000 seats Still in operation
1937	Bruin	Los Angeles, Calif. Fox West Coast and California Realty	876 seats Still in operation
1937	Inglewood	Inglewood, Calif. Harry Beaver and Carl Mattson	700 seats Unknown whether executed according to Lee's design
1937	Gentry	Compton, Calif. Sunbeam Theatre Corp.	1,000 seats Demolished
1937–38	La Reina	Sherman Oaks, Calif. Sherman Oaks Theatre Corp. and Fox West Coast	900 seats Converted into La Reina Mall 1988
1937–39	*Fox*	Redondo Beach, Calif. Redondo Properties	1,324 seats Unknown whether executed according to Lee's design
1937–39	De Anza	Riverside, Calif. Hunt's Theatres and Fox West Coast	800 seats Opened June 1939 Still in operation

continued

Year	Theatre or Project[a]	Location Client	Remarks[b]
1937–38	*Manchester*	Los Angeles, Calif. Southside Theatres and Arthur Gruenaer	600 seats Unknown whether executed according to Lee's design
1937–40	Theatre	Los Angeles, Calif. Alex Pavlov	Unknown whether executed according to Lee's design
1937–38	*Arcade*	Los Angeles, Calif.	800 seats
1937–38	Tujunga	Los Angeles, Calif. Edwards Theatre Circuit	843 seats Still in operation
1937	*Majestic*	San Francisco, Calif.	760 seats
1937	Richmond	Richmond, Calif.	600 seats Unknown whether executed according to Lee's design
1938	*Selma*	Selma, Calif. Seelee Theatre Co.	550 seats Destroyed by fire 1980s
1938	*Loew's State*	Los Angeles, Calif. Fox West Coast	2,422 seats Original 1921 Unknown whether executed according to Lee's design
1938–39	*Valley*	North Hollywood, Calif. Fox West Coast and Guy Weddington	Demolished
1938	Sierra	Delano, Calif. Frank Panero	700 seats Still in operation
1938–39	*Rosemead*	Rosemead, Calif. Edwards Theatre Circuit	706 seats Remodeled building into theatre Demolished
1938	*Alhambra*	Alhambra, Calif.	600 seats Unknown whether executed according to Lee's design
1938	Allena	Los Angeles, Calif.	700 seats Unknown whether executed according to Lee's design
1938	Reinhardt	Los Angeles, Calif.	Unknown whether executed according to Lee's design
1938	Hawthorne	Hawthorne, Calif.	350 seats Unknown whether executed according to Lee's design
1938–41	Hopkins	Oakland, Calif. Lawrence Goldsmith and Fox West Coast	914 seats Closed; being used as Love Center

continued

Year	Theatre or Project[a]	Location Client	Remarks[b]
1939	Academy	Inglewood, Calif. Manchester Blvd. Theatre Corp. and Fox West Coast	1,156 seats Converted into church ca. 1976
1938–39	*Cinema*	Los Angeles, Calif. Louis Berkoff	700 seats Opened 1939 Store remodeled into theatre Reconverted back into store
1938–39	Yerington	Yerington, Nev. Mr. MacPherson	350 seats Unknown whether executed according to Lee's design
1939	Tumbleweed	Five Points (El Monte), Calif. Edwards Theatre Circuit	750 seats Opened 1939 Demolished pre-1970
1938–39	Tower	Fresno, Calif. Fox West Coast	930 seats Opened 15 Dec. 1939 Restored to live theatre 1989
1939	Tower	Santa Rosa, Calif. Fred Rosenberg and Fox West Coast	900 seats Opened 5 Oct. 1939 Demolished
1939–40	*Roxie*	Los Angeles, Calif. Srere and Metzger	1,350 seats Box office 1948
1939–40	*Admiral*	Hollywood, Calif. Julius Stern	700 seats Later named Vine Closed
1939–41	Theatre	San Pablo, Calif. Fox West Coast	1,019 seats Unknown whether executed according to Lee's design
1939–40	Carlos	San Carlos, Calif. Peninsula Theatre Corp. and Fox West Coast	1,000 seats
1939	*Rivoli*	Van Nuys, Calif.	700 seats Unknown whether executed according to Lee's design
1939	*Wasco*	Wasco, Calif. Frank Panero	700 seats Unknown whether executed according to Lee's design
1939–40	State	San Diego, Calif. Fox West Coast	1,012 seats
1939	Encino	Encino, Calif.	Demolished
1939	Fox Venice	Venice, Calif. Fox West Coast	960 seats

continued

Year	Theatre or Project[a]	Location Client	Remarks[b]
1939	Grand	San Francisco, Calif.	800 seats Unknown whether executed according to Lee's design
1939	*RKO*	Los Angeles, Calif.	2,916 seats Unknown whether executed according to Lee's design
1939–41	State	Modesto, Calif. Redwood Theatres	800 seats Unknown whether executed according to Lee's design
1939–41	Vern	Los Angeles, Calif. Wyvernwood Theatres, Inc., and Jack Berman	800 seats Converted into Don Quixote Disco club
1939–40	Mayfair	Ventura, Calif. Jeanne and James Dodge	850 seats Opened May 1940 Still in operation
1939–41	Disney	Burbank, Calif. Disney Studios	600 seats Private screenings Still in operation
1940	Calvi	Lennox, Calif. E. S. Calvi	974 seats Unknown whether executed according to Lee's design
1940	*Alex*	Glendale, Calif. Fox West Coast	2,030 seats Original Alexander by Arthur Lindley and Charles R. Selkirk Opened 4 Sept. 1925 Renovation to performing arts center 1993
1940	Theatre	North Long Beach, Calif. Delux Theatres, Inc.	Unknown whether executed according to Lee's design
1940	Theatre*	South Pasedena, Calif. Edwards Theatre Circuit	1,000 seats
1940	Santa Maria	Santa Maria, Calif.	1,250 seats
1940	Temple	Temple City, Calif. Edwards Theatre Circuit	750 seats Demolished
1941–42	Theatre	Los Angeles, Calif. Fox West Coast and David Bershon	1,000 seats Unknown whether executed according to Lee's design
1940–41	Dinuba	Dinuba, Calif. Dunuba Theatre Co. and Tom Sharp	550 seats Still in operation as Maya Theatre
1940–41	Theatre*	Eureka, Calif.	

continued

Year	Theatre or Project[a]	Location Client	Remarks[b]
1940–41	Theatre	Ft. Bragg, Calif.	600 seats Unknown whether executed according to Lee's design
1940–41	Theatre	Modesto, Calif. Modesto Theatres	600 seats Unknown whether executed according to Lee's design
1940–41	Ukiah	Ukiah, Calif.	600 seats Still in operation
1941	American	Newhall, Calif. American Legion	374 seats Served as theatre and as American Legion meeting hall Theatre closed; still serving as meeting hall
1941	Bundy	Santa Monica, Calif. George Bourke and M. E. Baylis	900 seats Demolished
1941–42	Fremont	San Luis Obispo, Calif. SLO Theatres, Inc., and Fox West Coast	1,086 seats Opened 29 May 1942 Still in operation
1941	Laurel*	Otto Thum	Unknown whether executed according to Lee's design
1942	Mayfair	New York, N.Y. Charles Skouras and RKO	2,500 seats With Thomas Lamb Unknown whether executed according to Lee's design
1941	Theatre	Long Beach, Calif. Fox West Coast	Unknown whether executed according to Lee's design
1941	Tower	San Diego, Calif. Metzger and Srere	600 seats Demolished
1941	El Capitan	Mexico City, Mexico	2,082 seats Opened as Teatro Tepeyac 1943
1941–46	Mission	San Diego, Calif. Frank Ullman	Demolished
1941	Dixie Canyon	Van Nuys, Calif. Fox West Coast	800 seats Unknown whether executed according to Lee's design
1941	*Capitol*	Glendale, Calif. Fox West Coast	808 seats Closed March 1990
1941–42	*California*	Glendale, Calif. Fox West Coast	722 seats
1941	*Fox California**	San Diego, Calif. Fox West Coast	Proposed addition of 450-seat newsreel theatre

continued

Year	Theatre or Project[a]	Location Client	Remarks[b]
1941	Toys*	Helena, Mont. Lenora Roy	882 seats
1941	*Theatre*	Glendale, Calif. Fox West Coast	Unknown whether executed according to Lee's design
1941	*Florencita*	Los Angeles, Calif. Jack Mingus	600 seats Unknown whether executed according to Lee's design
1941	*Glendale*	Glendale, Calif.	1,024 seats Closed 1990
1941	Vogue	Oxnard, Calif.	Used as store
1941	Sacramento	Sacramento, Calif.	Unknown whether executed according to Lee's design
1941	San Jose	San Jose, Calif.	Unknown whether executed according to Lee's design
1941	Santa Cruz	Santa Cruz, Calif.	Unknown whether executed according to Lee's design
1941–42	Ramona	Los Angeles, Calif.	480 seats Unknown whether executed according to Lee's design
1941–42	San Pablo	Santa Ana, Calif.	
1942	Arcadia	Arcadia, Calif.	450 seats Unknown whether executed according to Lee's design
1942	Lido	Mexico City, Mexico	1,400 seats Opened Dec. 1942
1942	Linda Vista	Mexico City, Mexico Theodore Gildred	2,500 seats Opened Dec. 1942
1942	Long Beach 1	Long Beach, Calif.	1,000 seats Unknown whether executed according to Lee's design
1942	Oakland Newsreel	Oakland, Calif. Fox West Coast	560 seats Unknown whether executed according to Lee's design
1942	Pantages*	Los Angeles, Calif.	1,954 seats
1942–47	Arden	Lynwood, Calif. Hanson and Zimmerman	940 seats Demolished 1988
1943–44	Chapultepec	Mexico City, Mexico	2,390 seats
1943	Huntridge	Las Vegas, Nev. Huntridge Development	900 seats Still in operation
1943	De Cuba	Mexico City, Mexico	Unknown whether executed according to Lee's design

continued

Year	Theatre or Project[a]	Location Client	Remarks[b]
1943	Imperial	Los Angeles, Calif.	Unknown whether executed according to Lee's design
1944–45	Lakewood	Lakewood, Calif. Lakeville Corp.	1,124 seats Town Hall (Quincy) recycled Still in operation
1944–46	Loma	San Diego, Calif. Fox/Balboa Building	1,188 seats Still in operation
1944	Big Bear	Big Bear, Calif.	720 seats Unknown whether executed according to Lee's design
1944–45	*Rialto*	Cottonwood, Ariz. Frank Becchetti	250 seats
1945	Newsreel	Beverly Hills, Calif.	Unknown whether executed according to Lee's design
ca. 1945	*Globe Newsreel*	Los Angeles, Calif.	Original Morosco by Alfred Rosenheim Closed 1987; converted into swap meet
1945	Theatre	Managua, Nicaragua	2,000 seats
1945–46	Perris	Perris, Calif. Tom Sharpe	554 seats Still in operation
1945	Silverlake	Los Angeles, Calif. Whitson and Schaak	Unknown whether executed according to Lee's design
1946–47	Miami	Miami, Fla. Wometco Theatres	2,000 seats With Robert E. Collins Demolished
1946	*Central*	Los Angeles, Calif. Pacific Amusement	Unknown whether executed according to Lee's design
ca. 1946	Calico	South Gate, Calif.	Unknown whether executed according to Lee's design
1946	Long Beach 2	Long Beach, Calif.	Unknown whether executed according to Lee's design
1946	Lazarus Drive-In	Encino, Calif. Edwards Theatre Circuit and S. Lazarus	Unknown whether executed according to Lee's design
1946	Theatre	Los Angeles County Dave Rector	Unknown whether executed according to Lee's design
1946–49	Visalia	Visalia, Calif. Levin, Seligman and Cahen	Still in operation
1946	Picwood	Los Angeles, Calif. Earl Collins	1,500 seats Demolished 1990

continued

Year	Theatre or Project[a]	Location Client	Remarks[b]
1947	Chino	Chino, Calif. Anderson Bros. Theatres	780 seats
ca. 1947	Valley Village	Gilmore Village, Calif.	Unknown whether executed according to Lee's design
1947–48	Helix	La Mesa, Calif. Burton Jones and Frank Bleeker	825 seats Demolished
1947–48	Puente	Puente, Calif. Steve Chorak	700 seats
1948	Grand	Visalia, Calif.	Unknown whether executed according to Lee's design
1948	Harper	Fontana, Calif. Glenn Harper	700 seats
1948–49	La Tijera	Los Angeles, Calif. W. J. Kupper, Jr.	1,530 seats Opened 12 Jan. 1949 Converted into office building
1948	Reseda	Reseda, Calif. Charles Grenzbach	900 seats Still in operation
1948	Edwards Drive-In	Arcadia, Calif. J. Edwards, Jr.	750 cars Still in operation
1948	Rancho Drive-In	San Diego, Calif. SERO Enterprises and William Oldknow	672 cars plus 300 seats Demolished
1948	Avo	Vista, Calif.	Still in operation
1948	Burbank	Burbank, Calif.	Unknown whether executed according to Lee's design
1948	Holly	Los Angeles, Calif.	Unknown whether executed according to Lee's design
1948	Lazarus*	Woodland Hills, Calif.	With Clarence J. Smale
1948	Oxnard	Oxnard, Calif.	852 seats Unknown whether executed according to Lee's design
1948	Sunset	Los Angeles, Calif. Whitson and Schaak	Unknown whether executed according to Lee's design
1948–49	Bay	Pacific Palisades, Calif. Leland M. Ford	1,100 seats Remodeled into drugstore
1949–50	Garmar	Montebello, Calif. Alfred J. Olander	998 seats Opened 29 March 1950 Demolished
1949	*Cameo*	Los Angeles, Calif.	600 seats
1949	Fox	Inglewood, Calif. Fox West Coast	Opened 31 March 1949 Replaced Granada Theatre Destroyed by fire 1993

continued

Movie Theatres by S. Charles Lee, 1926–50

Year	Theatre or Project[a]	Location Client	Remarks[b]
1949	*Marcal*	Hollywood, Calif.	800 seats Unknown whether executed according to Lee's design
1949	Palm	Palmdale, Calif.	Unknown whether executed according to Lee's design
ca. 1950	Ken	San Diego, Calif.	575 seats Still in operation

[a] "Project" generally refers to theatres that were never developed beyond the design stage. These are indicated by an asterisk. Remodelings are indicated by italics. Listed in sequence according to job number.

[b] Information in this column varies. Facts were not consistently available, and no inferences should be drawn from the absence of data. Status listed as "still in operation" may have changed.

Notes

CHAPTER ONE: COMING ATTRACTIONS

1. John Updike, "The Dogwood Tree: A Boyhood," *Assorted Prose* (New York: Knopf, 1965), 174.

2. "Morgan Freeman: Creating a Character," *Los Angeles Times,* 18 December 1989.

3. Jerome Charyn, *Movieland: Hollywood and the Great American Dream Culture* (New York: Putnam's, 1989), 13.

4. Quoted in Neal Gabler, "For 25 Cents, Every Moviegoer Was Royalty," *New York Times,* 24 January 1989.

5. Note that when movies are taken seriously, they are called films. The history of the American motion picture industry involves three areas: production, distribution, and exhibition. Writers have studied the first category in depth but have ignored the other two, relying on the repetition of early accounts (see Terry Ramsaye, *A Million and One Nights: A History of the Motion Picture* [New York: Simon and Schuster, 1926] and Benjamin Hampton, *A History of the Movies* [New York: Coovici-Friede Publishers, 1931]). These early historians had access to documents that are no longer available and depended on the individuals who were making what is now film history. Other valuable contemporary sources include Joseph Kennedy, *The Story of the Film* (Chicago: A. W. Shaw, 1927), and various trade publications.

There are notable exceptions. Scholars who research distribution and exhibition, such as Michael Conant and Mae Huettig, tend to study the economics of the business. Anthologies that include original source materials and explorations of distribution and exhibition techniques include Tino Balio, ed., *The American Film Industry,* rev. ed.

(Madison: University of Wisconsin Press, 1985); Gerald Mast, ed., *The Movies in Our Midst; Documents in the Cultural History of Film in America* (Chicago: University of Chicago Press, 1982); and John Fell, ed., *Film before Griffith* (Berkeley: University of California Press, 1983). Joseph North's *The Early Days of the Motion Picture Industry, 1887–1909* (New York: Arno Press, 1949) includes exhibition techniques of that period. Contemporary film historians concerned with early exhibition in the study of business techniques include Douglas Gomeroy and Suzanne Mary Donahue, *American Film Distribution: The Changing Marketplace* (Ann Arbor: UMI Research Press, 1987). Gomeroy, Robert C. Allen, and Russell Merritt (all cited in the text) have each challenged the traditional visions and stereotypes regarding film attendance and studio and movie palace economics routinely accepted and repeated in earlier historical accounts. In 1990, the Cinema History Project began publishing, under the editorship of Charles Harpole, a scholarly, multivolume series entitled *History of the American Cinema,* which includes the role of exhibition.

6. Most architectural surveys give, at most, a condescending paragraph to the movie theatre. Encyclopedias of architects and building types, architectural dictionaries, and indexes ignore motion picture theatres and their designers, even their vocabulary. Those authors who do mention the movie theatre do so despairingly and disdainfully. The National Trust for Historic Preservation broke with this tradition in publishing the Guide to American Architecture series, including *Built in the USA* (1985), *Main Street* (1987), and *Great American Movie Theatres*

(1987), all of which contain short essays on the history of the American movie theatre and cite surviving examples.

• 7. Even those scholars who categorize history by building type have not yet included the motion picture theatre. Nicholas Pevsner devoted twenty-eight pages to the history of the Western theatre in *A History of Building Types* (Princeton: Princeton University Press, 1976). He mentioned the motion picture theatre only in the last paragraph, dismissing "that objectionable vein" as a "postscript." The implication of this deliberate disregard is that the movie theatre is of the bike shed variety, i.e., not architecture worthy of serious consideration.

8. Unlike vernacular architecture, which was accepted for its integrity and honest roots, popular architecture was created by architects operating out of a business ethic, and therefore critics could not view it as art. It was considered commercial and consumerist, designed to communicate with the public instead of with other architects and critics. Although popular architecture gained attention following Robert Venturi and Denise Scott-Brown's revolutionary look at Las Vegas, most of the literature has been filled with nostalgic and superficial accounts of building types, such as coffee shops, hamburger stands, and car washes. Notable exceptions to this attitude include David Atwell's *Cathedrals of the Movies: A History of British Cinemas and Their Audiences* (London: Architectural Press, 1980) and Ross Thorne's *Cinemas of Australia via USA* (Sydney: University of Sydney, 1981), neither of which is primarily about the American experience. Art historian Herbert Scherer wrote a brief essay accompanying an exhibition of drawings by theatre architect Jack Liebenberg at the University of Minnesota in 1982 (*Marquee on Main Street: Jack Liebenberg* [Minneapolis: University of Minnesota, 1982]).

9. Theatre historians also considered the movie theatre invisible or irrelevant within their discipline, which came out of centuries-old drama, not nouveau-riche film. Typical is Richard and Helen Leacroft's *Theatre and Playhouse* (London: Metheun, 1984), in which they present an analysis of legitimate theatre building with no mention of its relation to the motion picture theatre. Mary Henderson's examination of *Theatre in America* (New York: Abrams, 1987) includes architects as key players in the development of theatre, but her focus is strictly on the experience of live drama.

10. Knowledge of motion picture theatre history comes largely from books and articles written by nostalgia buffs, avocational historians, and theatre lovers; the reliability of these accounts varies widely. These texts, albeit classic because of their paucity, are usually not documented and have been based only on anecdotes or on other books within the genre. The authors nonetheless deserve credit for creating an awareness of these issues, providing valuable photographic and emotional descriptions, and motivating preservationists to pay attention. Ben Hall's *The Last Remaining Seats* (New York: Bramhall House, 1961) and David Naylor's *American Picture Palaces: The Architecture of Fantasy* (New York: Van Nostrand Reinhold, 1981) and *Marquee* magazine contain valuable descriptions. Such books also tend to focus on one type or one period of theatre building, omitting the overview of movie theatre evolution. Academics who have explored the field include Charlotte Herzog, whose dissertation in speech, "The Motion Picture Theatre and Film Exhibition, 1896–1930" (Northwestern University, 1980), presented a convincing argument linking the architecture of the movie palace with popular entertainment forms in the nineteenth century.

11. Lee's office literature credited him with over 400 theatres, 10,000 residences, and 5,000 factories. These numbers may be somewhat exaggerated, because they probably included designs that never became job numbers or got beyond the preliminary stages. In 1950, about the time he retired, he

claimed to have built between 167 and 300 theatres. I have verified fewer than 250 theatres, including many that remained unbuilt (see appendix B). But in all fairness, the office records did not survive. When I requested a list from him in the 1980s, he replied that the office no longer retained that kind of information and that my research and knowledge would be more accurate than his memory. Even so, he was very prolific. The claim says more about his carefully promoted image than about the veracity of his statements.

12. Lee adopted this motto to sell theatres to clients and to distinguish himself from other architects. It is unclear at what time during his practice he first began using this slogan, but it emerged in our conversations: "I used to say, 'The show started on the sidewalk.'"

13. See chap. 3 for a discussion of the Hays Office.

CHAPTER TWO: SHORT SUBJECTS

1. "The Show Started on the Sidewalk," an oral history transcript of an interview with S. Charles Lee conducted by Maggie Valentine (300/271), Department of Special Collections, University Research Library, University of California, Los Angeles (hereafter cited as Lee, Oral History). Unless otherwise noted, biographical information is from this oral history and from the conversations and interviews I had with Lee between 1984 and 1989.

2. S. Charles Lee, interview with John M. Grenner, 14 December 1984.

3. Ibid.

4. Lee, Oral History, 4–5.

5. Louis Sullivan, *Autobiography of an Idea* (New York: Dover, 1956), 312.

6. Robert Twombly, *Louis Sullivan: His Life and Work* (Chicago: University of Chicago Press, 1986), 381–82.

7. Willard Connely, *Louis Sullivan: The Shaping of American Architecture* (New York: Horizon Press, 1960), 235.

8. Quoted in Ramsaye, *A Million and One Nights: A History of the Motion Picture* (New York: Simon and Schuster, 1926), 475.

9. Garth Jowett, for the American Film Institute, *Film: The Democratic Art* (Boston: Little, Brown, 1976), 110.

10. To encourage unsuspecting lingerers to move along, Barnum posted a pretentious sign with an arrow that read, "This way to the egress," implying the promise of an exhibit of one of nature's oddities.

11. For a good overview of these popular nineteenth-century entertainment forms, see Robert C. Toll, *On with the Show: The First Century of Show Business in America* (New York: Oxford University Press, 1976), and Donna R. Braden, *Leisure and Entertainment in America* (Dearborn: Henry Ford Museum, 1988).

12. See Michael Forsyth, *Buildings for Music: The Architect, the Musician, and the Listener from the Seventeenth Century to the Present Day* (Cambridge: MIT Press, 1985).

13. See Harlowe R. Hoyt, *Town Hall Tonight* (Englewood Cliffs, N.J.: Prentice-Hall, 1955).

14. Alfred O. Tate, *Edison's Open Door* (1938), quoted in Gordon Hendricks, "The History of the Kinetoscope," in *The American Film Industry,* rev. ed., ed. Tino Balio (Madison: University of Wisconsin Press, 1985), 43–56.

15. Hendricks, "The History of the Kinetoscope," 53.

16. Ibid., 56.

17. Music halls featured musical entertainment to keep men on the premises and buying more drinks. Women were featured as singers but did not frequent these establishments as customers. Variety programs (without the drinking) were cleaned up in the 1860s and 1870s in an attempt to broaden the audience. This heritage of bawdy drinking songs and their accompanying rowdy behavior helps explain all the later references to "suitable for ladies" and Tony Pastor's introduction of "refined entertainment" in 1881.

The Gaiety Theatre in Boston (1883) is usually credited with being the first vaudeville theatre.

18. *Billboard,* 19 December 1900, 20 April 1901.

19. Ramsaye, *A Million and One Nights,* 232. Audiences had the same reaction to the introduction of 3-D, Cinerama, Circle Vision, and other wide-screen experiments in the 1950s.

20. Robert Grau, *The Business Man in the Amusement World* (New York: Broadway, 1910), 109.

21. For a general source on the role of film in vaudeville, see Robert C. Allen, *Vaudeville and Film, 1895–1915: A Study in Media Interaction* (New York: Arno Press, 1980).

22. Historians of vaudeville disagree about the role of the movies as a strike breaker. According to Robert Allen and Charles Musser, the strike was a "relatively minor event" promulgated and exaggerated in importance by early film historians. See *The Emergence of Cinema: The American Screen to 1907,* vol. 1 of *History of the American Cinema,* ed. Charles Harpole (New York: Scribner's, 1990), 276–77 and notes.

23. The "chaser" controversy continues. Early film historians argued that the film, always run as the last act on a vaudeville bill, was a sign to patrons to leave the theatre. Robert C. Allen disputes that interpretation in "Contra the Chaser Theory," in *Film before Griffith,* ed. John L. Fell (Berkeley: University of California Press, 1983), 105–15.

24. Robert C. Allen, "The Movies in Vaudeville: Historical Context of the Movie as Popular Entertainment," in Balio, *The American Film Industry,* 62.

25. The Palace (New York) has a rich history. In 1932, it was converted into a motion picture theatre; in the 1950s it again featured live entertainment in the form of concerts; and in 1966 it became a legitimate theatre in the Broadway theatre district.

26. The term "People's Palace" had also been applied to grand hotels, such as Boston's Tremont House (1828–29), New York's Astor House (1836, both designed by Isaiah Rogers), and Cincinnati's Burnet House (1850), when they were new. This new building type not only served the traveler but provided a civic gathering spot and showplace for the host city.

27. Edward Renton, *The Vaudeville Theatre: Building, Operation, Management* (New York: Gotham Press, 1918), 116.

28. Ibid., 12.

29. Edwin H. Flagg. "Evolution of Architectural and Other Features of Motion Picture Theatres," *Architect and Engineer* 57:2 (May 1919), 97–102.

30. Ibid.

31. *Los Angeles Times,* 10 April 1902; reprinted in Ramsaye, *A Million and One Nights,* 425.

32. According to Musser, *The Emergence of Cinema,* after six months, Tally converted the Electric into a ten-cent vaudeville theatre named the Lyric. Two weeks later, he closed the theatre and concentrated on traveling exhibitions, which he found more profitable (p. 299).

33. Flagg, "Evolution of Architectural Features," 100.

34. Q. David Bowers, *Nickelodeon Theatres and Their Music* (New York: Vestal Press, 1986), 51.

35. Although very few air domes were built in the United States, perhaps owing to the climate and the external noise from the city, they were common in Australia, Africa, and other countries with milder climates and fewer automobiles. They reappeared in the postwar period (e.g., the Cinema Tropical, Acapulco-Chauvet, 1949) and are directly connected to drive-in theatres.

36. Eugene LeMoyne Connelly, "The First Motion Picture Theater," *Western Pennsylvania Historical Magazine* 23 (March 1940): 2.

37. Barton W. Currie, "The Nickel Madness," *Harper's Weekly* 51 (24 August 1907): 1246.

38. "The Nickelodeon," *Moving Picture World and View Photographer* (4 May 1907).

39. Russell Merritt, "Nickelodeon Theaters, 1905–1914: Building an Audience for the Movies," in Balio, *The American Film Industry,* 86.

40. Bowers, *Nickelodeon Theatres and Their Music,* 43.

41. Balio, *The American Film Industry,* 16–17.

42. See Kathy Peiss, *Cheap Amusements: Working Women and Leisure in Turn-of-the-Century New York* (Philadelphia: Temple University Press, 1986), chap. 6, "Cheap Theater and the Nickel Dumps," 139–62.

43. George L. Rapp, "History of Cinema Architecture," in *Living Architecture,* ed. Arthur Woltersdorf (Chicago: A. Kroch, 1930), 57.

44. Lucy France Pierce, "The Nickelodeon," *World Today* 19 (October 1908); in *The Movies in Our Midst: Documents in the Cultural History of Film in America,* ed. Gerald Mast (Chicago: University of Chicago Press, 1982), 51–56.

45. Abel Green and Joe Laurie, Jr., *Show Biz from Vaude to Video* (New York: Henry Holt, 1951), 5; Bowers, *Nickelodeon Theatres and Their Music,* 45.

46. Lary May, *Screening Out the Past* (New York: Oxford University Press, 1980), 22.

47. *Cyclopedia of Motion Picture Work* (1911), quoted in Bowers, *Nickelodeon Theatres and Their Music,* 43.

48. Herzog, "The Nickelodeon Phase."

49. Bowers, *Nickelodeon Theatres and Their Music,* viii.

50. For example, see Chicago Vice Commission, "Cheap Theatres," in *The Social Evil in Chicago* (1911), in Mast, *Movies in Our Midst,* 61–63.

51. Flagg, "Evolution of Architectural Features," 97; P. R. Pereira, "The Development of the Moving Picture Theatre," *American Architect* 106:2022 (23 September 1914): 177–78.

52. May, *Screening Out the Past,* 56.

53. Robert C. Allen, "Motion Picture Exhibition in Manhattan 1906–1912: Beyond the Nickelodeon," *Cinema Journal* 18 (Spring 1979): 13.

54. "Development of the Moving-Picture Theatre," *Architect and Engineer* 40 (February 1915): 51.

55. *Moving Picture World* 4:5 (10 April 1909): 441.

56. See Bowers, *Nickelodeon Theatres and Their Music;* also Ross Thorne, *Cinemas of Australia via USA* (Sydney: University of Sydney, 1981).

57. Lee, conversation with author, 17 November 1988.

58. Ibid.

59. Lee, Oral History, 3–4.

60. Lee, Oral History, 8.

61. In 1940 the Armour Institute of Technology merged with Lewis Institute to form the Illinois Institute of Technology.

62. Lee, Oral History, 11.

63. Lee, interview with Marlene Laskey, 14 May 1980.

64. Lee, Oral History, 19.

65. Ibid., 12.

CHAPTER THREE: DOUBLE FEATURE

1. *Film Daily Year Book* (1929), 931, 933.

2. *Motion Picture News,* 6 December 1913.

3. Foster Rhea Dulles, *America Learns to Play: A History of Popular Recreation, 1607–1940* (New York: D. Appleton-Century, 1940; reprint, 1959), 103.

4. Robert A. M. Stern, Gregory Gilmartin, and Thomas Mellins, *New York 1930: Architecture and Urbanism between the Two World Wars* (New York: Rizzoli, 1987), 248.

5. Roxy Rothafel, in *Green Book Magazine* (1914), quoted in Ben Hall, *The Best Remaining Seats* (New York: Bramhall House, 1961), 37.

6. Roxy Rothafel, "What the Public Wants in the Picture Theater," *Architectural Forum* 42:6 (June 1925): 362.

7. Quoted in Hall, *The Best Remaining Seats,* 202.

8. The 1933 movie *Footlight Parade* is a humorous backstage look at the business of prologue production. In it, Jimmy Cagney races all over town producing packaged prologues for a theatre chain. The various prologues provide the vehicle for a musical comedy, performed by a repertory cast starring Ruby Keeler.

9. Charles Beardley, *Hollywood's Master Showman: The Legendary Sid Grauman* (New York: Cornwall, 1983), 25.

10. Quoted in David Naylor, *American Picture Palaces: The Architecture of Fantasy* (New York: Van Nostrand Reinhold, 1981), jacket back.

11. John F. Barry, "The Motion Picture Theatre," *Paramount Pep Club Yearbook* (1926); reprinted in the *Theatre Historical Society Annual* (1976), 2.

12. Advertisement, reprinted in Hall, *The Best Remaining Seats,* 44.

13. Craig Morrison, "From Nickelodeon to Picture Palace and Back," *Design Quarterly* 93 (1974): 13.

14. Terry Helgesen, "The Works of B. Marcus Priteca," *Marquee* 4:2 (Second Quarter 1972): 10.

15. Hall, *The Best Remaining Seats,* 136.

16. David Naylor, *Great American Movie Theatres* (Washington, D.C.: Preservation Press, 1987), 132.

17. W. A. S. Douglas, "The Passing of Vaudeville," *The American Mercury* 12 (October 1927).

18. Lee, conversation with author, 17 November 1988.

19. Ibid.

20. Lee, Oral History, 18.

21. Lee, conversation with author, 17 November 1988.

22. Lee, Oral History, 25.

23. Lee, conversation with author, 17 November 1988.

24. Lee, Oral History, 43.

25. Lee, interview with Marlene Laskey, 7 May 1980.

26. Lee, Oral History, 23; "Six Story Apartments Announced," *Los Angeles Times,* 28 July 1929, sec. 5, p. 3.

27. Lee, Oral History, 25.

28. Lee, conversation with author, 28 April 1985.

29. Lee, Oral History, 22–24.

30. Lee, interview with Marlene Laskey, 14 May 1980.

31. Lee, letter to author, 2 October 1986.

32. Lee, Oral History, 33.

33. Roscoe "Fatty" Arbuckle, an extremely popular star of silent films, including Mack Sennett's Keystone Cops, went on trial for manslaughter following the death of starlet Virginia Rappe. She died of a ruptured bladder after attending a drinking party at which Arbuckle allegedly sexually attacked her. He was acquitted at his third trial, after two hung juries, but was forced into retirement when his films were banned as a result of the scandal. The incident was seen as representative of Hollywood's wanton disregard for public mores and values and of the belief that innocent starlets were being devoured by evil forces on a routine basis.

34. Quoted in Harold B. Franklin, *Motion Picture Theater Management* (New York: George H. Doran, 1927), 22. Raymond Moley, *The Hays Office* (Indianapolis: Bobbs-Merrill, 1945), 41.

35. *Hollywood News,* 8 December 1928, 15.

36. *Los Angeles Times,* 9 December 1928, sec. 5, p. 2.

37. *Hollywood News,* 8 December 1928, 15.

38. Lee, Oral History, 36.

39. *Hollywood News,* 8 December 1928, 15.

40. Every few years, Radio City announces plans to end the Rockettes' reign because of failing economics. This news invariably elicits fund-raisers, subsidies, and

pleas to retain this last vestige of the movie palace era.

41. Victor Watson, *New York Times,* 11 April 1914.

42. John Eberson, "Reflections and Confessions," in *Film Daily Year Book* (1948), 671.

CHAPTER FOUR: TEASER

1. Lee, conversations with author, 8 February 1984, 28 April 1984); Oral History, 26.

2. Ibid.

3. The name of the architect on the building permit is S. Tilden Norton, who designed the office building on the block behind the theatre. According to Lee, a clause in the property deed specified that Norton, the son of the former landowner, be the architect for any building on that site. Gumbiner paid Norton a full fee and recorded him as the architect, even though Norton provided no services or suggestions whatsoever.

4. Harold B. Franklin, *Motion Picture Theater Management* (New York: Doran, 1927), 32.

5. Tino Balio, ed., *The American Film Industry,* rev. ed. (Madison: University of Wisconsin Press, 1985), 213.

6. The Broadway Theatre District in Los Angeles was the first and largest Historic Theatre District to be listed on the National Register of Historic Places. Between 1930 and 1960 the theatre district in Los Angeles moved to Hollywood Boulevard, and between 1960 and 1980 to Westwood.

7. C. Howard Crane, "Observations on Motion Picture Theatres," *Architectural Forum* 42:6 (June 1925): 381–84.

8. The clock tower was lowered slightly following the 1971 earthquake.

9. E. C. A. Bullock, "Theater Entrances and Lobbies," *Architectural Forum* 42:6 (June 1925): 369.

10. Lee, conversation with author, 8 February 1984.

11. *Los Angeles Times,* 12 October 1927, sec. 2, p. 11.

12. *Southwest Builder and Contractor* (10 February 1931): 47.

13. Edwin Schallert, "Premier Jams Broadway," *Los Angeles Times,* 1 February 1931, sec. 2, p. 7.

14. R. W. Sexton and B. F. Betts, eds., *American Theatres Today,* 2 vols. (New York: Architectural Book Publishing, 1927), 1:5.

15. Bullock, "Theater Entrances and Lobbies," 372.

16. Ibid.

17. Foster Rhea Dulles, *America Learns to Play: A History of Popular Recreation, 1607–1940* (1940; reprint, Gloucester, Mass.: Peter Smith, 1959), 106.

18. Draperies, known as teasers and tormenters, were used first in vaudeville and then in movie theatres to mask the front house curtain. In the early days they were made of painted canvas. Teasers refer to the elaborate swags and jabots hung across the top of the house curtain; tormentors hung along the side. There were usually two sets of teasers and tormentors on each side of the house curtain. The asbestos curtain, which covered the proscenium, was designed to prevent the spread of fire between the backstage and the front of the house.

19. Marvin Carlson, *Places of Performance: The Semiotics of Theatre Architecture* (Ithaca: Cornell University Press, 1989), 178.

20. Lee, interview with Karen J. Safer, 28 April 1980, quoted in Karen J. Safer, "The Functions of Decoration in the American Movie Palace," *Marquee* 14:2 (1982): 6.

21. Ralph Rugoff, "The Architect of Babylon: S. Charles Lee," *L.A. Style* (June 1987): 93. Television preacher Dr. Gene Scott acquired the United Artists Theatre in Los Angeles, patterned after a Spanish cathedral, to use as a church. He planned to recycle the famous L.A. sign "Jesus Saves" by adding it to the restored marquee. According to a mailed request for "Thanksgiving offerings," dated

February 1990, Mary Pickford, Charlie Chaplin, and Douglas Fairbanks, who built the theatre, "never dreamed that they were a part of a Destiny to provide this house of God."

22. Richard Houdek, "Sleeping Beauties," *Los Angeles Times,* 4 June 1978, suppl., 36.

23. Schallert, "Premiere Jams Broadway," 7.

24. *The Jazz Singer* opened in Los Angeles on 28 December 1927 at the Criterion Theatre, where it played for several weeks.

25. Lee, Oral History, 27.

26. See Douglas Gomeroy, "The Coming of Sound: Technological Change in the American Film Industry," in Balio, *The American Film Industry,* 229–51.

27. Robert Friedman, "The Air-Conditioned Century," *American Heritage* (August–September 1984): 20–32.

28. For years, movie theatres were one of the few building types that featured air-conditioning for the sake of comfort. The Broadway theatre season, lasting from fall through spring, reflects the original need to close live theatres in the summer because of the New York heat.

29. *Los Angeles Times,* 12 October 1927, sec. 2, p. 11.

30. Lee, Oral History, 27.

31. *Southwest Builder and Contractor* (20 October 1931): 47.

32. Charlie Chaplin, *My Autobiography* (New York: Simon and Schuster, 1964), 330, 332.

33. Rugoff, "The Architecture of Babylon," 94.

34. James Timmerman, "L.A.'s Forgotten Palaces," *Pasadena Star News,* 6 November 1987, 7.

35. Lee quoted in Sam Hall Kaplan, "L.A. Theatre Redefined the 'Movie Palace,'" *Los Angeles Times,* 21 February 1987, sec. 5, p. 1.

36. *Southwest Builder and Contractor* (10 April 1931): 51.

37. Los Angeles Conservancy, "Last Remaining Seats, Part III," program; Mike Hughes, "Palaces of Dreams in the City of Angels," *Hollywood Studio* (n.d.), 31; Jack Smith, *Los Angeles Times,* 30 September 1986. According to theatre historian John Miller, Gumbiner reportedly wound up selling suits at Barker Bros. department store.

38. Letter from H. L. Gumbiner to Lee, dated 28 August 1939, in S. Charles Lee Papers, Collection 1384, Department of Special Collections, University Research Library, University of California, Los Angeles.

39. See Frederick Jennings, "A Theater in the Egyptian Style," *Architect and Engineer* 72:3 (March 1923), 76–84. The Egyptian Theatre actually opened before King Tut's tomb did.

40. David Naylor, *American Picture Palaces: The Architecture of Fantasy* (New York: Van Nostrand Reinhold, 1981), 40–44.

41. Ibid., 107.

42. John F. Barry, "The Motion Picture Theatre," in the *Paramount Pep Club Yearbook* (1926); reprinted in *Theatre Historical Society Annual* (1976), 2–4. In a curtain-call speech at the premiere of *The Dancing Cavalier,* held at Grauman's Chinese Theatre, Lamont [Jean Hagen] "graciously" explains, "If we bring a little joy into your humdrum lives, it makes us feel as though our hard work ain't been in vain for nothin'." This 1952 movie also contains accurate descriptions and depictions of early movie theatre forms, including the nickelodeon and the palace, as well as often-humorous first attempts at sound.

43. Benjamin Hampton, *A History of the Movies* (New York: Coovici-Friede 1931), 204.

44. Garth Jowett, *Film: The Democratic Art* (Little, Brown, 1976), 61.

45. Franklin, *Motion Picture Theater Management,* 28.

46. Jowett, *Film,* 197. In 1928 Radio Corporation of America (RCA) absorbed what was left of the Keith-Albee and Or-

pheum vaudeville circuits to form Radio Keith Orpheum (RKO).

47. See Douglas Gomeroy, "U.S. Film Exhibition: The Formation of a Big Business" in Balio, *The American Film Industry,* 218–28.

48. *Billboard,* 16 January 1926.

49. See Douglas Gomeroy, "The Movies Become Big Business: Publix Theatres and the Chain Store Strategy," *Cinema Journal* 18 (Spring 1979): 26–40.

50. *Variety,* 7 August 1929, 4.

51. Gomeroy, "The Movies Become Big Business," 37.

52. The Majestic (San Antonio, John Eberson, 1929) has been restored to its opening-night glory, complete with stars that twinkle, clouds that drift across the sky, and hovering birds that appear ready to take flight. It is a wonderful opportunity to experience an atmospheric theatre and listen to the symphony under the stars.

53. Advertisement, reprinted in Hall, *The Best Remaining Seats,* 94, 102.

54. Unlabeled article found among Lee's papers, undoubtedly from an exhibitors' trade journal. See Lee Papers, UCLA.

55. Tom Owen, *Marquee* 4:4 (Fourth Quarter 1972): 16.

56. Quoted in Craig Morrison, "From Nickelodeon to Picture Palace and Back," *Design Quarterly* 93 (1974): 15.

57. John Eberson, "A Description of the Capitol Theatre, Chicago," *Architectural Forum* 62:6 (June 1925): 373.

58. Naylor, *American Picture Palaces,* 78.

59. P. Morton Shand, *The Architecture of Pleasure: Modern Theatres and Cinema* (London: Batsford, 1930), 19.

60. *Los Angeles Times,* 20 September 1930, sec. 1, p. 9.

61. "The Architects' Service to the Industry," *Motion Picture News,* 29 December 1928.

62. Lee, interview with author, 14 February 1984.

63. Walter Rendell Storey, "Picture The-atres Made to Fit Our Day," *New York Times Magazine,* 9 June 1929, 14.

64. Naylor, *American Picture Palaces,* 162.

65. The $2-million renovation, completed by Richard F. McCann, constituted half the cost of an equivalent new building and consisted mostly of cleaning up, painting, and bringing the building up to code. Modern stage equipment was installed, and the seats were raised for a better view.

66. The Fox Phoenix was razed in 1975.

67. Quoted in obituary, *Los Angeles Times,* 22 June 1981, sec. 1, p. 14.

68. Underground parking was added to Pershing Square in 1950–51, using Lee's idea and a similar plan executed by Stiles Clements.

69. Quoted in Russell Merritt, "Nickelodeon Theaters: Building an Audience for the Movies," *The Movie-Going Experience* (American Film Institute) 4:2 (May 1973): 8.

70. Quoted in Thomas and Virginia Aylesworth, *New York: The Glamour Years, 1919–1945* (New York: Gallery, 1987), 102.

71. For example, see Sexton and Betts, *American Theatres Today,* 1:14–16; Franklin, *Motion Picture Theater Management;* Eberson, New Theatres for Old," *Film Daily Year Book* (1929), 9.

72. "Modern Tendencies in Theatre Design," *American Architect* 131 (20 May 1927): 682.

73. For example, see J. H. Kurlander, "The Design of Theater Projection Rooms," *Architectural Forum* 42:6 (June 1925): 403–06.

CHAPTER FIVE: FEATURE PRESENTATION

1. David Bordwell, Jane Staiger, and Kristin Thompson, *The Classical Hollywood Cinema: Film Style and Mode of Production to 1960* (New York: Columbia University Press, 1985), 400.

2. See Robert Sklar, *Movie-Made America* (New York: Random House, 1975), 167–70.

3. See "Discussion of Physical Construction Aspects of Motion Picture Theaters," in *The Motion Picture Theater: Planning, Upkeep,* ed. Helen M. Stote (New York: Society of Motion Picture Engineers, 1948), 53–62.

4. S. Charles Lee, "Front Showmanship: Presenting the Methods Employed by S. Charles Lee," *Motion Picture Herald,* 8 February 1941, 16.

5. *Fresno Bee,* 14 December 1939, pp. 2B, 5B.

6. Lee, Oral History, 63.

7. Ben Hall, "The Crown Jewels," *Marquee* (June–August 1970), 6.

8. Lee, Oral History, 65.

9. "Items That Modern Buildings Contain," Lee Papers, UCLA.

10. *Santa Rosa Press Democrat,* 4 October 1939, 1. Vitrolite is a plate glass made of white opal, which was developed in 1934 and manufactured by Libby Owens Ford Glass Co. Its translucent quality and its ability to scatter light made it ideally suited for wall tile and other architectural treatments.

11. *Southwest Builder and Contractor* (19 January 1940): 10.

12. "Items That Modern Buildings Contain."

13. S. Charles Lee, "The Influence of West Coast Designers on the Modern Theatre," in Stote, *The Motion Picture Theater,* 34.

14. *Fresno Bee,* 14 December 1939, 2B.

15. The advent of the drive-in in 1933 (see chap. 6) also encouraged the pairing of popcorn and movies, making it financially and psychologically difficult for indoor theatres to say no. My grandfather was a popcorn broker in the early days of movie theatre concessions. He credited the theatre showmen Charles Spyros and George Skouras with helping to institutionalize popcorn and candy sales; they were influenced by a son-in-law in the candy business.

16. Lee, Oral History, 64.

17. There is a photo of this machine in the Lee Papers at UCLA. The machines were later replaced by popcorn factories that supplied prepopped corn in large bags; concessions merely warmed it and fanned the smell into the auditorium.

18. *Southwest Builder and Contractor* (19 January 1940): 8.

19. C. N. Cutler and H. J. Chanon, "The Uses of 'Black Light,'" *Theatre Catalog* 3 (1942): 12.

20. *Santa Rosa Press Democrat,* 4 October 1939, 10.

21. "Modeled for Flash and Luxury in a Compact Plan," *Motion Picture Herald Better Theatres,* 29 April 1939, 11.

22. *Southwest Builder and Contractor* (18 October 1940): 16.

23. Lee, conversations with author, 7 February 1984, 28 April 1985.

24. Lee, Oral History, 67–68; Guy Keeler, "Architect's Pride Is Still Quite Evident in Tower Theatre," *Fresno Bee,* 9 October 1987, F6.

25. *Santa Rosa Press Democrat,* 4 October 1939, 1.

26. Lee, Oral History, 70.

27. Stote, *The Motion Picture Theater,* 54.

28. The etched-glass mural was extant in 1989, although the building was being used as a church.

29. See Walter J. Boyne, *Power behind the Wheel: Creativity and the Evolution of the Automobile* (New York: Stewart, Tabori and Chang, 1988), 119; and Donald J. Bush, *The Streamlined Decade* (New York: George Braziller, 1975), 118.

30. Notes and letters found in Lee Archives.

31. Lee, Oral History, 52–53.

32. Tours of the Max Factor Beauty Museum in the building began in 1984. The tour captures the feeling of the period, from the architectural spaces and details to glamour photos, famous hairpieces, and makeup devices, such as the "Beauty Calibrator." Since Procter and Gamble's acquisition of the company, the fate of both the tour and the building has been in question.

33. Lee, Oral History, 85–86.

34. Lee, quoted in Stote, *The Motion Picture Theater*, 32.

CHAPTER SIX: NEWSREEL

1. See the *San Luis Obispo Telegram-Tribune*, 28 May 1942, for a twelve-page feature on the theatre.

2. *Daily Variety*, 22 June 1942, 6.

3. Liz Krieger, "The Theatre of the Future Goes to War," *La Vista, The Journal of Central Coast History* 4:2 (ca. 1982): 32.

4. Quoted in W. Young Lewis, "The Place to Go," unpublished memoir written by the chief projectionist at the Fremont Theatre (1942), 2; cited in Krieger, "The Theatre of the Future Goes to War," 31–32.

5. *San Luis Obispo Telegram-Tribune; Daily Variety*, 9 April 1942, 2; *Showmanship* (17 June 1942): 12. (*Showmanship* was the in-house magazine of National Theatres.)

6. "Post-War Plans by Theatre Architects," *Theatre Catalog* 4 (1945): 9.

7. See advertisement in *Theatre Catalog* 3 (1942): 301.

8. Allen G. Smith, 'The Physical Operation of Your Theater in 1944," in *Film Daily Year Book* (1944), 669.

9. "Dedication," *Theatre Catalog* 3 (1942): iii.

10. "Notes on Post-War Theatre Sound Service," *Theatre Catalog* 5 (1946–47): 434. "AA" was the highest priority allocation in a conventional wartime situation; "AAA" indicated emergency status.

11. "Foreword," *Theatre Catalog* 3 (1942): 8.

12. John Eberson, "Scene: Washington," in *Film Daily Year Book* (1944), 673.

13. *Film Daily Year Book* (1943), 150.

14. Walter T. Brown, "The Whole Industry in the War Effort," *Theatre Catalog* 4 (1945): xii.

15. *Theatre Catalog* 4 (1945): iii.

16. Lee, Oral History, 53–54.

17. *Southwest Builder and Contractor* (13 September 1935): 41; (1 November 1935): 51; (16 February 1945): 69.

18. *Southwest Builder and Contractor* (21 November 1941): 14.

19. Lee, Oral History, 59.

20. Lee, interview with John M. Grenner, 14 December 1984.

21. See Raymond Fielding, *The American Newsreel* (Norman: University of Oklahoma Press, 1972).

22. *New York Times*, 21 September 1930, sec. 9, p. 5.

23. *New York Times*, 16 March 1931, 25.

24. "Hearst's 'News of the Day,'" *Time* 26 (23 November 1936): 25.

25. William C. DeVry, "The Cooperative Plan for Local Newsreels," *Theatre Catalog* 5 (1946–47): 565.

26. Ivan Besse, owner of the Strand Theatre in Britton, South Dakota, in the 1930s, filmed everyday events and people along Main Street. To encourage patronage on weekends, he would narrate these "local newsreels" before presenting the main feature. When the theatre was sold in 1987, a box of fifty-year-old film clips was rediscovered, restored, and reshown at the Strand and on PBS. The film clips provided wonderful historic records and images of everyday life in a small town in mid-twentieth-century America.

27. Charles Hillinger, "Eyes and Ears of the World in the Arms of a Museum," *Los Angeles Times*, 18 July 1989, sec. 6, p. 6. This theatre is no longer in operation, but the newsreels have been deposited in the university library.

28. Lee, Oral History, 54.

29. Ibid., 56.

30. *Southwest Builder and Contractor* (5 January 1945): 170.

31. "Dividends Are Paid in Textile Progress," *Theatre Catalog* 4 (1945): 211–15.

32. See *Theatre Catalog* 4 (1945): 112–51.

33. John Eberson, "Prepare for Peace," in *Film Daily Year Book* (1943), 973–75.

34. "Editorial Foreword," *Theatre Catalog* 7 (1948–49): iii.

35. "Post-War Sketches from the Drawing Boards of S. Charles Lee," *Theatre Catalog* 4 (1945): 93.

36. Lee, Oral History, 64.

37. At 25 cents a squirt to the consumer, butter was an expensive commodity that earned the theatre another $78 in profit per pound of butter. Secretary of Agriculture and later Vice President Henry Wallace is credited with crossing yellow field corn with Spanish Jumbo popcorn to produce yellow popcorn. The kernels popped out large and appeared buttery when a yellow light bulb was shone on them.

38. Robert C. Switzer, "Use of Black Light in Theatre Decoration," *Theatre Catalog* 5 (1946–47): 223.

39. See "Drive-in Theatre, Camden, New Jersey," *Architectural Record* 7 (March 1934): 235; S. Herbert Taylor, "Drive-in Theater," in *The Motion Picture Theater: Planning, Upkeep,* ed. Helen M. Stote (New York: Society of Motion Picture Engineers, 1948), 40–46; and Lewis Beale and John Stanley, *San Francisco Examiner and Chronicle,* 5 June 1983; reprinted in *Landscape* 27:2 (1983): 22.

40. Mary O'Hara, "The Drive-in Theatres Achieve Their Own Place in the Sun," *Theatre Catalog* 3 (1942): 145–48; see also David Bruce Reddick, "Movies under the Stars: A History of the Drive-In Theatre Industry, 1933–1983" (Ph.D. diss., Michigan State University, 1984).

41. "Post-War Growth of Drive-In's," *Motion Picture Herald Better Theatres,* 1 April 1944, 71.

42. "The Use of the Quonset in Theatre Design," *Theatre Catalog* 5 (1946–47): 145.

CHAPTER SEVEN: INTERMISSION

1. Tino Balio, ed., *The American Film Industry,* rev. ed. (Madison: University of Wisconsin Press, 1985), 401.

2. David Bordwell, Janet Staiger, and Kristin Thompson, *The Classical Hollywood Cinema: Film Style and Mode of Production to 1960* (New York: Columbia University Press, 1985), 400.

3. Freeman Lincoln, "The Comeback of the Movies," *Fortune* 51:2 (February 1955): 130.

4. Ibid., 131.

5. Hy Hollinger, "Hollywood: Bigger Profits, More Headaches," *Challenge* (1955): 19.

6. *Theatre Catalog* 9 (1950–51): iii.

7. Ibid.

8. J. R. Popple, "Television: A Coming Amusement Industry," *Theatre Catalog* 4 (1945): 544; Nathan L. Halpern, "Theatre Television Today and Tomorrow," *Theatre Catalog* 8 (1949–50): 513; Laurence Urdang, ed., *The Timetables of American History* (New York: Simon and Schuster, 1981), 357.

9. Fred C. Matthews, "What's Wrong . . . with Our Theatres?" *Theatre Catalog* 9 (1950–51): xii.

10. Ibid.

11. Halpern, "Theatre Television Today and Tomorrow," 513.

12. "Theatre Television Progress," *Theatre Catalog* 10 (1952): 358.

13. "Theatre Television Goes Outdoors," *Theatre Catalog* 11 (1953–54): 70–73.

14. David Bruce Reddick, "Movies under the Stars: A History of the Drive-In Theatre Industry, 1933–1983" (Ph.D. diss., Michigan State University, 1984), 118.

15. Lee, Oral History, 78.

16. William R. Latady, "Cinerama Arrives," *Theatre Catalog* 11 (1953–54): 192.

17. Lincoln, "The Comeback of the Movies," 158.

18. "The Cinerama Dome Theatre" brochure produced by the theatre for its anniversary, 1988.

19. Lincoln, "The Comeback of the Movies," 129.

20. "Is Cinemascope the Answer?" *Theatre Catalog* 11 (1953–54), 209.

21. Ibid.

22. Lincoln, "The Comeback of the Movies," 158.

'23. The results of this compatible process, first utilized in *Ben Hur* (1960), won for Panavision an Academy Technical Award. Television adopted the old ratio of 1:33:1, and thus it became difficult to broadcast movies without distortion or masking, or without cutting off some of the picture. Bordwell, Staiger and Thompson, *Classical Hollywood Cinema,* 359–60.

24. Hollinger, "Hollywood: Bigger Profits, More Headaches," 16.

25. Robert Kimball, ed., *The Complete Lyrics of Cole Porter* (New York: Alfred A. Knopf, 1983), 312.

26. Lincoln, "The Comeback of the Movies," 131.

27. The origin of the term *ozoner,* commonly used in the industry, remains uncertain. According to Reddick, the term *passion pit* was first used in "Passion Pits with Pix," *Variety,* 1 April 1953, 1.

28. Bryce W. Anderson, "A Home in a Drive-In," *Theatre Catalog* 7 (1948–49): 222–26; "Another Home in a Screen Tower," *Theatre Catalog* 11 (1953–54): 84–85.

29. "The Unusual Fly-In Drive-In," *Theatre Catalog* 9 (1950–51): 221–22.

30. George M. Petersen, "Drive-In Theatres of Today and Tomorrow," *Theatre Catalog* 8 (1949–50): 236.

31. Jesus Sanchez, "Scene Change," *Los Angeles Times,* 7 August 1989, sec. 4, p. 5

32. Kelli Pryor, "A Night at the Drive-In," *New York,* 9 May 1988, 35.

33. John Dreyfuss, "Fantasy Found," *Los Angeles Times,* 29 October 1989, sec. L, p. 23.

34. Shauna Snow, "Dive In Movies," *Los Angeles Times,* 17 June 1989, sec. 4, p. 1.

35. W. W. Smith, "Drive-In Theatres and Their Construction," *Theatre Catalog* 4 (1945): 471.

36. James P. Cunningham, "The Drive-In Theater," in *Film Daily Year Book* (1955),

801. According to *Motion Picture Almanac,* as late as 1974 theatre owners could count on walk-in patrons spending an average of twenty-two cents per individual for refreshments, while drive-in patrons spent an average of forty-nine cents.

37. *Film Daily Year Book* (1949; 1950).

38. *Film Daily Year Book* (1949; 1957).

39. Samuel L. Lowe, "Designing for Modern Open Candy Display," *Theatre Catalog* 5 (1946–47): 510.

40. J. J. Fitzgibbons, Jr., "How to Get Those Sweet Earnings," *Theatre Catalog* 8 (1949–50): 503.

41. "The Second Box Office," *Theatre Catalog* 11 (1953–54): 346–47.

42. J. J. Fitzgibbons, Jr., "Theatre Confection Vending in 1952," *Theatre Catalog* 10 (1952): 336.

43. Robert Sklar, *Movie-Made America: A Cultural History of American Movies* (London: Chappell, 1975), 169.

44. "Frozen Foods in Theatre Lobbies," *Theatre Catalog* 4 (1945): 526.

45. S. Charles Lee, "Restaurants in Association with Theatres," *Theatre Catalog* 6 (1947–48): 518.

46. *Film Daily Year Book* (1953); "Second Box Office," 349.

47. "Second Box Office," 348–49.

48. Ibid., 342.

49. Matthews, "What's Wrong . . . with Our Theatres?" xvi.

50. *Los Angeles Times,* 17 February 1989, 1.

51. Lee, Oral History, 68–69.

52. Ibid., 83–85.

53. Lee, conversation with author, 14 February 1984.

54. Lee, Oral History, 84.

55. In 1970, persuaded by considerations of rent control and inflation, Lee sold most of the apartment buildings, preferring to limit his land holdings to business properties. Lee, interview with John M. Grenner, 14 December 1984.

56. Lee, Oral History, 85, 95. He had

originally sold the corner lot for $135,000; he bought it back for $1.5 million. Lee, conversation with author, 18 December 1985.

57. Leonard S. Hammel and S. Charles Lee, *Los Angeles Blue Book of Land Values* (Los Angeles: Land Value Book Publishing Company, 1932), 301.

58. Lee, conversation with author, 14 February 1984.

59. Ibid.

60. Peter Waldman, "Silver Screens Lose Some of Their Luster," *Wall Street Journal,* 9 February 1989, sec. B, p. 1; Damon Wright, "A Theater Full of Woes," *New York Times,* 23 July 1989.

61. Waldman, "Silver Screens Lose Some of Their Luster."

62. Ibid. In fact, the number of screens increased only 7 percent between 1989 and 1992, the last year for which figures were available. The number has remained fairly constant for the past several years (see appendix A).

63. Damon Wright, "A Theater Full of Woes."

64. Richard Turner, "A Showdown for Discount Movie Houses," *Wall Street Journal,* 18 July 1989, sec. B, p. 1; Bob Fenster, "Will Dollar Cinemas Soon Join the Dinosaurs?" *Arizona Republic,* 6 July 1989, sec. E, p. 11.

65. The first multiplex was created in 1962 when Stanley H. Durwood built a twin-screen theatre in a Kansas City mall. By 1972, of the 11,670 theatres operating in the United States, 798 had smaller, multiple screens. The first dual auditorium, however, was in the Alhambra Theatre in Alhambra, California, and was designed to accommodate double features. People could see both movies or go from one theatre to the other without waiting for the end of a film. James Edwards, Jr., "The Case of the Dual Auditorium," *Theatre Catalog* 3 (1942): 17–18.

CHAPTER EIGHT: EPILOGUE

1. Nikki Finke, "Theaters Go Upscale to Woo Baby Boomers," *Los Angeles Times,* 17 February 1989, sec. 6, p. 1. At the National Association of Theater Owners/ShoWest convention in March 1993, Mark Canton, chairman of Columbia Pictures, blamed the declining movie attendance in part on poor presentation in the theatres. According to a studio survey of eight hundred moviegoers, 16 percent had had a bad experience at one of the last three movies they saw in a theatre. Susan Spillman, "Moviegoing Slips: Audiences Growing Older," *USA Today,* 10 March 1993, 1.

2. Advertisement, *Los Angeles Times,* 27 October 1989.

3. Harold W. Rambusch, "The Decorations of the Theatre," in *American Theatres Today,* 2 vols., ed. R. W. Sexton and B. F. Betts (New York: Architectural Book Publishing, 1927), 1:29.

4. Lary Linden May, "Reforming Leisure: The Birth of Mass Culture and the Motion Picture Industry, 1896–1920" (Ph.D. diss., University of California, Los Angeles, 1977).

5. The term *marquee* comes from the French *marquise,* originally a large tent with open sides, similar in style to the carriage in which a marquis would ride. It was used by traveling troupes of entertainers and came to mean the canopy over the entrance to a theatre.

6. Charlotte Herzog, "The Movie Palace and the Theatrical Sources of Its Architectural Style," *Cinema Journal* 20 (Spring 1981): 16.

7. "The Box Office," *Marquee* 6:1 (1974): 4.

8. Herzog, "The Movie Palace," 29.

9. "Facts about the Uptown Theatre," *Marquee* 9:2 (Spring Quarter 1977): 8.

10. "The Exploitation of Theatre Construction," *Theatre Catalog* 6 (1947–48): 478–79.

11. Lee, conversation with author, 14 February 1984.

HISTORY OF THE MOVIES

Alicoate, Jack, ed. *The Film Daily Year Book.* New York: Film Daily, 1923–68.

Andreen, Paul H. *Main Street Today.* Rock Island, Ill.: Augustana Book Concern, 1941.

Balio, Tino, ed. *The American Film Industry.* Rev. ed. Madison: University of Wisconsin Press, 1985.

Batman, Richard Dale. "The Founding of the Hollywood Motion Picture Industry." *Journal of the West* 10 (October 1971): 609–23.

Bordwell, David, Janet Staiger, and Kristin Thompson. *The Classical Hollywood Cinema: Film Style and Mode of Production to 1960.* New York: Columbia University Press, 1985.

Charyn, Jerome. *Movieland: Hollywood and the Great American Dream Culture.* New York: Putnam's, 1989.

Conant, Michael. *Antitrust in the Motion Picture Industry.* Berkeley: University of California Press, 1960.

Curti, Carlo. *Skouras: King of Fox Studios.* Los Angeles: Holloway House, 1967.

Donahue, Suzanne Mary. *American Film Distribution: The Changing Marketplace.* Ann Arbor: UMI Research Press, 1987.

Fell, John L., ed. *Film before Griffith.* Berkeley: University of California Press, 1983.

Fielding, Raymond, ed. *A Technological History of Motion Pictures and Television.* Berkeley: University of California Press, 1967.

Franklin, Harold B. *Sound Motion Pictures from Laboratory to Presentation.* Garden City: Doubleday, Doran, 1929.

Gabler, Neal. *An Empire of Their Own: How the Jews Invented Hollywood.* New York: Doubleday, 1988.

Gomeroy, Douglas. "The Movies Become Big Business: Publix Theatres and the Chain Store Strategy." *Cinema Journal* 18 (Spring 1979): 26–40.

———. "Problems in Film History: How Fox Innovated Sound." *Quarterly Review of Film Studies* 1 (August 1976): 315–30.

———. *Shared Pleasures: A History of Movie Presentation in the United States.* Madison: University of Wisconsin Press, 1992.

Grau, Robert. *The Business Man in the Amusement World.* New York: Broadway, 1910.

Hampton, Benjamin. *A History of the Movies.* New York: Coovici-Friede, 1931.

Hollinger, Hy. "Hollywood: Bigger Profits, More Headaches." *Challenge* 4 (1955): 19.

"Introduction to the Photoplay: A Course in the Appreciation of Motion Pictures." Los Angeles: University of Southern California and the Academy of Motion Picture Arts and Sciences, 1929.

Jowett, Garth. *Film: The Democratic Art.* Boston: Little, Brown, 1976.

———. "The First Motion Picture Audiences." *Journal of Popular Film* 3 (Winter 1974): 39–54.

Jowett, Garth, and James M. Linton. *Movies as Mass Communication.* Newbury Park, Calif.: Sage, ca. 1989.

Kennedy, Joseph. *The Story of the Film.* Chicago: A. W. Shaw, 1927.

Kozarski, Richard. *An Evening's Entertainment: The Age of the Silent Feature Picture, 1915–1928.* Volume 3 of *History of the American Cinema,* ed. Charles Harpole. New York: Scribner's, 1990.

Bibliography

Lincoln, Freeman. "The Comeback of the Movies." *Fortune* 51:2 (February 1955): 127–31, 155–58.

Low, Rachel. *The History of the British Film, 1906–1914.* London: Allen and Unwin, 1949.

Mast, Gerald, ed. *The Movies in Our Midst: Documents in the Cultural History of Film in America.* Chicago: University of Chicago Press, 1982.

Moley, Raymond. *Are We Movie Made?* New York: Macy-Masius, 1938.

———. *The Hays Office.* Indianapolis: Bobbs-Merrill, 1945.

The Movie-Going Experience (American Film Institute) 4:2 (May 1973).

Musser, Charles. *The Emergence of Cinema: The American Screen to 1907.* Volume 1 of *History of the American Cinema,* ed. Charles Harpole. New York: Scribner's, 1990.

North, Joseph. *The Early Development of the Motion Picture, 1887–1909.* New York: Arno, 1949.

Ramsaye, Terry. *A Million and One Nights: A History of the Motion Picture.* New York: Simon and Schuster, 1926.

Rathbun, John B. *Motion Picture Making and Exhibiting.* Chicago: Charles C. Thompson, 1914.

Sinclair, Upton. *Upton Sinclair Presents William Fox.* Los Angeles: Upton Sinclair, 1933.

Sklar, Robert. *Movie-Made America: A Cultural History of American Movies.* London: Chappell, 1975.

Squire, Jason E., ed. *The Movie Business Book.* New York: Simon and Schuster, 1983.

Stanley, Robert. *The Celluloid Empire: A History of the American Movie Industry.* New York: Hastings House, 1978.

Thompson, Kristin. *Exporting Entertainment: America in the World Film Market, 1907–34.* Tonbridge, Great Britain: Whitefriars Press, 1985.

Thorp, Margaret. *America at the Movies.* New Haven: Yale University Press, 1939.

HISTORY OF THEATRE BUILDINGS

Architectural Forum (Motion Picture Theater Reference Number) 42:6 (June 1925).

Atkinson, Robert. "The Design of the Picture Theatre." *Journal of Royal Institute of British Architects* 3:28 (1921): 441–55.

Atwell, David. *Cathedrals of the Movies: A History of British Cinemas and Their Audiences.* London: Architectural Press, 1980.

Bode, Paul. *Kinos.* Munich: D. W. Gallwey, 1957.

Burris-Meyer, Harold, and Edward C. Cole. *Theatres and Auditoriums.* New York: Reinhold, 1949.

Callenbach, Ernest. "Temples of the Seventh Art: Notes on Cinema Design." *Sight and Sound* 50 (Winter 1965–66): 12–17.

Carlson, Marvin. *Places of Performance: The Semiotics of Theatre Architecture.* Ithaca: Cornell University Press, 1989.

Chase, Linda. *Hollywood on Main Street: The Movie House Paintings of Davis Cone.* Woodstock, N.Y.: Overlook Press, 1988.

Clute, Eugene. *The Practical Requirements of Modern Buildings.* New York: Pencil Points Press, 1928.

Design Quarterly 93 (1974).

"Development of the Moving-Picture Theatre." *Architect and Engineer* 40 (February 1915): 51–60.

Flagg, Edwin H. "Evolution of Architectural and Other Features of Motion Picture Theatres." *Architect and Engineer* 57:2 (May 1919): 97–102.

Forsyth, Michael. *Buildings for Music: The Architect, the Musician, and the Listener from the Seventeenth Century to the Present Day.* Cambridge: MIT Press, 1985.

Graf, Donald. "The Design of the Cinema" *Pencil Points* 19 (May, June, July 1938): 330–31, 337–40; 397–406; 443–51.

Grenner, John M. Interview with S. Charles Lee. 14 December 1984. Videotape.

Helgeson, Terry. *Grand Drapes: Tormentors and Teasers.* Washington, D.C.: Theatre Historical Society, 1983.

Henderson, Mary. *Theatre in America.* New York: Abrams, 1987.

"Here at the Dome." Souvenir notes on twenty-fifth anniversary of Cinerama Dome Theatre, Hollywood, Calif., 1988.

Hine, Al. "Film Palaces: Ornate Gingerbread Is Still with Us." *Holiday* 5 (May 1949): 23–27.

Kerr, Eleanor. *The First Quarter Century of the Motion Picture Theatre.* New York: Potter, 1930.

Klaber, John. "Planning the Moving Picture Theatre." *Architectural Record* (November 1915): 540–54.

Knight, Arthur. "Dawn Over Hollywood." *Theatre Arts* 34:9 (September 1950): 21–27.

Krieger, Liz. "The Theatre of the Future Goes to War." *La Vista, The Journal of Central Coast History* 4:2 (ca. 1982): 31–32.

Laskey, Marlene. Interview with S. Charles Lee. Beverly Hills, California, 14 May 1980. Tape recording.

Leacroft, Richard, and Helen Leacroft. *Theatre and Playhouse: An Illustrated Survey of Theatre Buildings from Ancient Greece to the Present Day.* London: Metheun, 1984.

Maddex, Diane, ed. *Built in the U.S.A.: American Buildings from Airports to Zoos.* Washington, D.C.: Preservation Press, 1985.

Margolies, John, and Emily Gwathmey. *Ticket to Paradise: American Movie Theaters and How We Had Fun.* Boston: Little, Brown, 1991.

Marquee. Washington, D.C.: Theatre Historical Society, 1970–85.

May, Lary Linden. "Reforming Leisure: The Birth of Mass Culture and the Motion Picture Industry, 1896–1920." Ph.D. diss., University of California, Los Angeles, 1977.

May, Lary, with Stephen Lassonde. "Making the American Way: Moderne Theatres, Audiences, and the Film Industry, 1929–1945." *Prospects* 12 (1987): 89–124.

Meloy, Arthur S. *Theatres and Motion Picture Houses.* New York: Architects' Supply and Publishing Co., 1916.

Mlinar, E. M. "Motion Picture Theatre Data." *Pencil Points* 3 (June, July, September, October, November 1922): 29–30; 10–13, 31; 13–15, 32; 32–34, 39; 27–30, 33, 37.

"Modern Tendencies in Theatre Design." *American Architect* 131 (20 May 1927): 681–90.

Motion Picture Herald, January 1928–December 1972.

"Motion Picture Projection Booths." *Architectural Record* 93 (February 1943): 83–84.

"Moving Picture Theatres." *Brickbuilder* 23:2 (February suppl. 1914).

Mumford, Lewis. "The Architecture of Escape." *New Republic* (12 August 1925): 321–22.

Naylor, David. *Great American Movie Theatres.* Washington, D.C.: Preservation Press, 1987.

"A New Architecture for the Movie Theater." *Architectural Record* 104 (November 1948): 120–47.

Pawley, Frederic Arden. "Design of Motion Picture Theaters." *Architectural Record* 71 (June 1932): 429–40.

Pereira, P. R. "The Development of the Moving Picture Theatre." *American Architect* 106:2022 (23 September 1914): 177–78.

Pictorial Survey of Marquees. Washington, D.C.: Theatre Historical Society, 1980.

Popper, H. R. "Palace Builder." *Theatre Arts* 32 (January 1947): 55–56.

Pridmore, J. E. O. "The Perfect Theatre." *Architectural Record* 17 (1905): 101–17.

Rapp, George L. "History of Cinema Architecture." In *Living Architecture,* edited by Arthur Woltersdorf. Chicago: A Kroch, 1930. Pp. 55–64.

Rugoff, Ralph. "The Architect of Babylon: S. Charles Lee." *L.A. Style* 3:1 (June 1987): 90–94.

S. Charles Lee Papers. Collection 1384, Department of Special Collections, University Research Library, University of California, Los Angeles.

Scherer, Herbert. *Marquee on Main Street: Jack Liebenberg.* Minneapolis: University of Minnesota, 1982.

Schlanger, Ben. "Motion Picture Theatres." *Architectural Record* 81 (February 1937): 17–24.

———. "The Theater Plan." *Architectural Record* 95 (June 1944): 86–94.

Schlanger, Ben, and William A. Hoffberg. "Effects of Television on the Motion Picture Theatre." *Journal of the Society of Motion Picture and Television Engineers* 56 (January 1951): 39–43.

Sexton, R. W., and B. F. Betts, eds. *American Theatres Today.* 2 vols. New York: Architectural Book Publishing, 1927.

Sharp, Dennis. *The Picture Palace and Other Buildings for the Movies.* New York: Praeger, 1969.

"The Show Started on the Sidewalk," an oral history transcript of an interview with S. Charles Lee conducted by Maggie Valentine (300/271), Department of Special Collections, University Research Library, University of California, Los Angeles.

Southwest Builder and Contractor (27 November 1924–10 May 1946).

Stern, Rudi. *Let There Be Neon.* New York: Abrams, 1979.

Stote, Helen M., ed. *The Motion Picture Theater: Planning, Upkeep.* New York: Society of Motion Picture Engineers, 1948.

Swasey, William Albert. "A Few Essentials in Theatre Construction." *American Architect* 1935 (22 January 1913): 53–62.

"Theatre Acoustics, Ventilating, and Lighting." *Architectural Record* 68 (July 1930): 87–96.

Theatre Catalog. Philadelphia: Jay Emanuel, 1940–57.

"The Theater for Motion Pictures." *Architectural Record* 95 (June 1944: 83–102.

Theatre Management. East Stroudsburg, Pa.: Exhibitors Review Publishing Corp., November 1927–January 1932.

Valentine, Maggie. Conversations with S. Charles Lee. 1984–89.

Vincent, Richard Charles. "The Cinema and the City: An Analysis of Motion Picture Theater Location in Selected United States Urban Areas." Ph.D. diss., University of Massachusetts, 1983.

Worthington, Clifford. *The Influence of the Cinema on Contemporary Auditoria Design.* London: Pitman, 1952.

POPULAR ENTERTAINMENT

Braden, Donna R. *Leisure and Entertainment in America.* Dearborn: Henry Ford Museum, 1988.

Csida, Joseph, and June Bundy. *American Entertainment: A Unique History of Popular Show Business.* New York: Billboard, 1978.

Dulles, Foster Rhea, *America Learns to Play: A History of Popular Recreation, 1607–1940.* New York: D. Appleton-Century, 1940. Reprint. Gloucester, Mass.: Peter Smith, 1959.

Hoyt, Harlowe R. *Town Hall Tonight.* Englewood Cliffs: Prentice-Hall, 1955.

Toll, Robert C. *On With the Show: The First Century of Show Business in America.* New York: Oxford University Press, 1976.

VAUDEVILLE

Allen, Robert C. *Vaudeville and Film, 1895–1915: A Study in Media Interaction.* New York: Arno, 1980.

Balaban, Connie. *Continuous Performance.* New York: A. J. Balaban Foundation, 1964.

Churchill, Allen. *The Great White Way: A Re-Creation of Broadway's Golden Era of Theatrical Entertainment.* New York: E. P. Dutton, 1962.

Gilbert, Douglas. *Vaudeville: Its Life and Times.* New York: Whittlesey House, 1940.

Green, Abel, and Joe Laurie, Jr. *Show Biz*

From Vaude to Video. New York: Henry Holt, 1951.

Laurie, Joe, Jr. *Vaudeville: From the Honky-Tonks to the Palace.* New York: Henry Holt, 1953.

Marsh, John L. "Vaudefilm: Its Contribution to a Moviegoing America." *Journal of Popular Culture* 18:4 (Spring 1985): 17–29.

Renton, Edward. *The Vaudeville Theatre: Building, Operation, Management.* New York: Gotham Press, 1918.

Snyder, Frederick E. "American Vaudeville: Theatre in a Package." Ph.D. diss., Yale University, 1970.

Stein, Charles W. *American Vaudeville As Seen by Its Contemporaries.* New York: Alfred A. Knopf, 1984.

NICKELODEONS

Allen, Robert C. "Motion Picture Exhibition in Manhattan, 1906–1912: Beyond the Nickelodeon." *Cinema Journal* 18 (Spring 1979): 2–15.

Bowers, Q. David. *Nickelodeon Theatres and Their Music.* New York: Vestal Press, 1986.

Connelly, Eugene LeMoyne. "The First Motion Picture Theater." *Western Pennsylvania Historical Magazine* 23 (March 1940): 1–12.

Currie, Barton W. "The Nickel Madness." *Harper's Weekly* 51 (24 August 1907): 1246.

Harter, Daniel C. "The Nickelodeon." *Marquee* 7:3 (Third Quarter 1975): 15.

Herzog, Charlotte. "The Nickelodeon Phase." *Marquee* 13:1 (Fall Quarter 1981): 5–11.

Peiss, Kathy. "Cheap Theater and the Nickel Dumps." In *Cheap Amusements: Working Women and Leisure in Turn-of-the-Century New York.* Philadelphia: Temple University Press, 1986. Pp. 139-62.

MOVIE PALACES

Adam, Nicholas. "The Last Picture Palaces." *Illustrated London News* 262 (April 1974): 41–43.

Atwell, David. "The Rise and Fall of London Picture Palaces." *RIBA* Journal 80 (January 1973): 8–10.

Aylesworth, Thomas, and Virginia Aylesworth. *New York: The Glamour Years, 1919–1945.* New York: Gallery, 1987.

Barry, John F. "The Motion Picture Theatre." *Paramount Pep Club Yearbook* (1926); reprinted in *Theatre Historical Society Annual* (1976), 2–4.

Beardsley, Charles. *Hollywood's Master Showman: The Legendary Sid Grauman.* New York: Cornwall, 1983.

Benton, Charlotte. "Palaces of Entertainment: Motion Picture Theatres in Great Britain in the 1930s." *Architectural Design* 10–11 (1979): 52–55.

Betjeman, John. "Pleasures and Palaces." In *Diversions: Twenty-Two Authors on the Lively Arts,* edited by John Sutro. London: Max Parrish, 1950.

Boyarsky, Bill, and Nancy Boyarsky. "Picture Palace Splendor." *Westways* (November 1971): 12.

Francisco, Charles. *The Radio City Music Hall: An Affectionate Look at the World's Greatest Theatre.* New York: Dutton, 1979.

Franklin, Harold B. *Motion Picture Theater Management.* New York: Doran, 1927.

Frausto, Robert. "The Decline of the Great Movie Palaces." *Planning: The ASPO Magazine* 40 (February 1974): 15–19.

Gomeroy, Douglas. "Movie Audiences, Urban Geography, and the History of the American Film." *Velvet Light Trap* 19 (1982): 23–29.

———. "The Picture Palace: Economic Sense or Hollywood Nonsense." *Quarterly Review of Film Studies* 3:1 (Winter 1978): 23–36.

Hall, Ben. *The Best Remaining Seats.* New York: Bramhall House, 1961.

Helgesen, Terry. "B. Marcus Priteca, 1890–1971: The Last of the Giants." *Marquee* 4:2 (Second Quarter 1972): 3–11.

Herzog, Charlotte. "The Motion Picture Theatre and Film Exhibition, 1896–1930." Ph.D. diss., Northwestern University, 1980.

———. "The Movie Palace and the Theatrical Sources of Its Architectural Style." *Cinema Journal* 20:2 (Spring 1981): 15–37.

Hughes, Mike. "Palaces of Dreams in the City of the Angels." *Hollywood Studio* (n.d.).

Lindsay, John C. *Turn Out the Stars before Leaving: The Story of Canada's Theatres.* Erin, Ontario: Boston Mills Press, 1983.

May, Lary. *Screening Out the Past.* New York: Oxford University Press, 1980.

Naylor, David. *American Picture Palaces: The Architecture of Fantasy.* New York: Van Nostrand Reinhold, 1981.

———. "Ticket to the World of Movies." *Historic Preservation* 31 (May–June 1979): 27–34.

"Portfolio of Theaters." *Architectural Record* 71 (June 1932): 421–28.

Ricketson, Frank H., Jr. *The Management of Motion Picture Theatres.* New York: McGraw-Hill, 1938.

Rothafel, S. L. (Roxy), as told to John Cushman Fistere. "The Architect and the Box Office." *Architectural Forum* 42:6 (September 1932): 194–96.

Shand, P. Morton. *The Architecture of Pleasure: Modern Theatres and Cinema.* London: Batsford, 1930.

Smith, Lucinda. *Movie Palaces.* New York: Clarkson N. Potter, 1980.

Stern, Norton B., and William M. Kramer. "G. Albert Lansburgh: San Francisco's Jewish Architect from Panama." *Western States Jewish Historical Quarterly* 13:3 (April 1981): 210–24.

Stern, Robert A. M., Gregory Gilmartin, and Thomas Mellins. *New York, 1930: Architecture and Urbanism between the Two World Wars.* New York: Rizzoli, 1987.

Thorne, Ross. *Cinemas of Australia via USA.* Sydney: University of Sydney, 1981.

Valerio, Joseph, and Daniel Friedman. *Movie Palaces: Renaissance and Reuse.* New York: Academy for Educational Development, 1982.

Wilburn, John Ashby. "Showstoppers." *Historic Preservation* 35 (March–April 1983): 16–31.

DRIVE-INS

Austin, Bruce A. "The Development and Decline of the Drive-In Movie Theater." In *Current Research in Film: Audiences, Economics, and Law,* edited by Bruce A. Austin. Norwood, N.J.: Ablex Publishing, 1985. Vol. 1, pp. 59–91.

Beale, Lewis, and John Stanley. *San Francisco Examiner and Chronicle* (5 June 1983); reprinted in *Landscape* 27:2 (1983): 22.

"Drive-in Theatre, Camden, New Jersey." *Architectural Record* 75 (March 1934): 235.

Pryor, Kelli. "A Night at the Drive-In." *New York* (9 May 1988): 35.

Reddick, David Bruce. "Movies under the Stars: A History of the Drive-In Theatre Industry, 1933–1983." Ph.D. diss., Michigan State University, 1984.

Buildings, including theatres, are listed by name; city, date, and architect are given in parentheses. *Pages with illustrations are italicized.*

Academy Theatre (Inglewood, 1939, Lee), 95, 96, 97, 102, 108, 110, *111–17,* 193
Acoustics, 14, *100,* 109, *158,* 187–88
Air conditioning, 69–70
Air dome, 23, *24*
Alex Theatre (Glendale, 1940, Lee), 119, *122,* 193
Arcade (parlor), 16
Arden Theatre (Lynwood, 1942–47, Lee), 153, *156,* 193
Art Deco, 47–52, 78–83, *80–82*
Atmospheric theatre, *41,* 54–55, 75–78, *77. See* Eberson
Auditorium design, *59–60,* 62, 65, *66–68, 67–68, 87,* 106, *107–08, 117, 152, 158,* 187, 193
Automobile, impact of, 83, 88, *97,* 147, 153. *See also* Drive-in theatre; Drive-through marquee
Avo Theatre (Vista, 1948, Lee), 147, 153, *154*

Ballroom lounge, 62, *64*
Bay Theatre (Pacific Palisades, 1948–49, Lee), 145, *150–51,* 193
Black light, 106–08, *107, 142,* 159
Block booking, 91, 164
Box office, 22, *96,* 102, *103, 105, 114, 120, 141, 173,* 186
Bruin Theatre (Los Angeles, 1937, Lee), 97, *101*

Candy sales, 26, 103, 153, 159, 171–72, 174, 176–77, 182. *See also* Concession stand
Carlos Theatre (San Carlos, 1939–40, Lee), *108*
Chaplin, Charlie, 70–71

Chapultepec Theatre (Mexico City, 1943–44, Lee), 139, *143*
Concession stand, 103, 153, 159, 169, 171–72, *174–75*
Consent decree. *See* Divestiture
Cry room, 106, 174

De Anza Theatre (Riverside, 1939, Lee), 118, *118*
Depression, 75, 90–92, 118–25
Dish Night, 90–91
Distributors, 24, 91, 163–64; film exchange, 24. *See also* Block booking
Divestiture, 163–64
Divorce decree. *See* Divestiture
Drive-in theatre, 159–61, 165, 169–70, 171
Drive-through marquee, 147, *147,* 153, *156–58*

Eberson, John, 39–40, *41,* 129
Edwards Drive-In Theatre (Arcadia, 1948, Lee), 160, *160*
Exhibitors, 26, 28, 29, 72–75, 163–64, 181; circuit-theatre chains, 55, 73–75; and Depression, 75, 90–92, 118–23; independent owners, 55, 73; itinerant exhibitors, 16, 22; oligopoly, 90–91, 181; studio-owned theatres, 55, 73. *See also* Gumbiner

Fox Florence Theatre (Los Angeles, 1931, Lee), 72, 83–85, *84–87,* 153, *190,* 193
Fox Theatre (Bakersfield, 1929–30, Lee), 72, 75–78, *76–77*
Fox Theatre (Phoenix, 1930–31, Lee), *81–82,* 83, 193
Fox West Coast Theatres (FWC), 73. *See* Appendix B
Fox Wilshire Theatre (Beverly Hills, 1928–30, Lee), *42, 43, 46–48, 74, 76,* 78, *79–81,* 83, 193

Foyer (interior lobby), 60–62, *61*, 103, *143*, 153, *174–75*, 186–87

Franklin, Harold, 92, 139

Fremont Theatre (San Luis Obispo, 1942, Lee), *96*, 128–29, *130*, 192

Garmar Theatre (Montebello, 1949–50, Lee), 147, 193

Globe Theatre (Los Angeles, ca. 1945, Lee), 135, 136, *136*, 193

Grand Lake Theatre (Oakland, 1936, Lee), 119, 123

Graumann, Sidney, 36–37

Gumbiner, H. L., 53–54, 69–71. *See also* Los Angeles Theatre; Tower Theatre (Los Angeles)

Hayden-Lee, 177–79

Hays Office, 47, 49

Helix Theatre (La Mesa, 1947–48, Lee), 147, 153

Hollywood Theatre (Hollywood, 1936, Lee), 127, 184

Hollywood-Western Building (Hollywood, 1928, Lee), 47–50, *48–51*

Hughes-Franklin, 92

Huntridge Theatre (Las Vegas, 1943, Lee), *191*

Keith, Benjamin Franklin, 17, 18, *20*, 42,

Kinetoscope, 16

La Reina Theatre (Sherman Oaks, 1937–38, Lee), *100*, 109, 193

La Tijera Theatre (Los Angeles, 1948–49, Lee), *147*, 153, *156–58*, 193

Lakewood Theatre (Lakewood, 1944–45, Lee), 131, *191*

Lamb, Thomas, 39, *40*

Lamella construction, 145–47, *151–52*

Lee, S. Charles, *6, 51, 117;* American Institute of Architects, 43–44; childhood, 12–13, 30–33; and Depression, 45; education, 31–32; factory design, 178, *178;* family, 12–13, 43, 180; marriage, 43; move to Los Angeles, 42–43; name change, 43; office building, 125; professional organizations, 43–44; promotional activities, 43, 179–80, 188–92, *189–91;* Rapp and Rapp office, 34–

35, 41–42; religion, 12; residential designs, 44–47; retirement, 163, 177–81; Society of Registered Architects, 44; theatres, 7, 197–208; U.S. Navy, 31–32

Lido Theatre (Mexico City, 1942, Lee), 139, *143*

Light trap, *105*, 106, *115–16, 142, 153*

Lighting, 97, *98–102*, 106, *112, 146, 155–57*, 186–87. *See also* Black light

Linda Vista Theatre (Mexico City, 1942, Lee), 139–44, *140–42*, 172

Lobby, exterior, 27, 95, *96*, 97, 186

Los Angeles Theatre (Los Angeles, 1930–31, Lee), 53–54, 56, 58, 61–68, *61, 63–68*, 70–71, 172, 192–93

Lyceum Theatre (San Francisco, 1935–36, Lee), 119, *121*

Marquee, 97, *98–102, 104, 160*, 186

Max Factor Office (Hollywood, ca. 1935, Lee), 123–25, *124–26*

Miami Theatre (Miami, 1946–47, Lee), 153, 172–74, *172–76*, 189, 193

Motion Picture Producers and Distributors of America (MPPDA), 47–49. *See also* Hollywood-Western Building

Movie palace, 34–42, *37, 39–41*, 50–52, 53–83, 88–89. *See also* Los Angeles Theatre; Neighborhood palace; Tower Theatre (Los Angeles)

Movie theatre: building type, 3–5, *7;* hierarchy, 28–29, 54–55, roots in popular culture, 5–6, *7*, 13–16, 23, 33; roots in theatre, 14–16; segregation, 62, 89, 170. *See also* Air dome; Atmospheric theatre; Drive-in theatre; Exhibitors; Movie palace; Multiplex; Neighborhood house; Neighborhood palace; Newsreel theatre; Nickelodeon; Storefront; Vaudeville

Moving picture theatre, 29–30, *30*

Multiplex, 182, 183–84

Municipal Light Water and Power (Los Angeles, 1930s, Lee), 123, *123*

Neighborhood house, 92–122

Neighborhood palace, 55, 83–88

Newsreel theatre, 134–36, *135–38*

Newsreels, 69, 134–36; Fox Movietone Newsreel, 69, 134–35; Hearst Movietone News, 135; local newsreels, 136

Nickelodeon, 23–28, *25–26*
Nursery, 62, *65*. *See also* Cry room

Organ, 23, 68; grilles, *66, 68*
Orpheum Theatre (Los Angeles, 1911, Lansburgh), 18, *18–19,* 56
"Ozoners," 169. *See also* Drive-in theatre

Parking lot. *See* Automobile
Picwood Theatre (Los Angeles, 1946, Lee), 153, *165*
Playhouse: building type, 3–4. *See also* Vaudeville
Poster cases, 97, 102
Priteca, Marcus, 40
Proscenium, 65, *68, 87,* 106, *108, 120, 152, 158,* 159, 187, 193
"Psychology of entertainment," 9, 95
Puente Theatre (Puente, 1947–48, Lee), 147, *151–52*
Pylon (vertical tower), 96–97, *98–100, 102, 104, 111–13, 132–33, 140,* 153

Quonset hut, 145

Rancho Drive-In Theatre (San Diego, 1948, Lee), 160
Rapp and Rapp (Cornelius and George), 34, 40–42
Regent Theatre (New York, 1913, Lamb), 33–34
Restaurants in theatres, 62, *64,* 172, *173*
Rothafel, Samuel "Roxy," 35–36, 71

Seating, 26, *67,* 95, 108–09, 187
Small-time vaudeville, 28–29
State Theatre (San Diego, 1939–40, Lee), 108, *102,* 109
Storefront theatre, 22–23, *22, 25*
Streamline Moderne, 78, 95, 110–18, *111–14, 117–19*

Studio Theatre (Hollywood, 1931, Lee), 92, *93–94*
Studios, 73, 90, 139, 163, 167–68; and Depression, 90–91, 163–64. *See also* Divestiture; Exhibitors

Television, 163, 164–65
"Theatre television," 165
Theatres. *See* Movie theatre; Playhouse
Tower Bowl (San Diego, 1941, Lee), 131–34, *132–33*
Tower Theatre (Compton, 1935–36, Lee), 97, *98–99*
Tower Theatre (Fresno, 1939, Lee), 96–97, *96,* 103, *104–05, 107,* 108, 109, 193
Tower Theatre (Los Angeles, 1926–27, Lee), 53–54, 56–62, *57–60,* 68–70, *76,* 189, *189,* 193
Tower Theatre (Santa Rosa, 1937, Lee), 97, 102, 109
Tumbleweed Theatre (Five Points, 1939, Lee), 109–10, *110,* 193

Vaudeville, 16–21; theatres, 17–21, *17–20, 25. See also* Small-time vaudeville
Vern Theatre (Los Angeles, 1939–41, Lee), *119–20,* 193
Vestibule. *See* Foyer
Visalia Theatre (Visalia, 1946–49, Lee), 147, 153, *155*
Visibility, 96–97, *98–102,* 185–86
Vogue Theatre (Oxnard, 1941, Lee), *103*

War: effects on movie industry, 128–31, 144–45, 153, 161–62, 164. *See also* Newsreels; Newsreel theatre
Westlake Theatre (Los Angeles, 1935, Lee), 119
Wide-screen film techniques, 166–69, *167*

Photo Credits

Photographs:

Maggie Valentine: figures 1, 30, 60, 65, 66, 68, 70, 92, 121

Witzel Photo: figure 4

Miss H. G. Reed: figure 5

Edward H. Mitchell: figure 6

Paul Gleye: figures 7, 24, 25, 26, 27

Reichner Bros., Boston: figure 9

Geo. Rice & Sons: figure 16

Teich Postcards: figures 20, 101

Luckhaus: figures 21, 67

Architect and Engineer: figure 31

Mott Studio: figures 36, 37, 38, 40, 41, 48, 97

W. P. Woodcock: figures 39, 54, 55, 56, 100

Folger Photo Service: figures 49, 53, 57

Watson Airfotos: figures 61, 62

Hoffman-Luckhaus: figures 64, 124

C. "Pop" Lavall: figures 69, 71, 72

Julius Shulman: figures 76, 77, 78, 79, 80, 81, 82, 85, 86, 87, 117

Nate Singer: figure 91

Merge Studios: figure 96

Luis Limon, Mexico City: figures 105, 106, 107, 108, 109

Javier Sivilla, Mexico City: figures 110, 111

Michael J. Greene: figures 120, 123

Alpheus A. Blakeslee: figure 125

Shorecolor: figure 130

Dwyer Studios: figure 139

Collections:

Maggie Valentine: figures 4, 5, 6, 8, 9, 10, 11, 12, 13, 14, 15, 16, 18, 19, 20, 101, 130

S. Charles Lee, Collection 1384, Department of Special Collections, University Research Library, University of California, Los Angeles: cover; figures 17, 21, 22, 23, 28, 29, 32, 33, 36, 37, 38, 39, 40, 41, 42, 43, 44, 45, 46, 47, 49, 50, 53, 54, 55, 56, 58, 59, 61, 62, 63, 64, 67, 69, 71, 72, 73, 74, 75, 76, 77, 78, 80, 81, 82, 83, 84, 85, 86, 87, 88, 89, 90, 91, 93, 94, 95, 96, 97, 98, 99, 100, 102, 103, 104, 105, 106, 107, 108, 109, 110, 111, 112, 113, 114, 115, 117, 118, 119, 120, 122, 123, 124, 125, 126, 127, 128, 129, 131, 132, 133, 134, 135, 136, 137, 138, 139, 140, 141, 142

Terry Helgeson: figures 34, 35